Enola: Or Her Fatal Mistake

Mary Young Ridenbaugh

ENOLA;

OR,

HER FATAL MISTAKE.

BY

MARY YOUNG RIDENBAUGH.

———•———

Oh, fatal day—oh, day of sorrow,
It was no trouble she could borrow;
But in the future she could see
The clouds of infelicity.

Illustrated.

———•———

PUBLISHED FOR THE AUTHOR:
WOODWARD & TIERNAN, PRINTERS AND BINDERS.
SAINT LOUIS.
1886.

Yours Truly.
Mary Young Ridenbaugh.

TO MY DAUGHTER,

Cora Baker Chouteau,

WHOSE FILIAL LOVE HAS BEEN THE BRIGHT SIDE OF MY LIFE,
AND WHOSE BEAUTIFUL WOMANHOOD IS THE FADE-
LESS CROWN OF A HAPPY HOME, THIS
BOOK IS AFFECTIONATELY IN-
SCRIBED, BY

HER MOTHER.

(3)

∴ PREFACE ∴

———•———

AS many of the late works given
to the public have been the out-
pouring of the author's vivid imagination, and works of fiction, the
writer of "ENOLA" feels secure in
vouching for the truthfulness of this
narrative, as it does not even bear
the semblance of being highly colored, but a plain, truthful story, TRUE
TO LIFE.

ONLY A DAILY STAGE COACH.

ENOLA.

CHAPTER I.

SITUATED in the midst of the most picturesque and fertile portions of the prosperous old State of Kentucky, was a small, quaint village, far removed from the busy, bustling world. The whistle of the iron horse had never invaded the quiet of this romantic and beautiful little town. Only a daily stage coach would come rattling up the "turnpike" road freighted with tourists, and bringing the mail from the outer world. Each day the busy farmer plodded along, oblivious to foreign news, and happy in his own seclusion, with no startling events to change the monotony of his quiet life, save the Saturday's trade, when scores of countrymen thronged the village to dispose of the products of this rich and prosperous land, for God's blessing appeared to rest upon everything connected with this, the land of plenty. Peace and harmony reigned supreme. Neighbors exchanged kind courtesies, and a feeling of love pervaded the entire atmospheric element around *Meadowville*. On that day many bargains were made; groups of farmers stood trading, buying and selling, and many fine blooded

horses changed owners,— noble animals that have made
Kentucky renowned for its fine horses, as well as its
beautiful women.

Saturday was always a gala day with the rural dis-
trict people, for on that day all the news was gathered
in from the surrounding country. Village belles prom-
enaded the long street (for there was but one thoroughfare) in search of dry goods, fashion and art; for in
those primitive days of Kentucky's early history, settled by the oldest and best families of almost every
State *then* in the Union, there was much taste and artistic
skill displayed in personal adornments, as well as the
decoration of their homes. Men that could boast of
owning five hundred or a thousand acres of this rich
soil, and a hundred or more slaves to cultivate their
land, were considered rich in the eyes of the world.
In the present age man counts his fortune up into the
millions; at that time gold was scarce and had not
flooded the world. California's rich mines, filled with
the precious metal, were comparatively unknown, although one of Meadowville's young attorneys ventured
with five hundred dollars in his pocket, *his all*, to ex-
plore and cast his fate in this far-away golden land—
with what results?—fortune smiled upon him, and to-
day, 1886, he is the richest man in that highly favored
country. His name is a household word in San Fran-
cisco. California claims him by adoption, though Kentucky is his place of nativity.

There were several very artistic and beautiful homes
around Meadowville. Two miles distant from the Old
Rock Court House, out on the rugged road known as

Ashton's Highway, was one of those rich blue-grass farms (a term used in those days to designate country homes), with broad expanse of wood and meadow, all of which were in a high state of cultivation. This magnificent body of land, thronged with its innumerable slaves, was owned by one of Kentucky's oldest and most aristocratic families, consisting of Col. William Baring, wife, and two small sons, Harry and Gene. Col. Baring, a tall, well-proportioned man, with large, steel-gray eyes, and indescribably colored hair, though the novelist might pronounce it a dark, poetic auburn, was a man that demanded great respect, from his dignified, austere bearing; a man his slaves feared as well as respected. He was a person not easily approached, yet, when you once knew him, he rapidly gained your confidence and esteem. To the stranger he seemed to have a cold, icy heart, yet no warmer impulses ever beat in man's bosom. He was a perfect agriculturist and devoted all his energies in the endeavor to render his country seat beautiful as well as his lands productive. Laburnums, with their golden blossoms, the variegated holly and copper-colored beech, spreading its graceful branches far over the pebble-washed brook, could but demand praise and admiration from the botanist or lover of the different species of trees.

The terraced lawn, ornamented with the rich scarlet passion flower, rare and exquisite, was pleasing to view ; while extending far in the distance, covering many acres, were observed fine milch cows, reveling upon the mellow clover meadows, with dewdrops sparkling from every leaf and flower. These blooded animals were hedged in this luscious (to them) enclosure, by a tall hawthorn hedge fence, artistic, at the same time substantial. As the illuminator of our world slowly sank beneath the western horizon, these fat, sleek Jersey cows came strolling through their beaten pathway, conscious of the hour termed "milking-time." More readily speaking, "creaming-time," for their milk was as rich and golden as the pure cream, freshly skimmed from the neatly prepared vessels. Faithful Mima and Dinah could be seen carrying their brazen-band cedar buckets, morning and evening, to the designated lot for them to milk the cows, soon returning with several buckets full of luscious, creamy, foaming milk to place upon the ice. The garden, too, was constantly supplied with fresh vegetables, growing luxuriantly 'mid such rich soil. Col. Baring had certainly succeeded in all his efforts.

This homestead was grand in every sense of the word, reminding one, as he viewed the hundreds of acres of green, velvety grass, with large fields of wheat representing a sea of waving gold, dazzling in the sunlight, of the old aristocratic English manorial. Faithful slaves were constantly kept busy cultivating the lands, grooming horses, and adding beauty with art, to make more attractive this lovely pastoral home. Col. Baring's great love for blooded horses caused many strangers to visit his stables, he being the owner of some very valuble animals. Among the most renowned were "Livingston" and "Pilot." The latter, a beautiful racer,

FAT SLEEK JERSEYS.

with flowing mane and tail reaching almost to the ground, was a perfect curiosity to the visitor, and a gem of beauty to those that admire a noble horse. His turf record was so fine that his owner repeatedly refused large amounts of money for him.

Col. Baring descended from one of the oldest families emigrating from Maryland to Kentucky, when the red man, in his savage nature, claimed the territory as his own, and defied the "pale-face" to invade its wilds. Notwithstanding these dangers and perils, two brothers (brave themselves), with vows and earnest prayers to God, that his mercy and protecting power would shield them from all savages, erected their crude homes in what is to-day the garden spot of the State. The traveler journeying along the Richmond pike will pause to view the heavy and substantial rock monument erected a century or two ago to the memory of one of these brothers (grandfather to Col. Baring), who was cruelly massacred by the Indians upon the very spot where the monument now stands to reveal his tragic death. Col. Baring's father settled near Bards-town, and it was there that he first opened his eyes upon this antiquated world. Mrs. Baring was a faultlessly beautiful woman, possessing every endowment that constitutes a noble christian. Her love and devotion to her husband and children was a subject of loving comment among her numerous friends, and her christian character shone forth to the world—as the sun to this old mother earth. Wherever she went she gave light and instruction to many, and her desire was that none might be lost.

She was the daughter of one of the greatest surgeons that has ever honored the profession, and to-day a handsome granite monument stands near London, England, to honor his sacred memory, for he was revered and loved by the English people. By his skill and great medical knowledge many valuable lives have been saved, and thousands relieved from suffering and affliction. He gave to his profession much information, and opened wide the gates to medical knowledge: his works are studied by all physicians to the present time. That he was a gifted man, no one would doubt; and could he but arise from his long resting-place, his mind would grasp and expand the wonderful strides science has made within the past century. But he quietly rests or sleeps beside another of Kentucky's most illustrious sons.

One cold, bleak day in the Ides of March, the wind whistling and sighing the anthem indigenous to this most-to-be-dreaded of all the months of the year, as the snow fell in fleecy purity over sombre nature, covering from view the cheering little "Johnny-jump-ups" that were peeping significantly from their snowy beds, a little daughter was born to Col. and Mrs. Baring, to become a member of this affectionate family. She was to be loved as few little waifs were ever loved. All the household were eager to get a glimpse into the face of this little stranger. Her diminutive pug nose, red face and bald head were anything but attractive to those who had expected to see beauty in its infancy—Gene exclaiming, "Take her to the kitchen," "Take her to the kitchen." Homely or pretty, it was all the same, for she took her part in life's drama. She was petted, loved and spoiled; brothers were pushed aside for baby sister; parents and family servants adoring the little loved "intruder." It soon became a question of great interest to family and friends as to what name they should give this infant daughter. After various consultations and many suggestions from interested relatives, the poetic Italian, the beautiful French, the soft, full English names hitherto unknown to the American vocabulary were freely discussed, and after a great effort in straining the imagination, distorting and twisting words, letters and sounds, "Enola" came forth in all its purity, and she was baptized "Enola Beatrice," in the Episcopalian faith. She soon grew to be a laughing, dimpled cherub, but not a beautiful child. The only redeeming feature she possessed were her large, soul-stirring eyes; beaming on all with tenderness and affection, she could but win the hearts of every one that looked into them. Her brothers, Harry and Gene Baring, she was particularly fond of, and she at a very early age displayed a firmness and determination of character not frequently observed in children of such tender years. Her brothers yielded to her every whim, which rather augmented her determination of asserting her rights with everybody and everything.

"Birchwood," the name of Col. Baring's homestead, was surrounded with many attractions to cause one to forget the cares or sorrows of life. Col. Baring and his devoted wife were truly blessed in all things, and the less fortunate could but sigh in drawing the un-

pleasant contrast.   Peace and a contented heart, which
is a greater boon than all else, seemed to fill every
bosom at Birchwood.   It was a home richly adorned
with all that wealth could possibly give.   God had remembered them in his choicest blessings ; in the cheerful, happy song of the returning slave from the field
after the day's labor ended, one could but detect the
spirit of contentment, even among them, that is frequently found wanting in the palace of the millionaire
of the present age.   We think that slavery never should
have existed, nor in any portion of the universe ought
it to be permitted; still, the slaves at Birchwood were
happy compared to the thousands of starving, miserable people that multiply and throng the great, busy
cities of the world.

The wail of agony and unavoidable suffering that
comes flashing upon the wires from land to land, across
the broad ocean, tells but too plainly each heart's own
tale of misery.   Yet who were more happy than the
slaves of Col. Baring, with not an anxious thought
about the future—all comforts in health as well as
sickness provided.   Family physician ever ready to
attend them upon the least complaint of illness, warm
comfortable cabins to shelter them from the chilling
north winds or noonday's August sun, with a great
abundance of substantial fuel to keep their rooms
warm in winter, good wholesome food prepared for
them by old Aunt Tillie, an experienced cook, placed
upon the table three times daily for them; say, what
slave, fettered by the yoke of bondage, could ask for
more to complete their happiness?

HUNTING SCENE NEAR "BIRCHWOOD."

THE SONG OF THE FREEDMAN WISHING TO RETURN TO SLAVERY, OR WAN-
DER BACK TO BIRCHWOOD, WHERE THEY HAVE SPENT SO
MANY YEARS OF TRUE HAPPINESS.

Sambo, we colored folks is free;
  I wish it hadn't ben,
For we was happier in the lea,
  Than now so crossed by sin.

I long for massa's good fat barn,
  I pine for slavery days,
All the joys we had on the farm
  Were bright and sunny rays.

Oh! place me back before I die
  In bondage's cold embrace;
I hear the wail, I hear the cry
  Of the colored, starving race.

Give me my old Kentucky home,
  With all I had so dear;
And let us reap what we have sown,
  For hard times ever near.

Alas! those days cannot return,
  For freemen we must be,
And yet within *some* hearts doth burn
  The song of liberty.

The slave knows not the life of envy or ambition;
is oblivious to its many strifes and anxieties; knows
nothing regarding the life of the aspirant to fame and
wealth; *they* escape its thraldom, but liberty is sweet
and freedom is glorious. Who are greater slaves than
the society leader? Fashion is a tyrant and governs
its subjects with an iron rod. It rides supreme over
all things, and casts aside the sweet boon of liberty.
The politician, too, becomes a slave to his constituents.
Strife, envy and bitter hatred often are engendered,
and like the anaconda, crushes all who come within the
baneful influence, dispelling the nobler traits in man.
Sardonic must become the politician of the present

age. Not an enviable life. Go, search the heart of the politician, and seek the woman of fashion in her gorgeous drawing-room. Her pale and society-worn face will answer the question, with "ennui" stamped upon every feature of her once beautiful countenance, now prematurely aged by dissipation. The politician, too, pleads for "an oasis in the desert-field of his over-burdened life."

What is their aim in life of this so-termed "fashionable society?" Swayed by a mighty force it impels one on and on in the vortex of pleasure, until suddenly its victim dies — dies from exposure. The frail body succumbs to the heavy burden imposed upon it, and goes down into the grave, soon to be forgotten, and its place filled by others. The companions of the lately deceased are soon whirling in the dizzy dance, and all, all is forgotten. A bubble upon the broad ocean of eternity. A moment known, then lost forever. Pause, dear reader, and try to fathom this word "eternity." Where shall *we* spend eternity? Has that question ever caused you to stop and think? Where shall we spend the summer? Where shall we spend the winter? 'Mid the shady dells or cooling breezes of northern watering-places, or 'mid the orange-scented homes of tropical climes? But where, oh where to spend eternity — that is the all-important question to be solved by all humanity.

Returning to the slaves at Birchwood, faithful "Chloe" was so accommodating and kind to everybody that the care and responsibility of "Enola" was given her, and she felt and appreciated the confidence

reposed in her. The redeeming trait in the character of the African or negro race is faithfulness toward those they love. Chloe was devotedly attached to " her baby Enola," and watched each day with much solicitude her development, hoping she would soon grow prettier; but in Chloe's eyes she was indeed beautiful already, despite her little pug nose and scarlet face.

Truly Enola's eyes opened on that memorable March day upon a beautiful home. Rich and heavy furniture, with rare and antiquated pieces of statuary, adorned the spacious rooms, whilst paintings by master artists decorated the daintily tinted walls. In the library hung life-like portraits of distinguished and far-famed ancestors, gazing upon you as if struggling to convince the curious spectator that canvas was a mockery, and *they*, the living faces, so cherished in life — faces that had long since yielded to the great destroyer, and paid the debt imposed upon all living creatures. With great force and striking resemblance hung the portrait of the illustrious " Henry Clay." With almost speaking eyes he follows from place to place your gaze, and with lips so expressive, and seemingly parted as if about to utter some grand, important thought to the nation. Ancient beauties, full of interest to the visitor, added much to the pleasure of the guests as they would stroll from room to room or hall to hall.

Standard works filled the library cases, and upon the mosaic table could be found such novels as Waverly, Festus, and Dickens' works.

Outside in the broad expanse of wood and lawn stood grand towering poplars, centuries old mayhap, stand-

2

ing in bold relief defying the mighty winds and bowing in grandeur to the great Omnipotent, whence some day all must bow in humility to *his* Mighty Holiness. Exotic flowers burdened the air with their rich perfume.

When the green and heavy foilage upon the maple, locust and elm trees put forth in early spring, the birds came with song from their sunny homes to add their music and charm to this quiet sequestered spot. The blue-jay keeping up a continuous chirp, defying the exquisite singer, the southern mocking-bird, the thrush with its discordent notes too chimed in, whilst in the rosebushes a cat-bird thrills you, so much resembling the domestic or house cat in its notes that for a moment one starts, expecting the animal to spring upon its prey. A perfect concert of birds. Suddenly a hawk, most dreaded by all small birds, pounces down among them, and bears away one of the little band of songsters, crushed in his strong and cruel talons. He has a feast of bird !

Acre upon acre of luxuriant verdure covered the broad lawns, dotted with the variegated sycamore so rare in this country. In the distance a lake of clear running water, fed by an everflowing spring, filled with diving, jumping fish, always ready for the breakfast fry, cattle quenched their thirst from the crystal beverage. Fruits, delicious in flavor, grew in great abundance, sufficient to supply the family, servants and neighbors. Everything that could satisfy the taste and please the eye could be found at this beautiful home. In the autumn the Golden Pippin, Russet and English Belle, together with many other fruits, were gathered and safely stored in cellar for winter use. The entire atmosphere around Birchwood was filled with the richness of their mellow perfume, luscious grapes hung in clusters from the burdened vines, bidding all to come and taste of their sweetness.

Who could but desire such a home? The park of deer, at no great distance from the mansion, was an object of some interest. Terror would seize one while looking through the tall worm fence, at the great, strong, bounding buck; with hair reversely turned, aroused to anger by the spectator's admiring gaze, he would come rushing toward you only to be stopped by the substantial barricade. Fawns in all their innocence skipped and played with each other, unconscious of their doom. Suffice it to say, this most delicious of all dishes often graced Col. Baring's table.

Many of the beautiful animals to which we have previously alluded, grazed leisurely upon the mellow clover, drinking from the freshly running brook, sheltered from the heavy night dews by closely boarded sheds and firmly built stables, groomed by most competent hostlers, until their bodies seemed clothed in silken hair. Such is a meagre description of this famous old homestead, two miles distance from Meadowville. God has in truth seemingly blessed some of His people more than others, but let us not question one act of *His*, for "He doeth all things well." All things work together for the good of those that love Him.

"A bright, frosty day," said Col. Baring. "I must arrange for my maple-sugar camp. The sap will soon be in the trees, and travel upward to nourish the bare limbs, and then the sweet water will not flow. My spiles are all ready, and from present appearances we will have a rich harvest." Sugar-making season was always a time of pleasure and interest to the slaves —especially those that attend the "camp." The spile is made from the elder-bush, a shrub abounding through the rich lands of Kentucky—being hollow, the tube makes a funnel, which is cut about twelve inches long and placed into an auger-hole that has been bored into the trees an inch or two ; a rough trough is hewn from clean logs or trunks of trees; these troughs are soon filled with clear sweet water which is emptied into huge iron kettles, hung up on a crane. After boiling for several hours a rich and most delicious syrup is made. From whence comes the real germ of the maple tree being extracted. Col. Baring usually attended to the sugar-making in person, and great quantities of waxy, creamy-looking cakes were stored away for future use. A very peculiar feature of the maple forest is, that no other tree grows or ever thrives among them. As we are not well versed in *Treeology*, can give no particular reason for this freak of nature. We only know it to be a fact, from observation.

CHAPTER II.

IT is well that man in his finite state cannot define the inscrutable mysteries of the great Creator. Were it so, Birchwood with its many happy hearts and delightful surroundings would be thrown into the most awful despair, for a dark cloud full of sorrow is hovering over this homestead, awaiting to rain misery upon the cherished ones of this household.

The Angel of Death has borne the message to a member of the Baring family. Which will answer the summons? Which of those dear ones will be the subject? Surely neither can be spared. The family circle is now complete. Why break asunder such sacred ties? Why does the owl, a strange, weird bird, continuously sit upon the window-sill of Col. and Mrs. Baring's room? Does he warn them by his nightly whoo too-too-too that a dreadful calamity is about to crush this affectionate family? He is the bird of ill omen. How harsh his midnight cry! It seems to shriek, in mournful sounds, *Death! Death!* A particularly strange feeling of awe creeps upon one when listening to his doleful notes, borne upon the silent stillness of the night. When all nature is in quiet repose, he stalks from his cavern home to awaken the sleeping inmates of the forest by his unearthly song.

May, the month of all the seasons, the *month* to invite the very gods from their ethereal abode, to drink

(21)

from dew and flowers their sweetness, is with us.   To
enjoy the many beauties of this microcosm, compared
with God's planetary system Mother Earth sinks into
utter insignificance.   May, the time for birds and song,
is upon us.   Sun and dewy grasses shedding a network
of silvery thread over flower and shrub.   The month
when all insects are busy, especially the industrious
little bee and spider weaver, the bee culling the
sweetness from flower to flower, whilst the spider spins
his silken web to form his treacherous parlor.   It is
the season when frail man clings tenaciously to life;
for how beautiful all nature seems, throwing asunder
the icy, wintry garb for one of flowers and beauty.
Man, in roaming through the grand old forests or 'mid
the flowery dells, exclaims, " *I could not die just now.*"
When God speaks, alas ! who can stand?   The beautiful, sainted mother, with so much to endear her to life
—devoted husband, with loving children, and faithful,
obedient servants—has awakened to the presentiment
that *she* has been called by the angelic messenger, and
without one murmur from her pure lips, so full of the
beautiful hope taught within the sacred pages of God's
Book, with a heart ready and willing at the great Redeemer's appointed time to yield to his decree, yet
yearning to have full assurance that her motherless
little children will be conscientiously and religiously
instructed in their rearing.   She prays a deep and
earnest prayer for God to give the required strength
necessary to bear the final separation, or until the
resurrection morn, when all that are asleep in Jesus
will be raised incorruptible.   So young, so beautiful

in face and character, but yet ripe and ready for the kingdom of heaven.

Mrs. Baring had been ill with a malignant fever, and sinking slowly but surely; her friends, with great anxiety of mind and hopeful hearts, tried to banish from their thoughts her true condition.

She had often pictured, whilst in health, the joy and comfort she would realize when "Enola" became matured to womanhood, and with exultant pride she looked upon her two noble sons, Harry and Gene. Busy fancy blended them with all that was honorable and good in man. She cared not for fame, so they made honest and christian citizens, beloved and respected by those that surrounded them by family ties or business connection. She desired, most of all, that their christian influence should be felt, and by their good example, set to young men, they would be known and remembered by their works. They loved their mother with great devotion and tenderness, and would listen with willing ears to all her good precepts, and in their youthful minds they could not realize that their loved mother could die. Death had never visited " Birchwood " — the grim monster was unknown to them.

On the tenth day of May, 18—, a glorious morn it was—sacred, for it was God's day—yet, " thou shalt do no labor " on the seventh day, saith the fourth commandment of God; but *Death* did its work on that day, so eager to claim its own. Mrs. Baring, on this most beautiful morn of all mornings, as the early spring birds chirped their silvery notes, as the cock crowed to announce the dawn of day, as the stir of the awakening world came flowing into this chamber of suffering and death, and thronged with invisible angels to bear away on snowy wings the spirit so soon to join them, Mrs. Baring, in a feeble voice, called around her bedside all the loved ones (including faithful servants), pressing mother, husband and children closer to her bosom as she realized how rapidly she was sinking; at last, with some effort she bade each and every one a long farewell. Tenderly kissing the dear ones over and over again, and at last in her dying struggle, as if the blessed Lord had inspired her, for her lovely face shone radiant with the glory of angels surrounding her deathbed, she exclaimed with a loud and fervent voice: "Mother, husband, children and servants, I beseech you, each and every one of you, to lead such lives as will enable me to meet you at the gate of the city. Away in the distance I catch a glimpse of the new earth, and myriads of angels are coming to accompany me thither; see, see them; husband, all"—and with outstretched arms to meet them, as it were, her spirit passed away. Yes, the darling mother is dead. Hush, hush, keep silent, for the angel of death hovers still over Birchwood.

The wail of mourning that goes out from this once happy family can better be imagined than described by our feeble pen.

Inconsolable Col. Baring treads silently the chamber of death, with only the sound of the old grandfather's clock that stood in the hall to mar the stillness of Birchwood. It struck or tolled its doleful sound as if in sympathy with the weeping, mourning family. Tick, tick, tick, seemed clearer and more distinct than ever before, as if reminding the remaining friends that time is rapidly rushing on to eternity and *they* in the "valley of decision." "No time to be lost," speaks plainly the old clock.

Harry and Gene fully realized the great loss they had sustained in the death of their mother as they stood weeping over the casket, that was so soon to close from view all that pertained to earth of their loved mother, but baby Enola, too young to appreciate a mother love and loss, clings to nurse "Chloe" and laughs to see father, grandma, brothers and servants weeping. It seems to strike *her* childish fancy as ludicrous. Mrs. Baring, robed in her snowy shroud, looking the picture of angelic loveliness, was arrayed for the grave. A long last kiss by dear ones is impressed upon her icy lips and all is ready for the funeral service, which was solemn and impressive, many friends following her to the silent tomb in the old churchyard at Meadowville, where she was laid to rest under one of the church windows, with the lilac and the honeysuckle to bloom continually above her narrow bed. The obsequies ended, the deeply distressed family in silence wended their way back to Birchwood, now the home of desolation and sorrow. God must surely give the grief-stricken heart strength to bear the burden He inflicts upon weak man, to purify him in the crucible of affliction, as the blower or refiner refines the gold.

What a desolate feeling comes over Col. Baring as
he anticipates the separation that must shortly take
place between him and his idol Enola ! Mrs. Bancroft,
the mother of the lamented Mrs. Baring, is arranging
for her departure to her home, some two hundred miles
distant. Enola, having been left to her care to be
reared, is to go with her and be " grandma's baby"
henceforth. Aside from all family ties, no more suitable person could have been selected. Mrs. Bancroft
was a superior woman, with a gigantic intellect, and
gifted in various ways, being a sweet writer, combined
with great excellence as a housewife, fine business
qualifications with purity of christian character, her
propinquity to perfection could but be remarked and
commented upon by those well acquainted with this
most gifted woman. She was commanding and a little
inclined to be austere, but since her ancestors were
known to have descended from old royal families, she
must be forgiven her apparently haughty manner.
Suffice it to say, she was a good and noble woman,
with few her superiors.

" To-morrow," said Mrs. Bancroft to Col. Baring,
" I purpose to return with my *protege* Enola. I have
arranged everything, so that you can have but little
trouble after I am gone. I have placed in the blue
room all articles belonging to our darling departed one.
All her clothing you will find in the large armoire and
drawers of the bureau; her jewels, which are rare and
costly, I have securely packed away in the morocco
case, and placed in the secret drawer of the bed-
stead. Here are the keys to the door of the room;

also keys to the other locks. And the tress of raven hair I clipped from our darling I have placed in the little gold jewel-box on the stand. I explain to you fully these little particulars, that after my departure you will have no trouble in finding anything that once belonged to my dear child.''

"Mrs. Bancroft," said Col. Baring, in a sad tone of voice, "I shall not unlock that sacred room until my daughter is grown and returns home to preside as mistress of Birchwood. I will then give to her her mother's jewels and lock of hair. *Enola* is my life, my all, *now*," said Col. Baring, rapidly brushing the scalding tears from his eyes. "I will live for *her*, though my love is buried with my wife. I feel, Mrs. Bancroft," he continued, "that God has dealt unfairly with me. I do not deserve such a punishment; it is more than I can bear. My soul is rebellious. I will drown my inexpressible grief in worldly affairs. I will plunge recklessly into business and devote the rest of my life, my entire energies, to the accumulation of wealth. I will live henceforth to make my children *rich*. What do I care for the pleasures of life now? Truly, life at best is hardly worth the struggle.''

Mrs. Bancroft replied, in her dignified, quiet way: "You should not rebel so much against God and His mysteries. He is just and merciful; His decrees are beyond the comprehension of weak man; He, the great Ruler of unknown worlds, the creator of man — that holds eternity in the hollow of His hand—*His* acts should not be questioned by human beings groveling in the dust of earth, under condemnation at this moment. If you will turn to God, Col. Baring, and in humble prayer ask for strength to be given you to bear this heavy affliction, He will comfort you in the darkest hour of despair, and *time*, the great soother of all affliction, will in a measure cause you to regard this calamity as a blessing in disguise from the 'Ancient of Days.' "

" I wish I could feel as you do," said Col. Baring, " but *this* is my heart-breaking grief—I am too frail to stand the test."

" Unless you have such a supporter as Christ, who took upon Himself our nature that He more fully could enter into our sorrows with us, you will forever be miserable and eventually lost—lost—lost," said Mrs. Bancroft.

"Have I been more sinful or wicked than others, that the great God should lay the chastening rod more heavily upon me?" asked Col. Baring.

Mrs. Bancroft replied : " No, it is not for your sins alone that this great affliction is sent upon you; you should remember that God plainly tells us that He is a jealous God; search your heart, and *there* you will find the true cause of this deep affliction. God saw that you loved our dear departed one more than you did your Creator ; hence, to draw you to Him, He knew it were best to remove the object of your adoration, in order that your soul might not be lost."

"A very strange way to lead one to God," said Col. Baring, " and I feel convinced that this chastisement will only alienate me more and more from Him."

"You should not express yourself thus, for the Divine Father may, in his wrath toward you, remove your idol, 'Enola,' from you; be guarded how you reproach your Maker, Col. Baring. You stand upon slippery ground where fiery billows roll beneath you.''

"I cannot help it if I am lost, but I am rebellious, and must be toward one who has so distressed me," reproachfully answered Col. Baring.

The family carriage, drawn by handsomely capari- soned horses, with the driver—a tidy colored man— and footman—trim and neat—stood at the door of Birchwood to bear Mrs. Bancroft, Enola and " Chloe " to Mercer, their destination. " Good-byes " affection- ately said, with showers of kisses impressed upon Enola's infant lips, and soon this little party were qui- etly rolling away on their journey. A sad ride for Mrs. Bancroft, but baby lips and baby smiles must and will cheer the heart of the grandmother. She seems to have taken a new lease upon life; all her thoughts are now centered in Enola. Let us leave Mrs Bancroft and her infant charge for a while, and return to Birchwood.

Col. Baring, true to his word, turned his entire attention to accumulating wealth. He engaged in mercantile pursuits, banking, and various other avo- cations, to attract his mind away from sorrow. Harry and Gene attended school regularly, and seemed to promise much for the future. The former was a tall, delicate youth, with flaxen hair, alabaster com- plexion, and violet eyes, of a most amiable and gentle disposition, religiously inclined and very free from guile. The latter was quite the opposite in appear- ance. Large, sparkling eyes, with a peculiar sadness about them that soon attracted one toward him. He was firm and daring and had many noble impulses. These two brothers, being entirely different in disposition, both loved their little sister with great tenderness and affection. We will now pass over a few years until Enola pays her first visit to Birchwood.

It is almost a decade since that memorable day when Mrs. Bancroft, with "Enola Beatrice Baring," left Birchwood for her home, to rear the motherless babe as her own, and but few changes have taken place to note the stride of time; only the babe of ten years ago is now a bright and interesting girl, very tall in stature for her years. The beauties of this quiet place, the home of her infancy, were unknown to her. Each year Col. Baring had taken his sons to visit their grandmother and sister. They always enjoyed their trips to "Locust Lawn," the homestead of Mrs. Bancroft; an air of comfort and neatness pervaded the entire household. Everything was arranged for a visit to Birchwood, and with joyous rapture Enola is to return to her birthplace and spend her vacation. With child-like eagerness she watched and counted every day, knowing that at the close of June her father would come for her. Mrs. Bancroft, loath to give her up for two months even, at last consented for her to return with her father to the home of her infancy.

Along the old State road, a carriage drawn by beautiful dapple-gray steeds, containing father, sons and sister, might be seen rolling on toward their destination. The road was picturesque and full of interest to the traveler. Passing through the charming little village of Harrodsburg, where the far-famed watering-place known as "Harrodsburg Springs" is located, where hundreds of Southerners come to while away the summer days and drink from Elixir's Spring the Waters of Youth; passing on they viewed rich, golden fields of grain ready for the harvest; Indian mounds, no doubt the resting-place of many brave warrior-chiefs, covered with the wild rose, twining its tender vines over stumps and wood; the running clematis and sweet pea, vieing for the ascendancy in fragrance, one could but pause, and in imagination see the chieftain, with tomahawk raised, ready to bury it in the head of some defenceless citizen; passing on, the cliffs of "Rolling Fork," a muddy, turbulent stream of rushing water, with wild and desperate stories connected with it, now rolls before us. When Kentucky was first settled by the white man, a strange and sad legend ran thus:

"There was a fair and beautiful girl who lived in the depths of the great deep forest. She often strolled away from her father's house into places never trodden by even the native savage before, to gather the gorgeous wild flowers that decked the trees. Upon one occasion, 'Vesta' was suddenly startled by an Indian war whoop; a moment more, and before she could spring from her mossy seat, a youth, perhaps twenty years old, stood before her. He was the son of an Indian chief. Far away from home, it was useless for her to scream or give an alarm. Her first impulse was to flee, when, with undaunted courage, this erect, commanding red-face approached her, and in a moment he gave the savage signal, and five hundred warriors answered him and surrounded the terror-stricken girl; fainting, she fell prostrate at the feet of the youth. He immediately bore her away to their savage wigwam village on the banks of the Rolling Fork, and she was never again seen alive, but after many days her body was found floating upon the muddy bosom of the silent stream.''

She no doubt attempted to escape and failed, and becoming desperate at her wretched condition, resolved to end her young life by plunging into these angry waters. The huntsman and rover vow that the beautiful form of ''Vesta'' can be seen any night walking alone upon the banks of the Rolling Fork. Death to her was truly preferable to the life spent with a savage tribe.

The afternoon was sunny and bright, the lovely farmhouses, golden fields, and grassy valleys dotted with the wild red strawberry, was a kaleidoscopic picture. Soon a small black cloud was seen flying high in the western sky, curling and writhing in its fury; rapidly it gathered and increased in its size, until the entire heavens were dark and threatening, while the vivid lightning, fierce and fiery, began to hold high carnival, flashing and forming a network of golden cord; the deep roaring thunder became appalling. It seemed as if the very gates of eternity swung open on electrical hinges. Crash—crash—the falling forest trees came tumbling to the ground; trees that had braved the mighty winds of many centuries succumbed to this formidable tempest. The frantic horses stood appalled for a moment and with a sudden bound or leap dashed away, unmindful of driver or footman. The faithful coachman lost all control of the frightened steeds. Enola clung to Col. Baring and buried her face in her hands that she might not see the blinding lightning. Every instant seemed an hour to this terror-stricken party, when, with a terrific crash, a large poplar tree fell immediately across the road, just in front of the carriage, which brought the horses to a sudden halt. Immediately Tom, the driver, sprang from his seat, and with an iron grasp held them firmly by the bit until Col. Baring could alight from the carriage and come to his rescue. The flood-gates of heaven being unlocked, the water came to the earth in torrents; not rain, but rivers fell from the watery clouds above. It is strange to note the many mysterious ways in which Providence interposes to save and relieve mankind. The falling of this tree certainly was the means of preserving the lives of this entire party, otherwise they all would have been dashed to pieces.

These mid-summer electrical storms are usually of short duration, and in an hour all traces of such a tornado were dispelled by the brightness of the sun; only the fallen timber and the drenched, washed earth bore any indication of such a recent disturbance. It brought forcibly to our minds the old adage, "No cloud without its silver lining."

It has long been a mooted question with students of the Bible—"Does God cause the fury of these cyclones; is it His angry voice speaking to man in thunder tones, or does the 'Prince of Darkness,' as the Evil One is termed, govern and control our mundane

3

sphere?'' The Prince of the Air certainly causes them, since he has control of our atmosphere. They are displays of his wrath. Oh! eternal woes! Deliver us from the '' Prince of Darkness.'' Deliver us from his fiery embraces. Rather fear *Him* that is able to destroy both soul and body.

'' Enola,'' said her father, '' do you know where we are?'' as they approached '' Birchwood,'' with its broad woodland drives through the dark, rich forest trees. '' Do you know that we are approaching the place where you were born, my little pet? See yon house in the distance, among the vines and clustering evergreens.'' Eagerly she caught a glimpse of ''Home''—'' there is no place like home.''

'' Oh papa,'' she enthusiastically cried, '' do let me get out and walk through these pretty green lawns.''

'' Be quiet,'' he said; '' in a moment we will be at the door.''

Not waiting to be assisted out, with a juvenile bound she stood upon the broad stone steps, for the first time since her mother's death. All seemed strange and new to her. With wild delight she ran from room to room, with Harry and Gene as companions with her in her every pleasure. Was ever girl so happy? Were ever brothers so overjoyed to have '' sister '' with them once more.

Col. Baring had lived almost a hermit's life since the death of his dearly beloved wife. With the exception of his various business relations, his constant thought was, that Enola should have all that wealth could lavish upon her. How he planned for her a brilliant future!

SCENES AROUND BIRCHWOOD.

How his fond paternal heart would swell with pride as he looked upon his daughter, growing in stature, improving in form and face, with rapid strides toward knowledge. All a father's pride and ambition centered in her.

One morning Col. Baring came in and announced that he had purchased a beautiful blooded horse, " a perfect racker," he said. " I have also for you a handsome English saddle and Comstock bridle."

"Oh papa," she passionately exclaimed, jumping upon his knee; " you are so kind, dear, good papa. Do I merit such kindness?"

" Yes, my own sweet child, you do deserve more. You have been studious, and your grandma gives such a good report of you that I resolved to surprise you, knowing your fondness for horses," he said.

Enola had her mother's handsome piano, and was quite a performer, yet so young.

Two months rapidly passed at Birchwood, with fishing, riding on her beautiful pony, gathering wild berries, and all the amusements that children so much delight in, were indulged in to heart's content. Brothers did everything for the pleasure of sister, and thus time glided on until the hour arrived when Mrs. Bancroft was expected at Birchwood to accompany Enola on her return to her home and school.

At the expected time this dignified personage arrived. The very first piece of news Enola had to impart to her grandmother was the beautiful gift from her father.

" My pony is called ' Nickema,' after a famous Indian chief, that bore away the lovely girl on the rushing Rolling Fork," she said.

" Well, Enola, I hope you have not had such a charming visit that you do not wish to return with me," said Mrs. Bancroft.

" I am ready at any time to go, grandma; I have indeed enjoyed my visit to my papa and brothers. When shall we leave here, grandma?" said she.

" To-morrow we must start in order to get home in time for your school."

The following morning, Enola, clad in her closely-fitting traveling dress, entered the library, and drawing a chair close beside her father, said: " Papa, I am soon to leave you; will you think of your little daughter when she is gone? I want you to promise that my beautiful Nickema will be carefully attended to, and when I return home you and I will have many a jaunt together."

She talked so rapidly and with such determination that Col. Baring, being an attentive listener, could but quietly sit and drink in her every word. Continuing, she said: " Papa, I am coming home when I complete my education; I will then be mistress of Birchwood, and won't we all be happy."

With a merry laugh she tossed aside her head coquettishly, and said: " I will make everybody happy. I will dance and I will sing, and I will play upon my piano, and we shall have a merry household. Papa, you shan't go around moping and sad; I will not let you."

" Stop and take a long breath," said Col. Baring, stroking her glossy raven hair. Smilingly he said: " Now, let *me* talk a short while, my little girl. I do promise not to forget my Enola; I do promise to have your Nickema receive all necessary attention, and you shall be mistress of Birchwood as soon as you are fully grown to womanhood,"

"Come, Enola," said Mrs. Bancroft, "the carriage is waiting at the door, and it is time we should be off; we have a long day's drive before us. Chloe, place the lunch-basket in the carriage. Here Tom, are our trunks ready to be placed upon the carriage rack?"

"Yes, ma'am," Tom answered.

"Run, Enola, and get your hat and gloves, you enthusiastic little girl, and we will then be ready for our journey. You have been so much engrossed in your father's conversation that nine o'clock has stolen upon us unawares.

Soon everything was in readiness for their departure. Enola skipped into the garden and gathered a large, rich bouquet of brightly tinted flowers, and threw them on the seat of the carriage.

"Now, grandma, I am ready to kiss papa, Harry and Gene good-bye, and shake farewell hands with old Aunties Tillie, Dinah, Susan and Caroline; then there is Henry, Ben and Walter, all faithful house-servants, who have been so polite and attentive to me during my two months' stay at home."

Enola did not forget to drop into each one of their hands a small gold piece as a keepsake and a happy remembrance of her when she would be far away. School-girls have a great idea that they must carefully be remembered by everybody that chance may happen to throw in their way; but with many in after life, acquaintances are made to-day and forgotten to-morrow. And such is busy, jostling life when we take a retrospective view. What a panorama each one's life is, anyway. This stage-world with its myriad of tableaux being daily presented, some in palatial mansions, some in poverty's deepest degradation, urged to desperate acts of violence by pleading, starving children, perishing at the half-frantic mother's feet, dying for want of nourishing food. Such tableaux are calculated to curdle the blood in the veins of those reflecting, charitable minds that go out in sympathy toward poor suffering humanity. Tableaux as diversi-fied as the flowers that deck the broad prairie fields in the summer months. Happy hearts, broken hearts, poverty, wealth, crime in its various forms, all are crowded into the short space of one day. Oh ! wonder-ful, mysterious world ; that has caused the student of science to become gray in trying to investigate thy deep-planned mysteries ; he that has burned the mid-night oil, hoping to search into thy gigantic wonders, but with futile attempts ; at last sinks upon his bed weary and in despair, brain exhausted, mind perplexed, and body worn out, till tired nature's sweet restorer—balmy sleep—comes to his relief.

CHAPTER III.

MRS. THORNE, the sister of Mrs. Bancroft, sent a hasty note to Colonel Baring (to whom she was not particularly partial) announcing the sad intelligence of Mrs. Bancroft's sudden illness, and stating her intention of starting immediately for "Locust Lawn," to her sister's bedside; requesting a reply, should he see fit to send one.

Relatives arrived and soon surrounded the sick bed. Enola came from school to watch beside her grandmother, who was so ill. Though the family physician gives great encouragement to the friends that she will recover, still a slow fever is so treacherous, one hardly dares hope until the crisis is past. Weeks she lay upon her bed of illness, with no apparent change in her condition, except constantly growing weaker and weaker. Typhoid fever with its enervating power had taken a strong hold upon her. Her life seemed to be so near gone that even a sudden start would snap its brittle thread and waft her spirit away.

'Twas the hour of midnight. The silent watchers in the sick chamber observed her rapid and painful breathing. Quickly rushing to her bedside they found her in the throes of death: the last struggle was upon her. A few brief moments more and all was over with this pure and noble woman. Enola, poor girl, felt keenly the death of her grandmother, for she realized that

she had lost one who had been, though firm, ever kind
to her, and had instilled into her youthful mind
precepts never to be forgotten.

As Mrs. Bancroft lived so she died, honored and
beloved by all. She descended from one of Kentucky's oldest and most distinguished statesmen—a
man known to history and fame, away back in the
past years when Kentucky's blood-stained soil was the
home of the savage Indians, when the white man had
to fight to hold his homestead, when the Pequods and
other hostile tribes threatened annihilation to the pale-
face invader of their land.

Mrs. Bancroft's father was given the highest and
most responsible position within the gift of the people,
and to-day she sleeps beside her renowned parent and
distinguished husband in a quiet family burying-
ground, away from the public cemetery, away from
the village and city — a lonely spot of ground known
as "*Traveler's Rest*," with none to disturb the silence
of these sacred graves save the singing of the forest
birds and the moaning of the turtle-dove. Loving
hands still 'tend this lonely graveyard, and roses in all
their sweetness bloom, solitary and alone, with only
the pansy and morning glory as companions. All
strangers or tourists, as they wend their way along
this historic road, pause in silent praise over the last
resting-place of this gifted woman, so pious, so noble,
so true.

Enola is again bereft of female influence, and after
due consideration it is deemed best that she should
return to Birchwood with her father, and under his su-

pervision, with a scholastic tutor, her education can be completed. She will be a great comfort to him.

Perhaps just a little selfishness was connected with her removal from her school, for Mrs. Onstead was considered a superior teacher, with many young ladies from the West and South constantly under her motherly care. Her school dated back a great many years.

Enola's life would necessarily be a lonely one. So young, and removed from gentle feminine influence, to pass her girlhood days in the country, be it ever so attractive and full of beauties, the monotony must become irksome, and life bereft of many charms. The young, so full of hope, look upon life as a garden of roses without the thorns ; as a bed of lilies without the thistles. But how is it with the aged and infirm? A field of stubble, where the germ of life has been gathered, stranded along the shores of time, and naught left but a barren waste, ready for the burning day. Some shudder as old age creeps upon them, and with the aged time flies with lightning speed. How important to define these points, for the change will surely come, be it soon or be it late.

Enola had been religiously trained by her devout grandmother. Col. Baring being a Universalist, she could not hope for much from him concert with herself. The seed of scepticism had never been permitted to grow within her bosom. Infidelity knew no resting-place in her young heart. Her nature was one particularly trusting and confiding. All that was ever told her she believed. She doubted no one. Being true to herself and her friends, she judged them accordingly.

Her standard was, "If true to yourself, you will be true to others." She had a most generous and sympathetic heart. Though an over-sensitive organization, trusting all and doubting none, spirituality composed a large share of her childish nature. Although she had inherited from her father strong prejudices, she was devotedly attached to those she loved. She possessed the attributes to make a very noble woman. A great pity that Mrs. Bancroft could not have been spared to have seen Enola in her fully developed womanhood. Many traits of her character would have been brought out, perfected and cultivated, with the evil crushed and changed. But God in His all-wise providence chose to remove her from earth — from Enola and all loved friends.

With weeping eyes and a heart full of love for her schoolmates and teachers, she bade them a sad farewell. Enola, with her father, must return to Birchwood. After several weeks at home, she sat in her tastily arranged chamber, alone, musing. "And I am at Birchwood again; I am mistress of my father's house; I have come to spend my girlhood days at this beautiful home, with maid and servants to attend my beck and call, with the lovely flowers as my companions, with my noble Nickema to fondle his head upon my shoulder; and this too is the anniversary of my sainted mother's *death*; it is as fresh in papa's memory on this heavenly May morn as though we had just laid her to rest. To-day must be kept sacred to her memory. I will not open my piano to-day. We will keep holy *this* day. It is papa's custom.

I shall observe it. Poor, dear mother, I would that *she* had been spared to be with her Enola. I would appreciate so much a mother's love; but, alas! that happiness has been denied me. I am alone. Papa, Harry and Gene I do love; but I crave more— a mother's love. I am pining for some sweet female voice to cheer me in my gilded home.

" I wish I could be content. I do not wish papa to see me unhappy. Yet I should have no concealment from him; that would not be right:" and returning from " Museland," she arose, and bathing her eyes and face, to freshen up her expression, she resolved to go at once and tell her father all, how desolate she felt; how she longed to have some female associations, and I must have a " male tutor," too, papa says. " Well, well," and Enola burst into tears. Her maid Chloe came into the room and found her weeping.

" Oh, Miss Nola!" she said. " That won't do. I knowed you would not be happy lone here, but after while you will get used to staying by yerself, and you will like it then."

Her large, lustrous black eyes glistening through the pearly tears, she raised them to Chloe, and sadly answering her, said: " I do not think, Chloe, that I will ever become accustomed to being so isolated. There are *some things* one's nature can never get entirely enured too. I have a social nature, and love my girl friends at school. Don't I, Chloe?"

" 'Deed you do, Miss Nola. I think old master might permit you to go back there," said kind-hearted Chloe.

"Well, Chloe, I am going down stairs and talk with papa."

She found him very much engaged in his business calculations. How much clear money he had realized within the last month—the advance in his bank stock, and so forth. His whole mind absorbed in how to accumulate property. So great had become his desire to acquire riches, that even Enola seemed for a time lost sight of, in his planning for the future wealth that he expected to realize upon certain investments.

She noiselessly tripped behind him and startled him for a moment. She took her seat beside him, and commenced by saying:

"Papa, don't you get very tried all day long at your business? and when evening comes to take your ledger book and begin your calculations, money, money, money. Why, papa, not go far away, somewhere with me? Let us go across the broad ocean, and oh! then papa, I will be so inexpressibly happy," she passionately said.

Laying down his business papers he replied, "Why are you not happy, Enola? I have tried in every way to render you cheerful and contented, and your brothers yield to you as though you were their little queen. I could not leave my business or the duties of life sufficiently long to go abroad, my dear child, and a hurried trip of that kind would be no pleasure to you or me; besides, you know your education is not completed, and then think how lonely *I* would be were you to go away. I cannot even make up my mind to let you return to Mrs. Onstead's."

Papa, Enola answered pleadingly, "I am a caged bird. All day I am alone, with no one to exchange a word with. Harry and Gene at college, and you attending to your business, or when at home so much absorbed in money making that you forget me."

"No, my child, you misjudge me. I only strive to obtain money so that I may leave you wealthy, above the frowns of this cold, wicked world. You are ignorant of its craftiness, and were I to die and leave my little Enola penniless, what could she do to make her living? No, my innocent little daughter, papa knows best; he has your interest at heart, and you shall never, while I live, and, I trust, after I am dead, be dependent upon any living being. It is a dreadful thing to feel your dependence, and one of your peculiarly sensitive nature could never endure such a life."

"Don't think," said Enola, "papa, that I am reproaching you; I am not. I understand fully all you have said to me, and know you have my interest at heart; but I do get very lonesome, and sometimes *blue*. I do pine so for cheerful, bright girl companions."

"My dear child," said Col. Baring, "I will at once order the carriage and let Tom drive you to Cloverdale to see your cousins and aunt." He immediately arose and went out to find Tom to give the order to get the carriage in readiness, and Enola went to her room to prepare for the little trip.

Cloverdale was only about ten or twelve miles distant from Meadowville, and the homestead of Mrs.

Robert Thorne. She frequently paid them visits and always enjoyed the society of her aunt and cousins, but Mrs. Thorne was not upon the best of terms with Col. Baring. Still he was not opposed to Enola visiting her aunt, and her two charming young lady cousins, Bertha and May Thorne.

Accompanied by her brother Harry, who was at home for a short time owing to a slight indisposition, they soon were snugly seated in the carriage, rolling down the great macadamized State road. Soon to be drawn up in front of the long lawn, reaching away in the distance, with the tall waving *gloria mundi* with bough clasped with bough, forming a perfect canopy overhead. Along the roadside wild-wood flowers decked in richest colors the fence corners, and the very atmosphere was laden with ther odoriferous perfume. Merrily the fond brother and sister chatted as they approached Cloverdale. The great gate hung upon its iron hinges and opened wide as the heavy wheels of the carriage rolled upon the spring. The approach to Cloverdale was indeed beautiful; a large, old-fashioned brick mansion stood at the end of the avenue, almost entirely concealed by grand old forest trees that had stood the storms of many seasons; the pathway to the house was a perfect labyrinth of shrubs and roses, interspersed with gorgeous beds of flowers—tulips, hyacinths, verbenas in every shade and color, when in the remote corner of the garden one could catch a glimpse of the gay sunflower, bidding good morning to the day-god and light of the world.

" We are at Cloverdale," said Harry.

AVENUE LEADING TO CLOVER DALE.

Aunt and cousins greet us warmly and affectionately, and once under this hospitable roof all anxious
thought is swallowed up in bright and pleasant conversation. Enola was never happier than when
with her aunt and cousins. Cloverdale was always
sunny and cheerful, charming in mid-winter and delightful in summer. Mrs. Thorne, with the girls, soon
arranged for pleasant drives and horseback rides, for
all must be gaiety when Enola is their guest. May, a
petite, sparkling brunette, with exquisite form and cultured manners, was the admiration of all the beaux
in and around Meadowville, whilst Bertha, a dashing,
romping, coquettish maiden, with mischief playing in
every feature of her laughing, dimpled face, was a true
type of the Kentucky girl. Enola, tall and stately,
must too claim her share of beauty and admiration.
Since the death of her grandmother she had developed
into a beautiful girl, and relatives and friends had already linked her fate with a brave and gallant cousin
who idolized her, and was only waiting for her to
finish her education when he would claim her as his
wife. As children they had exchanged vows of cousinly
love—a dangerous love—that was fast ripening into a
feeling so lasting and binding that nothing but death
could sever it : and, kind reader, let me pause here in
my narrative and say death did at no distant day sever
this love, for young Ernst Hawthorne was cruelly shot
down whilst defending the honor of a loved friend.
He died the instant the ball penetrated his brain and fell
bleeding, a lifeless corse, before his adversary. No truer,
braver heart ever beat in man's bosom. The announce-

ment of the murder stirred the very community in which
he lived to desperation, and groups of earnest friends
armed themselves and searched for the assassin. He
made his escape and was never again heard of. He
perhaps now may be an infirm old man, passing his
life in a distant land under an assumed name, away
from home and family; a miserable murderer with a
stain upon his character that *time* cannot erase. It was
a terrible blow to his cousin Enola, who loved him with
a strange tenderness. Being so very young and light-
hearted, as her brief years had dealt tenderly with
her, after the horrible impulses connected with the
crime had passed from her mind, she could scarcely
realize the grave import of the murder, and being surrounded by his family lessened the acute sting of grief
and anguish caused by his untimely death, though at
times her maiden, girlish heart would dwell upon her
noble cousin's untimely end, and sympathetic tears
would flow.

Let his sleep be not disturbed. Ernst Hawthorne
died with his face to his foe. None ever for one moment doubted his bravery.

Let us return to "Clover Dale" and peep into that
charming little circle, and see what those three lovely
girls with Harry, so manly and agreeable, are planning
to do:—yes, a visit up to "Meadowville" to attend
the annual college exercises. It is a time of much
interest to friends and patrons, there being three
large and widely known schools located in this inland
village—a male college and two female seminaries,
each one conducted in the most thorough manner;

where after Colonel Baring's close investigation of schools decided to enter his daughter in Madam Nold's school the coming session.

"Come, girls, said Mrs. Thorne, we will all drive up to the "Shelby College."

"Hours well spent," said Harry.

The college building was an imposing old edifice, with spacious grounds and attractive scenery, situated upon the slope of the hill that hugs the stream of clear, limpid water that so gracefully flows through Meadowville.

Shelby College was quite renowned, as some of our most gifted and honored statesmen were educated there, and grace, to-day, the senatorial chamber at Washington with great ability and success.

Standing amid a group of Southern boys was one particularly striking. He was tall, with cold steel-gray eyes, manly brow, with rather a swarthy complexion, so frequently observed in the tropical States. His face was one of sadness when in repose. Save a nervous twitch of the eye when speaking, his whole bearing was that of a gentleman of refinement and culture, with cleanly shaven face that more clearly defined his classic features. He stood erect, with dreamy eyes resting upon the group of beautiful girls that had just entered the school hall. Those girls were May, Bertha Thorne and Enola Baring, chaperoned by Mrs. Thorne and a mutual friend, Mrs. Judge Prescott.

Soon Mr. Enders, an old acquaintance of Judge Prescott, approached the bevy of ladies, and asked permission to introduce a friend. Each in her ex-

4

quisite toilet, best suiting her particular type of beauty, reminded the beholder of newly plucked roses, fresh from the dew-washed bush.

May, arrayed in a most dainty French muslin dress, in color vieing with the sea-shell pink, with a jaunty hat, and gloves to blend with this ethereal costume, her sparkling black eyes flashing amid this labyrinth of rose-color. Bertha, robed in an azure blue, with a rich combination of colors to heighten her complexion, with a lovely little bonnet of crape, tied carelessly under her chin. And standing beside her was Enola, whose dress was of spotless white, thin and zephyr-like, falling in graceful folds around her willowy form. Her face, a beam of sunshine and happiness, peeped out from her snowy little hat, her cheeks vieing with the carnation pink for the ascendency in brilliancy of color, her glossy raven hair, smoothly brushed from her well-developed brow, was noted by all for its extreme silkiness.

This trio of girls were observed by every one in the great hall. After due compliments to each young lady, Mr. Enders said, "And now, girls, I wish to present my young friend, Mr. Claude Vernon, of Florida, to you. He has requested me to see if an introduction would be agreeable."

"Certainly," replied Mrs. Thorne.

In a moment more, Mr. Claude Vernon, with his friend, Mr. Enders, stood before the party, when a formal introduction was given each one of the ladies. They were soon joined by other friends, and passed into the room where the valedictory was to be delivered, a farewell to classmates, teachers and college. One of the brightest students in the academy spoke the final adieus to all.

The party returned to spend the evening with Judge and Mrs. Prescott, where a large number of friends were unceremoniously invited. Mr. Enders and Claude Vernon were also invited to meet the three young ladies, May, Bertha and Enola. Harry was quite interested in the last named gentleman, and there seemed to be at once an affinity between them. Strange there should have been; they were so unlike in every respect.

All spent a most enjoyable evening. Claude Vernon was most assiduous in his attentions to Enola, and seemed madly in love with her upon so brief an acquaintance, judging from outward appearances. He expected to have returned to his Southern home the following day after the college closed, but he lingered and lingered around Meadowville, as the moth lingers around the light. Enola was his light, and he frequently met her, with other friends and her fair cousins, but seemed oblivious to all beauty save that of Enola. He saw no other eyes but hers; he heard no other voice but hers; he was unmindful of all beauty but hers. His friends pronounced it a genuine case of love at *first sight*. When the time came for Enola to return to Birchwood, Claude asked that he might be permitted to call at her home and meet her father and Gene. He expressed a very great desire to form their acquaintance, and had entirely that he was expected to return to Florida.

No sooner had Enola returned to Birchwood than Claude Vernon called out at her own residence to see her. He became a frequent visitor, and it was soon whispered around among the busy gossips that Enola Baring and Claude Vernon were betrothed.

Days and weeks passed, and still he could not bear the idea of leaving Meadowville; or at least some particular star near there chained him closely to the locality. Enola was becoming to him his life-dream. Wretched away from her presence, unhappy when in her society, contemplating the separation that must at no distant day take place between her and himself.

His father had repeatedly written him to return home, and as the autumn was rapidly approaching, with its yellow leaf and chilling blasts, he would be compelled to do so, as his father wished him to determine upon some business, now that his college days were ended. He would have to engage in some avocation.

Col. Baring could but notice the growing affection ripening between his daughter and this Southern youth; but he did not wish to allow himself to think for one moment that Enola would ever love anybody enough to leave *him* desolate, consequently he sought to banish all such ideas.

" But what did this devotion on Mr. Vernon's part mean?" thought Col. Baring. " He would have left here long ago I am sure if Enola had not encouraged him to remain." Finally, he grew so anxious to know when these constant visits would end that he called Enola to him, and put the plain question to her.

"Enola," he said, "you have never deceived me in your life, in the most trivial matter, and I feel assured you will answer me truthfully, as I am about to ask you a very grave question."

With an anxiously beating heart Col. Baring continued :

"Enola, has Mr. Vernon been trying to win your affections from me, from home, from all that love you?"

"Papa," she calmly replied, "Claude Vernon has not avowed his love to me, however much he may appear to love me. Had he done so, I should have told you; for I have never yet deceived you or told you an untruth, and, pray God, I never may."

"Oh, my darling child, you will never know the inexpressible joy your words give me; how consoling to my heart, Enola. I have never liked this young Vernon; I do not like his face; I am sure that he is not worthy one so good and lovable as my own daughter. But I can now rest contented," he continued, "for I *know* you would not tell me an untruth."

"No, papa, were I ever to deceive you, I feel that there could be nothing but sorrow and remorse in store for me. I could never be happy to know in my own mind that I had betrayed your confidence, the sweet confidence you have always reposed in me. You will know, papa, when Mr. Vernon or any one else expresses his love for me."

"Love is a queer commodity: it comes unbidden, unsought. I remember once of reading a pathetic little verse, prompted by the disappointed hopes, no

doubt, of some poor lovesick swain," mused Enola.
"It read as follows :

> No more we can be friends, no more;
>   When love once leaves the heart,
> It enters near the closing door,
>   From which its steps depart.
> No more the bond can reunite;
>   When snaps the silken chain,
> Love flies on freedom's wings of light,
>   And ne'er returns again.

"Papa," she continued, "did you ever love more
than once? I mean sentimental love."

" No, my daughter, I never loved but one woman,
and she was your sainted mother, that lies in the
lonely churchyard. Your pure good mother was the
choice of my heart. She was all and all to me, and
when God called her to rest, and they buried her in
the cold, damp ground, I felt then that my love was
buried too. You should, Enola, try to imitate her example, for she was one of the salt of the earth. You
sometimes remind me, my child, of your mother, only
you are not so perfect in your nature, nor are you so
handsome. She was gentle, and oh! so amiable. If
ever one were ripe for heaven she certainly was."

Colonel Baring's heart's desire was to dwell upon
the lovely character of his departed wife, and was
never more pleased than when listening to the eulogies
of his friends in regard to her many noble qualities.

CHAPTER IV.

ENOLA, I must return to my far Southern home in a few days, since fate so ruthlessly forces me away. I have much to say to you before I go. Listen to me, my beautiful girl, now that this opportunity has presented itself to my anxious heart. From the very first moment my eyes beheld *you*, *I loved you;* I have lingered here three months to tell you of my love. I love you as never girl was loved. You are my life, and without your love in return, life will be a blank to me. Enola, O speak to me, and tell me from your own pure lips that you love me; that you will never forget me. You will not let me go without one-word of encouragement, will you my dark-eyed beauty? O say that you reciprocate my affection for you, and that I may soon return to claim you as my bride. You ought to have known long ago that it was only *you* that detained me here. Oh how I dread the separation from you! how I will miss your bright and merry laugh. Speak to me, Enola, some word of hope, that I may bear it away with me through the painful months that I must be absent from my idol, my beautiful girl."

Such were the words of Claude Vernon, as he tenderly clasped the hand of the girl he loved.

"Claude," said Enola, with her calm, gentle voice, "you know I am to commence school very shortly.

I have listened to all you have said. Is it proper for me to conceal from papa what you have said to me, Claude?"

"O Enola," he said, "if you will but give me hope, I will go at once and relate to Col. Baring our conversation. I will do as you desire, if you will only tell me that you love me — that you will at some future day be my little wife. I know you will not let me go so far away without one word of hope or encouragement. Only give me some assurance that you will not forget me when I leave you. I can then bear this dreadful separation."

"Claude," said Enola, her face suffused with blushes, and raising her dark, lustrous eyes to his, she said, in a timid voice, so gentle you could scarcely hear it, "Claude, I want to ask you again, would it be treating my father honorably to give you my love, heart and life without ever consulting him?"

"Yes, my Enola, it would be right. I would not do anything to give you pain, or advise you wrongfully. I will at once repair to the library and tell him of *our* engagement, Enola. Will you agree to my proposition?"

Hesitatingly she said, "Claude, you can join papa and tell him — that I — well — you know what to say.

Clasping her soft, tiny hand more tightly, and pressing it passionately to his lips, with sacred vows of love, *undying* love, Claude Vernon repaired to the library to join Col. Baring, who was busily engaged looking over some business papers.

It was something unusual for Claude Vernon to leave Enola and seek the presence of her father on his previous visits to Birchwood, but he had a motive, a very important mission to perform. A gentle knock at the door, and Claude Vernon stood face to face with the only man on earth he dreaded to meet.

"Good evening, Col. Baring," Claude spoke in a serious voice, "I hope that I am not intruding or interrupting you."

"Be seated, Mr. Vernon," said Col. Baring in his same dignified manner.

"I expect to leave for the South to-morrow," said Claude, "and would like to claim your attention for a brief time."

"Certainly, Mr. Vernon, I will be all attention to your remarks." Col. Baring fully anticipated what was coming, for he was a man full of discernment.

"Col. Baring," said Claude, "you must have long since noticed my constant attentions to your daughter; I cannot deny that I love her, and have sought her heart and hand in marriage. She has engaged herself to me, and I deem it *our* duty to advise you of the fact, which only occurred this evening."

Continuing, Claude said: "I am aware that Enola expects to return to school shortly; I believe she intends to prosecute her studies with Madame Nold; I do not desire to interfere in any way with her scholastic plans for the future; I felt it *our* bounden duty and with all due respect to you as her parent, to consult freely with you and make known to you my expectations in life, together with my future business prospects. Col. Baring, I can give you the very highest testimonials regarding my family and pedigree."

Col. Baring, interrupting him in his forbidding manner, curtly answered him thus: "Mr. Vernon, I expect my daughter to complete her education before I discuss this subject with any one; there is time enough to think of matters of so grave an import when the youthful mind knows and appreciates the momentous truth. There are two steps or scales in life man or woman should ponder and weigh well; the scales of matrimony and the balance scales of death, and if found wanting in either, woe, woe, woe, will be the portion of the unfortunate. Man is not fully matured until he is thirty years old, and woman until she arrives at the age of twenty-one years; none know their own hearts, their loves, or hatreds. The mind is an expanding power, capable of containing untold worlds of thought, knowledge and wisdom. The heart, when matured, is susceptible of great love, constancy and perception; but to fill either with imaginary love or hatred, no one could fathom the wretchedness so sure to follow such a course. I have spoken to you plainly, Mr. Vernon, and let me in the closing of my remarks say to you, return home to your parents and in due course of time, after you as well as my daughter have tested and studied your own hearts, and are thoroughly convinced from every standpoint that you both really do love each other, with all things made satisfactory to *me*, I could not, as a true father, refuse to sanction the consummation of such holy vows as you both are willing to take upon yourselves, but until then I can give neither of you any encouragement in a matter involving the future happiness of both of you. I have traveled along the pathway of life, through years of gilded hopes and bitter disappointments, culminating in the death of one dearer to me than my own life, and if I did not feel and know the importance of my words my lips would be silent.''

"Col. Baring," said Claude, "I fully appreciate all you have said to me, and agree with you in every respect. I shall return to my home, and it shall be the aim of my life, not only to convince you of my worthiness to claim the hand of your daughter, whom I know I love, but in every way to make myself worthy of her; and after I convince you of all you desire, regarding my family prospects, habits and character, I shall then claim Enola, at your hands, as my wife. Thanking you for your kind remarks and treatment to me, I will say farewell until some future day.''

Arising, Col. Baring clasped Claude Vernon's hand with friendship's grip, when Claude hurriedly left to join Enola in the drawing-room. He related to her the conversation that he so recently had with her father, on the all-important subject, and after many protestations of undying love—love that even the grave could not crush out, but would perpetuate and bloom on, and on, in the new earth—Claude arose to say the farewell word, so painful to many, when quietly and gently he whispered into her ear these beautiful vows of undying love :

" Forget *thee*, no, never, among the light-hearted,
  Love may sink to decay, when the fond ones are parted;
But affection like *mine* is too deep and sublime
  To be chilled in its ardor by absence or time.
I will not forget *thee* 'till life's latest day,
  Till the dark hour of death shall have vanished away.''

"Enola, my dear girl, remember these lines when I am far away among the orange-blossoms and sunny breezes, wafted from a thousand roses, that fan my anxious brow. O Enola, think of me in your happy school-days, with your young companions. I go to make myself worthy of you, my expectant wife, and to enter into a new life of business, but will be happy in knowing that I am working for my absent girl, so dear to my heart, and ever shall be. Farewell, Enola, farewell."

Enola watched him until she saw him drive through the large road gate that led into the country thoroughfare. He was soon out of sight, bound for Meadowville, where he was to take the stage-coach that would bear him to the city of Ashville, where he would secure passage on board one of the numerous floating palaces that traverse the waters of the Mississippi river, bound for New Orleans.

The time was rapidly approaching for Enola to resume her studies at Madame Nold's. Her aunt, Mrs. Thorne, invited her to spend a week or so with her, that she might have all the necessary clothing prepared previous to her entering school.

Colonel Baring was very proud of his daughter, and indulged her in spending money more freely in those days than most parents permit in this age of extravagance and folly. I deem this *a golden age*, when in one single day untold wealth has been made, and as liberally and recklessly spent. It is an age of gain, and never was this land supposed to be that of " Sheshach " (o'er-shadowed with darkness) referred to in the twenty-fifth

LAND OF "SHESHACH" O'ERSHADOWED
WITH DARKNESS.

chapter of Jeremiah, in such a state of plenty and prosperity, this boundless western territory, so full of its precious metals, pouring into the lap of the Treasury millions of dollars, until the rafters of the building are propped to support the heavy weight imposed upon it.

That God has blessed our land no one can doubt, when contrasting it with other countries. When the mind wanders back to the ancient times presented to us in sacred Scripture, the blight and curse that God had placed upon those lands rebellious to Him and His laws, we can but praise His holy name for all His goodness to us. Do we owe our prosperity to christianity? to our morality, or our religious culture? to the piety of the inhabitants? to the attempt to crush out infidelity, that is now spreading over our beautiful land, so blessed? Let your own heart answer these questions. God promised the rain to fall upon the wicked as well as the righteous; and not a sparrow falls to the ground unobserved by His all-seeing eye.

A very learned divine, an expounder of God's word, once exclaimed from his pulpit: "Oh that God would lift the veil from my mortal eyes, and let me view with an immortal eye thy great mysteries," and a moment more his body quivered, and reeled to and fro an instant, and he fell a lifeless corpse before his loving congregation. Every idle word is heard by God's omnipotent ear, hence, how guarded should we always be in our language. Let that thought ever be uppermost in our mind.

Even the changing seasons fill the soul with wonder
and admiration, and are a study to the closely reflecting mind ; there is wonder in the smallest leaf, indeed,
nature becomes a miracle when we try to comprehend,
with our finite minds, God's supreme wisdom. The
philosopher's mind becomes dazed, and sinks into utter
insignificance when trying to investigate even the
minutiæ of God's creation. Science has almost arrived
at its acme of perfection, but alas ! it fails whenever
trying to unravel the mysterious putting forth of the
leaves when spring is at hand, or from what cause the
tiny sprig of grass is expelled from the hard-crusted
earth, and from the soil the richest-tinted flowers
spring and grow to full perfection. Alas, what is man,
that he should for one moment doubt a living God ;
the controller of the universe. Space, eternity,
worlds and might must yield to Him, the Alpha
and Omega.

The family circle is again complete at Birchwood,
for Harry, Gene and Enola are basking in each other's
society. It is the season of vacation for the student in
college, and the school-miss returns to the loved ones
at home and the long summer days are upon us.

"Enola," said Harry, "I had a long letter from
Claude to-day. Would you like to read it, sister?"

"No, I have also had one from him, that came no
doubt in the same mail-bag with yours, and as I do not
purpose to let you read mine (clasping it more firmly
in her hand), I cannot be so extremely selfish to make
such a demand upon your very generous heart, Harry,"
said his sister.

"How sweet in you, sister, to judge me as being so unselfish. I am sure I do not deserve such praise, for I think I am selfishness intensified."

"Oh, no, Harry, you are the kindest and best of brothers. But tell me, Harry, what did Claude say in his letter to you?"

"I thought you did not care to know, sister, since you, too, hold a letter in your hand, from him. Sufficient to say that Claude intends to visit his friends in Meadowville the coming year."

"How charming that will be," said Enola, who had read and re-read the letter she clasped in her hand, and she dwelt upon that portion of the epistle where Claude Vernon wrote: "I feel that your father has had sufficient opportunity and time to investigate fully all my habits, my family history, and everything connected with me and mine; and I rejoice in the thought, dear Enola, of being able to prove myself worthy of you, and I hope at no very distant day to be allowed to return to Birchwood and claim you as my wife. Oh how my thoughts dwell constantly upon you, and sooner let the sun forget to shine or the wanton eagle its crested mate, than I forget my own Enola. You must never doubt me, will you? Never love any other—Why taunt you with such cruel questions? for I am convinced that *our* love is built upon such a firm basis that even the green-eyed monster, with all his subtlety can never invade our confiding bosoms. We must trust each other, and an abiding faith, watered with the dews of love, and cherished by hope's radiant beam, can but find a resting-place in our cozy home."

"Enola," said Col. Baring, who had just that moment entered, "I am going to drive over to Meadowville; will you accompany me?"

"Yes, papa, cheerfully, for I do wish to see my friend Mrs. Prescott. It always makes me feel so bright to spend a few hours in her charming society."

Mrs. Prescott was an ardent admirer of Enola's, and often expressed herself in glowing terms of her beauty. She regarded her youthful friend as a girl of much promise.

The day was most delightfully passed, and in the shade of the evening, Col. Baring and his daughter returned to Birchwood.

During the conversation between father and child, he asked her if she had ever heard from Mr. Vernon, and if her teachers at school permitted the young ladies to correspond with gentlemen.

" Candidly Enola replied to her father, that she had heard more frequently since she returned from school, but upon several occasions Claude had written her, but she would always let the teacher see the letters, as it was one of the regulations of the school."

"Papa, have you made any inquiries about Claude's family, as he requested you to satisfy yourself fully about him?" she asked.

"No, he promptly replied, nor do I intend to trouble myself in the least regarding him."

" But, papa, do you think that you are treating Claude with fairness, when he was so very desirous that you should ascertain everything connected with his life? He is proud of his family, and his mother and sisters have written me such a sweet and loving letter."

"What, Enola," said Col. Baring, "have you arrived at that stage of your child courtship where *they write you?*" and in a sardonic manner continued, "I suppose you fancy this youth *loves* you, and you, in return, *love him?*"

With a trembling voice, Enola said, "O, papa, don't be sarcastic with me, for I would not do or say anything to displease you; but, papa, you must give Claude justice, and I know he will do what is honorable and right. I heard that his family were most charming people, and they already love me, and I, in return, can but reciprocate their love. Claude Vernon is a gentleman, papa, and if you will permit me, when we arrive at home I will show you letters from some of the most prominent gentlemen of the South, speaking in the most exalted terms of Capt. Vernon's family."

"My daughter," said Col. Baring, "I wish you to cease this conversation—it is very disagreeable to me—and I prefer that you never mention this young man's name to me again. I do not care to discuss with you a subject so distasteful to me, however pleasant it might be to *you.*"

Enola knew just how far to go with her father, and so great was her love and respect for him that she could never do or say anything to displease him; at the same time she felt a great wrong had been done Claude, and how her proud young heart yearned to convince her stern father that Claude Vernon was not the wicked, low man he pictured him to be.

5

Col. Baring was a man of the strongest prejudices,
and so positive and obstinate in his nature that he frequently allowed his dislikes to carry him beyond reason. He was a man of firm friendship and ardent in
his attachments, which were few. He did not make
friends easily, and when he once disliked a man nothing
could change the first impressions stereotyped upon his
mind. He was blind to all the good, and clear-sighted
to the bad. Hence it was difficult to get him to yield
to justice; yet with his friends no man would go further to serve them.

Enola sat motionless beside him in the carriage until
they arrived at Birchwood. She retired at once to her
chamber, perhaps to weep, maybe to resolve to love
Claude Vernon even with a more determined will, for
she was of that disposition, when she saw that wrong
had been done a friend (especially Claude), her sympathetic nature became aroused in his behalf, and she
would brave the storm for him. She had her father's
firmness, with her mother's devotion toward those
whom she loved. She drew from her pocket Claude's
last letter. She read over his mother's and sister's kind epistles, and, brushing a tear from her
eyes, she said, or musingly whispered: "Since papa
will not give poor Claude justice, I will see that no
wrong be done him by any of *my* family. If papa
only did but know that his course toward Claude only
causes the flame to burn brighter and brighter in my
heart, I am sure his prejudices would soften. Shall
I write to him and tell him what a conflict I am
having? No; I cannot cause him one pang, poor. dear

Claude. I wish I could see him this quiet summer evening; but he is far away. I know he is thinking of *me*."

A loud rap at the door, when she was startled from her reverie. " Come in," she said.

Harry entered, with his kind, cheery manner. " Come, sister," he said, ".I missed you from the table and sought you, and what do I see? A tear glistening in your eyes? Such eyes as yours, sister, should never be dimmed by tears. Who did or said anything to wound your sensitive pride? "

" Oh, Harry," she said, bursting again into weeping, "I think papa is so unjust and cruel to Claude; he will not even permit himself to inquire or learn anything about him. And you know, Harry, how earnestly Claude urged him to write South and get a good report of him. Harry, what am I to do? Shall I let Claude know how bitter my father feels toward him? "

" I don't think, if I were in your place, that I should annoy him; but when you meet him, you could more fully explain satisfactorily everything to him," replied Harry, kindly.

" I am sure," continued Enola, " were papa to read the letters that I have received, extolling Claude and his family, that papa would yield, and not be so bitter against him, but, Harry, he will not even permit me to talk about him, or tell any favorable reports I hear,' she said, pressing Harry's hand.

" Cheer up, sister, all will yet turn out for the best, I trust," he said.

"Oh, Harry, you are ever so hopeful, and always can see a silvery lining to every cloud. I am sure if I could be as you are, Harry, I could illuminate many a dark day."

"I am very fond of Claude, you know, sister," said Harry, "and I intend to answer his letter shortly ; he writes interesting letters, to the point and full of wit. I like him anyway, for I view him as a cultured gentleman. You know father is strong in his prejudices, and we know he has disliked Claude from the first hour he ever met him, and I really think, Enola, the least said about Claude or anything connected with him, the better for you. Beside, it will have no effect upon father."

"You are correct, Harry."

"Well, shall we go down into the drawing-room and have some music, sister?"

"Yes, in one moment, Harry. I don't want papa to see that I have been worried."

It was one of those balmy summer evenings when village friends love to drive to the country and enjoy the delicious fruits that have made Birchwood famous, and, too, the pure creamy milk and ices were enough to tempt the most fastidious.

May and Bertha Thorne, with some other friends were announced. Soon all was brightness and mirth at Birchwood; some cake and ices were handed, and a row upon the cool lake was proposed, for it was an oppressive eve within doors.

The party were soon out upon the clear, smooth lake, indulging to their heart's content a sail. May's sweet, full voice sounded over the waters, entrancing the heavens. Bertha kept the party laughing by her repartee — she was a bright, vivacious girl, full of wit and humor — when the gay party was suddenly broken up by the announcement that a favorite little servant had been killed by an infuriated buck that had made his escape from the park, and not until he had been shot could they conquer him. The poor little slave was an object of pity to look upon, and there was great weeping and wailing among the numerous slaves that belonged to Col. Baring. Death soon came to the little sufferer's relief and he was quietly laid to rest in the colored people's graveyard, just over the hill. After this dreadful catastrophe Col. Baring decided not to indulge any longer in keeping up this beautiful park of deer, as the bucks had become so unmanageable that not infrequently with one bound they would leap over the tall worm fence that enclosed them from the public. So with time passed away one of the attractions of Birchwood.

Enola, being a warm-hearted and confiding girl, greatly attached to old Aunt Tilly, the cook, deemed it her duty to impart the secret to her. Just as soon as she had consented to become the wife of young Claude Vernon she sought this old woman, feeling that she could find comfort in her crude advice; she who had served many a dainty dish to grace the table of Col. Baring, and was even then dressing a large fat turkey, that had fed upon the wild nuts of the forest until its juicy flesh partook of the beech and hazel nuts in its flavor; as Enola entered the kitchen, Aunt Tilly's salutation was: "La bless my soul, Miss 'Nola, what bro't you here? Of course, you cum to see your old Aunt Tilly. Didn't you?"

"Yes, Aunt Tilly, I sought you, and found you busy, as usual, preparing nice things to eat. You must certainly grow weary of such sameness," said Enola, gently patting her upon the shoulder.

"I does git mighty tired some days, and wish I hadn't bin born a slave; then I looks round, and sees many poor devils wus off than I is, and it kinder cheers me, and I takes comfort. Old massa's good to us, which you know, Miss 'Nola, is a good thing with us slaves."

" Never mind, Aunt Tilly, said Enola, I am going to get married soon, and I am determined to take you, and you shall have a home that will suit you exactly."

With an astonished look, and bracing herself firmly before her young mistress, with arms a-kimbo, she stood statue-like, viewing Enola, from her head to her feet. At length she said, "Ise older than you is, Miss 'Nola, and my advice is, you jist let mar'ing alone."

"Why, Aunt Tilly, shouldn't I marry, as well as other girls?" asked Enola.

" *You* marry and leave old massa, and all this 'ere easy life, and ever'thing. These things you is sure of, but t'other change you ain't. Who's you gwine to 'spouse, Miss 'Nola?"

"I am engaged to be married to Claude Vernon, the handsome young gentleman from the balmy South," replied Enola, in her coquettish manner."

"Worse still, Miss 'Nola: that thar young man don't

know how to take care of a wife, like you's been pampered up. I's peeped at him time and agin, when you's bin walking wid him in de flower garden, and I ses to myself: 'I wonder if he tinks he's gwine to get our young missus,' and if you marries him, I can't cum and cook for you, No ! No !"

"Aunt Tilly, you are not the least encouraging. What has caused you to dislike Mr. Vernon? He is one of the best and noblest men in the world. He likes you, Aunt Tilly, and everybody but papa respects him."

"Miss 'Nola, tho' I's an old colored woman, and has known you since the hour you was born; you feels as near to me as one of my own chillen, and I knows I would grieve to see you marry a man, and him not provide everything that he could for you. You is got a nice home here, and my poor little missus might not have all these servants to wait on her. It is a 'sponsible persition, and you must not marry in haste, but t'ink about it ten or twelve years. Then you will know your own mind, child; thar is nothing like knowing one's own mind, and I is sure, it takes time to know that, 'specially if your mind is big. Don't you believe me, Miss 'Nola?"

" You talk very sensibly, Aunt Tilly, upon the subject, and in many cases your words would be most appropriate; but with such love as Mr. Vernon has for me, and my devotion for him — I say, with such *unadulterated* love as ours, there can be no sorrow or storms through our devoted life; all will be sunshine," said Enola. " Strewn with roses our life's pathway will be."

"Stop, Miss 'Nola. Did you ever t'ink there isn't no sunshine without rain? There isn't no joy without pain. There isn't no rose, 'less you stick yer finger. Everything in this here world won't be true to you, and you can't 'pend on all the folks you meet with, Miss 'Nola. You always believed everything people said. You mustn't do that, chile, for people will deceive one another. It is the truth, Miss 'Nola. Don't smile at me that way."

Enola felt and appreciated the force there was in her words, and she thought, in her young mind, "Perhaps I might be more happy were I not to love Claude more than father and brothers. How can I control the impulses of my heart? Can I bid love come at will and go to suit circumstances? I love, love. How strange for me to love," thought she.

"Aunt Tilly, why do you think that Claude Vernon would not make a good husband? You must have some reasons for your prejudices."

"Miss 'Nola, I can read a man if I can git a good look at him in the eye, and I did git a chance to see Mr. Vernon, and I s'pose my 'pinion was based on that. I hope my poor little chile will change her mind before she leaps."

"Oh Aunt Tilly, you make me feel badly, but my mind is made up. I know that Claude Vernon loves me, and his love, based upon principle, will make him ever faithful as a husband."

"Does you trust a stranger, Miss 'Nola? You don't know his people; you hain't saw any of them but him. S'pose they hain't the same kind of folks

as yourn? What would you do, then? Jist cry, I
s'pose."

"Aunt Tilly," said Enola, " I am troubled at heart,
and papa's dislike for Claude pains me no little."

" Poor chile, I does sinterthise wid you, Miss
'Nola, but I know ole massa is a good teller of charac-
ter, and then he knows what is best for your good.
You come to me, chile, for my 'pinion and words. I
say, mind all the time what ole massa bids you do.
Why, chile, you is purty enough to catch a little
Prince, and all that ar kinder thing."

" So, Aunt Tilly, you advise me not to marry, do
you?" said Enola.

" Of course I does; you is nothing but a chile yit,
and what does you want to bring 'sponsibilities on you
fur? You hain't seen no young-lady days yit. Old
massa is rich, and when you git to be a young lady he
will pick you out a grand man for a husband, Miss
Nola. If you must git married, wait till you gits about
thirty, then plunge into the lake of matrimony.
Them's old Aunt Tilly's sentiments, they ar'."

" Well, Aunt Tilly, you and I can't agree upon the
marriage subject, so I will have to bid you good-bye,
but I will come in another day, for you may change
your mind; besides your turkey needs your attention."

"Bress your soul, chile, I'se can cook and talk too."

Enola felt to some extent the old cook's words, but
smothered her feelings and went tripping out of the
kitchen to join her friends.

" Good-bye, Aunt Tilly, I will pay you another visit
soon." She was soon out of sight.

Tilly said aloud to herself: "Poor dear chile, I loves her terrible; she is a puty little gal and I's gwine to try and coax her not to marry." Shaking her head wistfully, continued—"Poor chile, if she marries that ar young fellur, it will kill old massa, sure it will."

May and Bertha passed the week with Enola, when Mrs. Thorne came over to accompany them to their school. Months passed without anything of interest transpiring either at Cloverdale or Birchwood. The three young ladies were constantly in school, with an occasional visit to their respective homes, each applying the hours to the best advantage, to their music, drawing, languages, and various other studies appointed for them.

Harry and Gene, having completed their education, returned to their father's to decide what kind of business they preferred to engage in. After due deliberation Harry decided to enter into the banking business with an old, trusted friend. I say trusted, because Col. Baring had known him intimately for many years, and he had proven himself deserving the name *friend*. How much is implied in that term, so often applied to an acquaintance.

Gene, a heavy-built, robust young man, declares he can never be suited in any mercantile business; but he would be a tiller of the ground. He loves the forest, game and the pleasures a farmer's life affords.

Each having fully marked out his course through life, Col. Baring felt quite a responsibility lifted from him, and at once decided to purchase a tract of land for Gene, who bids fair to become a model agriculturist.

The soil of this comparatively new country was loamy, and tempting to the cultivator. Gene was eager to see the inky earth curling beneath the plow preparatory to sowing the seed. In his vivid imagination he pictured vast fields of golden grain; meadows of sweet-scented, dewy clover, with its army of busy bees culling from leaf and flower the substance to make their honey.

Winter, with its icy touch and snowy garb, is upon us again, and the farmer, with a long-drawn sigh, and melancholy face, proclaims "a terrible winter." Why should he be wiser than the learned lawyer or scientific investigator? Has God given him an all-seeing eye? No, but nature speaks to him from every point. No sibyl voice, but the ear of corn, says, "I am provided with a greater supply of shucks;" the tripping little rabbit. answers and proclaims his unusual quantity of warm fur, and the wild geese echo, "Feel my downy crest, and see its fullness"—all provided for the certainity and intended severity of the approaching winter. The busy farm-hand's ax echoes and re-echoes through the boundless forest; and birch, ash and hickory finally yield to the cutting strokes, and with a loud crash fall to the earth, to be burned, root and branch; and the places in the forest that knew them will know them no more.

And thus will perish this microcosm of ours, for the "Ancient of Days" has warned us, through His holy prophets, of the end, when the wicked, together with man's works, will be destroyed "root and branch"—

"clean dissolved;" and the righteous are promised
a new heaven and a new earth.

What comforting words to the weary traveler as he
journeys on toward the close of his pilgrimage, being
tempted, as he is, along the broad wayside of life, to
realize the beauties and rest in store for him. He can
almost hear the anthem of hosts of angels, bearing to
God, on silvery notes, the praises of the Most High—
"Glory to God."

Another Christmas, with its festivities and gaieties,
rolls around. Enola, with flushed cheeks and merry
heart, rushes in upon loved ones at home, wishing
a "Merry Christmas" to one and all. She is unusually happy this holiday. Why? Because Claude
Vernon has arrived in Meadowville, and she had already
passed several hours in his charming society before she
left her school.

Claude comes, laden with all the required testimony of his worthiness to aspire to the hand and heart
of Enola Baring, and, not knowing the bitterness that
lurks in the heart of her father toward him, feeling
secure in his own merit and Enola's valued promises, immediately procures a cutter and drives out to Birchwood.

Enola had longed to explain to him her father's feelings, but trusted, as time passed on, she would be able
to overcome all obstacles, and then Claude would never
know the struggle she had passed through to gain her
desired point. It was now too late, and they would
have to abide the consequences and brave the worst—
"Sufficient unto the day is the evil thereof."

A moment more, and Claude Vernon turned his horse and cutter over to the hostler and was ushered into the great drawing-room. He was soon seated before a large wood fire, blazing so cheerily, he warmed his hands while waiting to greet his idol.

Enola, in a dress of rich maroon cashmere, with snowy-white cuffs and collar, looked the perfection of loveliness; her girlish beauty, in all its purity and freshness, dazzled the eyes of Claude Vernon as he looked upon her, and he could but compliment her upon her handsome appearance as he extended his hand to her, wishing her "Merry Christmas," at the same time placing upon her tiny third finger a beautiful diamond ring—a perfect gem—with this expression:

"Enola, as this ring is endless, so is my love for you. Accept it as a small gift upon this happy Christmas day; and, oh, may you live to see many, many returns of the season, and ever be as free from care and sorrow as at this present moment."

Looking earnestly into the very depths of her dark, expressive eyes, he noticed a glistening tear. "What," he passionately exclaimed, "troubles you, my beautiful betrothed? Why this tear? You surely do not regret our engagement? Tell me, dear Enola, what causes your heart to feel heavy? This, of all other times, when everybody should smile; this, the advent, as the Christians say, of their Redeemer. You have some secret sorrow that you never wrote me; do not have any concealments from one who loves you so devotedly, who has your every interest at heart, but speak your thoughts to me."

Enola (leading him to a chair, for they were still
standing) said : "Claude, what I am about to say pains
me as much as it can you ('What can be the matter?'
thought Claude); I should have kept you posted in regard to papa's feelings toward you, but oh, Claude, I
could not bear to cause you one pang; hence I concealed everything from you till our meeting."

"I do not understand you, Enola, for I have every
proof your father desired and requested me to procure
to satisfy him as to who I am. My credentials are good.
Don't be so distressed; it will all come out right. As
soon as I see Col. Baring I can satisfy him in regard
to everything he wishes to know. Did you give him
mother and sisters' letter to read, Enola?"

"No, Claude, I did not," replied Enola, "for several reasons, which I will explain. Papa, I am thoroughly convinced, will never consent to our marriage.
He refused to read any letters from you or any of your
family. You don't know my father's peculiar disposition, or his unforgiving feeling toward you. He will
not listen to reason, Claude, and since I ascertained
that he was so bitter toward you, especially, I have
never discussed the subject with him. I have been
constantly at school since you left, with the exception
of two months' vacation spent at Birchwood."

"Have you seen your aunt, Mrs. Thorne, lately?"
said Claude, "she might aid you in a reconciliation
with your father toward me."

"Oh, no, "replied Enola, "Aunt Nannie Thorne
never liked papa, and as he never particularly admired
her the influence that she could have over him would

not have much weight. We will have to meet him together, and I will now excuse myself a few moments
and let him know that you are here.''

Enola left the room to search for her father. She
met Harry in the hall, and told him that Claude was
sitting in the parlor. Harry immediately joined him,
and was only too happy to welcome him back to
Meadowville. After a half hour of nervous anxiety,
on the part of Claude, Enola returned, saying:

''Papa will be in to meet you, within the next ten
minutes.'' All chatted pleasantly, until Col Baring
walked into the room. He offered his hand to
Claude, but with freezing dignity welcomed him, appearing quite surprised to think that he should leave
his sunny home at *this* season of the year, and seek so
frigid a clime. Claude in his quiet, gentlemanly manner, assured him that as he had spent several years in
a northern climate, he rather preferred the chilling
winds to the sultry sun.

''How long do you expect to remain in Meadowville?'' asked Col. Baring.

''I can scarcely answer that question, Colonel, as
my visit here is both for pleasure and business,'' answered Claude.

After some few other remarks, Claude proposed to
Harry to drive down with him to Cloverdale, to see
Mrs. Thorne and the young ladies. It was a cold
frosty day, and the horse and cutter glided along so
smoothly that one could hardly perceive that the sleigh
was moving. Arriving at Cloverdale amid a blinding
snow-storm, Claude and Harry with but very little

persuasion consented to remain over night, and not
face the snow for a ten-mile drive. The house
was warm and cozy, and after a most enjoyable
six-o'clock Christmas dinner the party retired to
the music-room, where "May" sang some exquisite
little ballads. She had a plantive voice and sang with
much feeling and pathos. She was a bright, dear little
girl, and won many hearts. Bertha, a regular romp,
toyed and played pranks upon old and young. Claude
and Harry were fond of both the girls, and always
enjoyed to the fullest extent the time passed in their
charming society.

Claude and Enola's engagement was freely discussed
by the whole family. At length he resolved to lay
his case once more before Col. Baring, regardless
of consequences; he was determined to do his duty.
Accordingly he visited Enola the following day, and
imparted to her what he intended to do. With her
consent they both agreed to be present when he
talked with her father upon the subject, and to decide
upon something more definite for the future. Enola
soon sought the latter, and making known to him
Claude's desire to have a conversation with him, he
followed her into the parlor, where the dreaded Claude
sat like a statue.

"Did you wish to see me, Mr. Vernon?" coldly
asked Col. Baring.

"I did, sir," as coldly replied Claude Vernon.

"What is the nature of your business, sir?" he
asked.

Claude (in quite an excited manner, for it was

almost more than his timid nature at this moment could endure) answered: "Col. Baring, Enola told me that you did not wish to accept any credentials from me, nor did you approve of our engagement; now, Col. Baring, when I left here, you treated me very nicely, and said that if I could satisfy you·of my worthiness of your daughter's hand and heart, that at some future day we could be married. Now, you perfectly ignore me and all of my family. You will not even read a beautiful letter my devoted mother has written to Enola, in which she gives our family pedigree and social standing. I appeal to you as a gentleman, Col. Baring, do you think that this is treating me with justice—not even permitting me to vindicate my family or myself?"

Col. Baring, in a freezing manner, replied: "I did not think, sir, that love, or imaginary love like yours, would ever ripen into anything serious. Enola is too young to think of marriage. Beside that, you are not the style of man I wish my daughter to espouse. I am sure it will not cause the death of either, to part and never meet again."

"Col. Baring," retorted Claude, "I am astonished at your remarks. They are cruel in the extreme. Can you read *my* heart, or the heart of your innocent young daughter, that *you* should be the judge of our feelings? No, Col. Baring, you have wronged me from the beginning, and I can never receive justice at your hands."

And rising to take his departure, but being prevented by Enola, stood for a moment in silence.

6

"Oh, papa," cried Enola, "how can you treat him
in such a manner, when he has acted so honorably toward
you? He is a perfect gentleman, and does not merit
such treatment, especially from *you*, papa."

In an imperative manner Col. Baring bade Enola
retire to her room. At the same time, addressing himself to Claude, he said: "Mr. Vernon, your visits to
my daughter will no longer be agreeable to me, sir,
and I desire you, from this moment, to banish all
thoughts from your mind of ever making her your
wife, however foolish she may be to wish to become
so."

"Col. Baring, one word more I propose to say to
you on this all-important subject. *That none other
than Enola will ever be my wife.* Good morning, Col.
Baring," said Claude.

He hastily drew from his pocket a slip of paper,
and standing on the great cold marble porch, he
wrote:

"MY DEAR ENOLA: I must see you to-day. Get your
brother Harry to bring you to your aunt's, and I will
meet you there. In haste.   Lovingly,

"Dec. —, 18—.   CLAUDE."

Handing the slip of paper to "Chloe" (who stood
on the porch) to give it to her mistress, he was
soon driving at a rapid rate toward the village, a
miserable man, his mind completely at sea as to the
best course to pursue. He had come to Meadowville
with the full determination of marrying Enola, and
had advised his family to that effect when leaving

home, supposing that all matters had been satisfactorily arranged with him.

Enola sought Harry, bearing the little note in her hand; she soon made known their wishes to him, he fully agreeing to anything she suggested. He loved his sister tenderly and was wretched whenever he saw a shadow resting upon her fair face. It was arranged that they should go to Cloverdale as Claude had suggested.

Mrs. Thorne, Enola knew, would come to her relief and advise her for her own good: she having daughters herself, could know just how she would act under similar circumstances.

Let the reader go with me—it will be no intrusion—and listen to this family group discussing the pros and cons of this all-absorbing topic just now.

"Mrs. Thorne," said Claude, "we have sought you for advice in this matter. We have explained fully our dilemma, and knowing your strong clear mind, feel secure in trusting to your judgment wholly."

"Since you ask my advice, I freely give it," said Mrs. Thorne, "and want you to feel, Enola, that your interest is as dear to me as that of my own daughter's, and I would not advise you wrongfully, for I know if any misfortune were to befall you or Claude, you would ever reflect upon me. I must be guarded how I give counsel upon so grave a subject. Now listen to me attentively, both Claude and Enola. I feel," she continued, "that you have done what every obedient and respectful child should do, under the circumstances. Mr. Vernon, you have acted honorably, and Enola I fully estimate

your worth. You are a girl of great firmness and
strong will-power—once your mind is fully convinced
of right—I know, with undaunted courage you act.
Now, I believe when two young persons love as ardently as Claude and yourself, they should marry.
I would seek my father once again, and tell him
plainly of my intentions, and if he still persists in refusing the boon I ask, then put your *will*-power into
force and demand your rights. You are both, my
children, young, your prospects glowingly bright, and
if you will be true to yourselves and to each other,
your fate will be happy; but, on the contrary, if
either of you deceive the other, naught but misery and
wretchedness will be your portion the remainder of
your life. The wife has her duties, binding upon her;
these neglected, will be ruinous. The husband has his
demands to fulfill; if both do their part no discord
can ever arise between husband and wife. They must
have full confidence in each other. Without this,
there can be but little happiness. I think now,
if you both follow the advice I have given you, that
you can have no fear for the future. May God bless
you, my children." Harry sat listening attentively to
all his aunt had said, and endorsed the ideas advanced
by her.

"Well, Aunt Nannie," said Enola, "I will return
to Birchwood, and will have a long, kind talk with
papa, and then advise you of our future plans."

Enola was seated in her father's room, before a
glowing hickory fire. A bright and cheery room,
with very many pleasant surroundings to place

one's mind at ease. The day was one of those peculiarly chilling days, that appeared to freeze the very marrow when exposed to such piercing winds, though the pale rays of the sun tried in vain to do their duty. Enola looking so sweet and pretty with downcast eyes addressed her father, for she dreaded this conversation.

"Papa," she said affectionately, "have you forgiven me, if I have done you a wrong?"

"I have not been offended with you, my darling daughter," he kindly answered.

"O papa," she continued, "why have you taken such a dislike to Claude Vernon?"

"My child, you are now asking me a question cal-calculated to arouse my indignation. I do not care to hear Mr. Vernon's name mentioned."

"But, papa, however painful this subject may be to you, I must defend the man I intend to marry. You have not given Claude a fair opportunity to convince you of his worth. He does not wish I should marry him without your approbation, but since you will not reason upon this, to us, important subject we will be constrained to act with more determination of character than you suppose I possess."

"What," said Col Baring, "do you propose to elope and marry this strange youth, without my consent? Never, no, never, can I see a man so utterly unworthy, marry you, with my consent;" and Col. Baring grew livid in the face. "I have loved you, Enola, as few fathers love their children; all my hopes have been centered in you, and until you knew this *stranger*, you

never caused me an anxious moment. Now, all is unhappiness and sorrow for me in the future. Begone
from my presence, Enola, and woe be to you if you
ever marry Claude Vernon. An *irate father's curses
will rest upon you.*"

"Enola, weeping bitterly, fell at her father's feet
and implored him to forgive her if she had wounded
his feelings, but he pushed her from him in anger
and hurriedly left the room, and her to her own sad
reflections, and in an evil moment just then she vowed
to marry Claude at all hazard. Had Col. Baring
counseled with her differently, she might have yielded
to his advice, but Enola, inclined to be a little self-
willed and indulged to a great extent, became aroused
to Claude's wrongs and full of sympathy for him, resolved to listen to his earnest entreaties and elope with
him. So, after she recovered from her spell of bitter
weeping, with a burning headache she penned two letters, one to Claude Vernon and the other to her aunt,
Mrs. Thorne. In due time the letters arrived at their
destination, with contents most carefully noted. Claude
could not again visit Birchwood, but daily a letter in
some manner from him found its way into Enola's
hands, and almost the entire remainder of their meet-
ings were arranged by proxy.

Col. Baring had studiously avoided his daughter, but
meeting her alone in the library one morning, he ac-
costed her in the following manner:

"I hope, Enola, you have concluded to be influenced
by your good common sense, and have studied your
own heart, and upon mature reflection have decided to

give up this young man. He is unworthy of you, my child, and should you ever be so reckless as to unite your fate with his, you will spend the remainder of your days in repining. He is a man that will soon grow weary of you, and cast your love aside for others. Enola, you are young, and ignorant of the wiles and vices of this cold and heartless world. Remember, my child, when you entrust your happiness, your life and everything to another, and leave the paternal roof against your parent's will, there can be no brightness in the future for you; nothing but remorse, remorse, black remorse. Weigh well the step of matrimony before taking it," he said.

Enola remained sadly quiet until she could listen no longer to her father traducing Claude.

"Papa," she pleadingly said, "you wound me sorely. I love Claude Vernon, and, oh, you do not know what bitter pangs rend my heart to hear you speak so cruelly of him—one who has never injured you in any manner or form. Papa, it is not just, and you are only—but unconsciously—urging or driving me to disobedience. I also love you, but—"

" I will not permit you in my presence, willful girl, to defend a man I despise. So no more from you on the subject. I have warned you, and already I feel that my curses are resting upon you. Take your own disobedient course;" he said, and hastily left the library.

Enola, more wretched than pen can describe, sought Harry, her panacea. After a long and earnest conversation between the devoted brother and sister, Harry left for Meadowville, to bear a note to Claude in answer to his proposition. What a terrible conflict is passing, between love and duty, in poor Enola's heart. She does not wish to cause her father any pain, or does she wish to disobey him, yet most keenly she feels and appreciates the injustice with which he had treated Claude. With a woman's true devotion she loves Claude Vernon, and from the very innermost recesses of her heart, love for him has quietly crept and prompted her to acts of defence in his behalf.

CHAPTER V.

IT was the hour when slumbering nature became absorbed in stillness and darkness—not a sound to mitigate the obfuscation that surrounded this quiet country home, save the barking of the ever faithful watch-dog, Nero, who braved the northern winds to keep vigil over Birchwood and its sleeping inmates.

Hush! What sound is that vibrating through the midnight air? Only the ringing of the horses' hoofs upon the hard, frozen earth as the wagon is driven cautiously round to the side gate to receive Enola's trunks. Never before did faithful Nero practice his lungs so vigorously. Never had Col. Baring slept so soundly; in Lethean's arms he did repose.

It was a bitter cold night. The wintry blast sang its chilling, weird song, and echoed back from tree to tree its desolate notes as if in mockery of Birchwood scenes. The frosted panes of glass, in ferns, flowers and scenes, sketched with nature's pencil, speak plainly how the thermometer stands.

"Oh, Harry," whispered Enola, "I am so cold; I am so cold. Will I be able to reach the carriage that stands at the great road gate?"

"Yes," kindly spoke Harry. "Brave up, my dear sister; we are almost there, and once safely in the carriage you will become warm. The wind is very piercing, particularly after nightfall."

"Harry, I am having a chill, I fear, a nervous chill," she said.

"Take this heavy shawl I have and wrap it closely around your quivering form," said Harry.

"Harry, it is my disobedience to papa. Will he ever forgive me?"

This conversation occurred during the walk from the house down the lawn to the waiting carriage, where Claude Vernon sat, anxiously watching for Enola and Harry. No sooner had he noticed the forms peering through the icy, leafless wood, than with a bound he sprang to Enola's side and bore her almost prostrate form to the carriage. A moment more, and the party were rapidly being driven down the hard, frozen road to Gersterville, where Claude Vernon was to lead to the sacred marriage altar, Enola Baring.

Harry, ever the devoted brother, could not bear the thought of his sister being driven to such desperation that her marriage had to be consummated in such a manner; yet he, as a true brother, pledged himself to accompany them wherever they went. True to his word, his sister's happiness was his only thought. Several times in the flight Enola gave up in despair, and by his cheering words, her timid nature had strength to brave the worst.

Safely reaching Gersterville, the bridal party at once drove to the hotel, where a minister of St. John's Episcopal Church was summoned to perform the solemn ceremony that would make Claude Vernon and Enola Baring man and wife. A sad and imposing obligation, so lightly entered into by too many of the present age.

Claude had promised to love and cherish his wife; Enola had vowed before the three or four witnesses, with God's all-seeing eye resting upon this act, to love and obey Claude. Yes,

"I said I would love thee in sickness, in health,
    Through clouds and through sunshine, in poverty—wealth.
    Then doubt not my love, though my spirit be weak,
    The vows I have taken I never will break."

After the Rev. Dr. White had pronounced the sacred vows and congratulations, he said : "My children, you are, from all appearances, very youthful; you have taken upon yourselves the grave responsibility of marriage. The married state is not a road strewn with roses, smiles and love always, but it, too, has its cares and sorrows. From this clandestine marriage it seems that you have deceived your parents, and as a father in Christ I appeal to you both, my children, to never deceive each other in the most trivial events connected with life. Love, happiness and prosperity will then be your portion. May God's choicest blessings ever rest upon you. Let us have a moment of prayer before I part from you," said the Rev. Dr. White.

"O divine Father, since it has been Thy will to join by fate this young couple, Enola Baring and Claude Vernon, in the holy bands of matrimony, we beseech Thee, O blessed Father, that it may please Thee to continue Thy blessings upon them, watching and guarding them continually from dangers and from the various temptations that must surely come to all. Be with them as they traverse the pathway of life together,

and finally, after this life is ended, take them to Thy
heavenly fold. We ask in the name of our blessed
Redeemer. Amen.''

The party then dispersed to their respective homes,
while Claude, Enola and Harry busied themselves for
their journey southward, the future home of Enola.
Dressed in her closely fitting traveling suit of dark seal-
brown cloth, with hat and gloves to correspond, she
looked the perfect type of beauty. Her complexion
of dazzling brilliancy was admired by every one, and
often Claude would ask his wife to draw down her veil
that the inquisitive stranger might not feast his eyes
upon her beauty.

Reader, go with me to the home of Col. Baring;
a perfect scene of anxious dismay. Breakfast being
announced, neither Enola nor Harry could be found.
In vain the servants flew from room to room, to be
disappointed in their fruitless search. Each of the
house-servants were arraigned and closely questioned,
but no one knew anything about the missing trio. At
length, in wild despair, Col. Baring sent a messenger
to Meadowville, to inquire if his daughter could be
with any of her lady friends. No trace of her, only
a small impress of a No. 1 shoe in the snow told the sad
tale of her elopement: but Col. Baring would believe
nothing of the kind; his own devoted child would not
leave her happy home, to risk her fate and happiness
with almost a stranger. He said, "*never, never,*"
and in utter wretchedness he walked the long hall floor
muttering to himself words of the keenest agony.

"I shall never, no never, see my own loved Enola

again ; she is forever gone, gone from me; can I live without her? It is like tearing out my heart to think her married to one so unworthy of her. I know he will not be kind to her. And oh! such a sensitive nature she unfortunately has. Can she, my Enola, brave the storms of life? Can she bear neglect and harsh treatment from this man? No, her pure young life will soon fall a victim to her unwise choice, and in despair will pass out, like the blighted rose. Poor chld.''

At length his grief changed to anger and he vowed to never again see her, to disinherit her, forever banish her from a heart she had so cruelly deceived. Gene and neighbor-friends tried to console him, but in vain. His heart was sorely tried; he could not bring himself to think Enola would so willfully disobey him, until a friend or an acquaintance handed him a newspaper containing the following paragraph:

"Married, on December—— 18——, at Gersterville, by the Rev. C. L. White; Enola, daughter of Col. Wm. Baring, of Meadowville, Kentucky, to Claude M. Vernon, of New Orleans, La. Long live the happy couple.''

It passed through Col. Baring's heart like an electric shock. All hope sank now within him; she was beyond his reach.

"Poor child, how I feel for her! but I will yet live to see her return to me in distress and poverty. Can I then refuse her shelter? can I turn away from my precious child and leave her to struggle among strangers? can I banish the sweet memories of the past? No, no,'' and burying his face in his hands he wept long and bitterly; it was the wail of an agonized father's heart.

"How keener than a serpent's tooth 'tis to have a thankless child. In one single day all my fondest hopes blasted; for I had pictured much joy in my dear child's society, I had given up all to accumulating riches that she might enjoy."

It was not altogether a selfish feeling that caused Col. Baring to feel so acutely the wrong, but he loved his daughter with great tenderness, and being greatly prejudiced against Mr. Vernon, magnified the injustice until a frenzied state of mind completely took possession of his unrelenting condition.

"I can only now seek happiness in living over memories of the past. Wife long since resting in her lonely bed, and daughter torn from me by the insidious artifice of a stranger. I wish I were a christian; I could then seek comfort in my religion; but alas, my deep afflictions have made me rebellious, and strange to say, carried me farther away from God, filling my soul with doubts and scepticism."

"Gene," said Col. Baring, "I have resolved to leave Kentucky as soon as I can profitably dispose of Birchwood. All, everything reminds me so of the past. If I wander into the parlor, Enola is there; I cannot look upon Nickema but a sadness o'erpowers me; all, all are sad reminders of the past. I can never again enjoy that fullness of contentment I did of yore, when Enola was with us. Alas! poor child, she is no doubt thinking of Birchwood this moment. I long to fly to some far-away country."

"Oh, father," said Gene, "you will in course of time become reconciled to your troubles and look upon life differently. I blame Harry for influencing sister to take such a step."

·'Yes," said Col. Baring, "Harry no oouot accompanied them in their flight, for he, too, is gone."

Steaming down upon the bosom of the Father of Rivers, on board the floating palace "Stonewall," was a bridal party consisting of three persons. All seemed apparently happy, but the young wife would, unobserved, steal quietly to her own state-room and give vent to the bitterest weeping. Strange coincidence for a bride to weep, but remorse of conscience seemed to haunt her and she could only find comfort in tears. "Claude," she said, "if I could only see papa and clasp him to my disobedient heart and ask his forgiveness, it would be the delight of my soul. It would lift an indescribable burden from my mind; only think of his desolation."

"Enola, you should not feel so distressed. Remember how your father treated both you and me. He will not grieve long for you."

"Oh, Claude, do not speak so against my deeply wronged parent. You will drive me mad," she continued; "I am drifting away from all that was dear to me at home; I am longing to have papa say he forgives me; longing to fall upon his bosom and ask to be forgiven. Several times I have resolved to write to him, but my heart each time has failed me, but some day, Claude, when I am in an agonized frame of mind, I *will* write him and ask his forgiveness."

"Noble, forgiving girl," said Claude. "Do you think, Enola, that I cannot provide for your wants and pleasures as well as your father?"

"Oh, yes, my own Claude, I never doubted you or your ability; it is remorse I am suffering from. Did I treat my only parent right in this act of disobedience to his wishes? And then, Claude, almost the last thing papa said to me was, 'my curses will rest upon you;' and you know that was a dreadful imprecation, wasn't it?"

"Well, Enola," said Claude, "you must not permit your mind to dwell upon the past; only look to the bright and happy future before you. Think of your home amid loved ones, each one willing to add to your happiness; all my friends will love you, and your life will be one long sunny dream, my love, so constant will be the foundation to build your hopes upon. So cheer up."

A week spent pleasantly on board the "Stonewall" brought the party safely to their destination — the "Crescent City," or City of Flowers. Garden spot of fruits and roses, bright and sunny homes to gladden the heart, with loving friends to greet them, all joined in to add pleasure to the newly wedded pair.

Loving mother and father, with charming sisters and brothers, make the Vernon family complete, and Enola, true to all the noble impulses that go to form a good woman, soon became very fond of Claude's family. She frequently expressed to Harry her fondness for them, and often exclaimed to Claude: "If I only had papa's forgiveness I would be so blessed. Every-

"STONEWALL" ARRIVING AT NEW ORLEANS.

thing would look so differently to me; the flowers would smell more fragrant, the birds would sing more merrily, and I would feel happier.''

After weeks and months passed in gay revelry, admiring all the beauties of this charming city—this tropical city, so different in every respect to Mrs. Vernon's former home—kind manners, abounding love, with every other attraction to endear her to her new sphere, still her heart yearned to be forgiven. No kind letter yet from papa. "Has he forgotten me?" was her daily question asked.

Days and weeks unconsciously rolled by, surrounded by many things to bring contentment. Notwithstanding, the dreaded season—to the unacclimated—will soon be upon them.

"Enola,' said Harry, "you know that you and I are strangers in this tropical clime; we are not acclimated, and we will necessarily have to hie away to some northern country, to escape from old "yellow-jack."

"Oh, how I wish we could return to Birchwood," "but papa has forgotten me," she mournfully said.

Reader, have you ever experienced one of those hot, dry days, indigenous to a southern country—the air a simoon? It was upon one of those peculiar days that Claude Vernon returned home from business much earlier than his usual custom. He was greatly agitated, having heard there were several cases of yellow fever in the city. He was most desirous to send his wife away to some healthy retreat.

7

"I wish you to prepare yourself as soon as possible to go with Harry to some locality out of the city."

"Why?" inquired Enola innocently.

"Because," said Claude, "neither you nor Harry are acclimated to this hot, feverish climate."

"Very well," she replied. "Mother Vernon, will you accompany me down street to-morrow, to make some purchases?"

"Certainly," replied her mother-in-law.

The following morning, bright and early, the ladies wended their way to the dry goods stores, and soon made the necessary purchases, and returned home as quickly as possible, as Enola complained of a very singular aching in all her bones, different from anything she had ever experienced before. She grew steadily worse, and by evening had a raging, burning fever, cheeks a flushed scarlet, and pulse very high. She could not divine the cause of this sudden illness. Claude, with many an anxious foreboding, knew too well what it meant; he had seen too many cases like hers. She rapidly grew worse. Dr. Chanfra was called in, and pronounced it a violent case of yellow fever. By midnight, Enola was raving with delirium. She called for her father constantly, and begged for a cooling draught of water from the running spring at Birchwood. Three physicians constantly attended her bedside, and for five long days her life hung upon a thread, the silvery cord liable at any moment to be snapped asunder. Tender and loving hands administered to her, in vain trying to relieve her sufferings, and every means on earth, all medical skill, was resorted to, to restore her to health, and snatch her from death's cold embrace.

Dr. Chanfra had told Mr. Vernon that if his wife could only live till past the midnight hour she would recover, as that would be the crisis. With what silent anxiety the friends watched and waited for the dreaded hour. Just before the great town clock chimed the twelve strokes that spoke the time, Enola sprang up in her bed, declaring her mother (who had been dead for years) was in the room with a host of angels. What a beautiful smile suffused her face, as she in her wild feverish vision saw the spirit of her departed mother.

"She lives," said Mrs. Vernon to her son, "the crisis is past, your sister will now recover, Mr. Baring," she encouragingly said.

The color had left Enola's cheeks, and she lay upon her bed of illness very weak and exhausted from her struggle between life and death. Life, the victor this time. As soon as she became convalescent she inquired for two or three young lady friends, and wanted to know why they were not to see her during her illness. Not dreaming the cause of her sickness, when her friends told her that they were dead, that they had died with yellow fever, and Claude said :

" Enola, you too have had the dreaded scourge, and thanks be to God, you are spared to me, for oh, Enola, had you been taken away from me, I never could have forgiven myself for having kept you in the city so long."

" Did any one write to papa and let him know I was ill?" she inquired.

"Yes, Harry wrote him all about your dangerous illness, and we are daily expecting an answer from him. He will surely answer Harry's letter, and when my Enola hears from her father she will be happy, won't she?"

There is joy in the Vernon household, for Enola has just received an affectionate letter from her father, in reply to one written by Harry. The letter ran as follows :

MY LONG-ABSENT DAUGHTER : — It is with feelings of the deepest anxiety I write you, my loved child. I did not learn of your illness until you were convalescing. I want you as soon as you are sufficiently strong to come, with Mr. Vernon and Harry, to Birchwood. Come, feeling that all is forgiven. Let bygones be bygones. I long to clasp you to my heart, my child. I know you will enjoy your country home once again. Everything is just as you left it, waiting for your return. I shall expect each one of you to accept of my invitation. Enola, Claude and Harry, as soon as you can consistently do so, *come.*

With love to all, your devoted father,

WILLIAM BARING.

Wild with delight, Enola could scarcely wait to gain strength, so as to enable her to fly to her forgiving father.

"Oh, Claude, I always told you that some day papa would forgive me. He is so kind and good. I shall now improve so rapidly in health that we can all soon be ready for the journey.

"I will go with you up to your father's," said Claude, " but can only remain a short time, on account of my business claiming my attention here, but you can stay until the autumn, and I will return and accompany you back to our cozy little home."

All the necessary arrangements were made for the expected journey, and once on the great swelling stream, the three will soon arrive at their destination. With many a tourist on this water palace, and many a happy heart, none enjoyed more ardently the trip than Claude and Enola. Many pleasures were planned and joys discussed.

Safely on shore again, the merry party now have to take the old stage-coach, that plods its way up the turnpike road to Meadowville. A quiet road, with no changes within the last few years, visible fields, farm-houses and meadows dot the wayside; acres of golden wheat, ready for the harvest. Reapers, mowers and binders, all busy gathering in the grain from Kentucky's richest soil. When once it is garnered, the farmer feels his wealth is in his barn.

As the stage-coach nears the village of Meadowville, Enola's heart pulsates rapidly—not that she expects to meet her father in the town, but the very idea of once more being at " home."

Col. Baring, knowing the time the coach would be due, ordered the carriage to be driven up to meet them at the hotel. He did not care to gratify the curiosity of an idle throng that daily crowded around the stage-coach and hotel. Did you ever observe what interest a lonely stage-coach's entry into an inland village pro-

duces? Every one eager to hear the news. Well, be
it so.

Birchwood, with its broad woodlands, its graveled
road, leading from the great heavy gate down to the
mansion, is in sight. Flower-beds, full of blooming,
richly tinted tulips, hyacinths, pansies, and a score of
other plants dot the garden, and add beauty to this
enchanted place. When Enola was once within her
father's enclosure, she insisted upon walking through
the thick, green grass, and being met by Col. Baring,
she fell into his arms, a forgiven daughter. Claude
and Harry alike receive a hearty welcome from him.

He kindly extended his hand to Claude, saying,
" Mr. Vernon—I mean my son Claude, I wish you to
make yourself perfectly at home. Harry, my son, I,
too, welcome you back. All, all are my prodigal
children," he said, smiling. " I must say, Enola,"
addressing himself to her, " that this is (with one exception) the happiest moment of my life."

The family servants, too, all had to crowd around
to see their young mistress, Enola.

" La, bless my soul;" chimed in old Aunt Mima, the
housekeeper, " Miss 'Nola looks the same. That way-
off, strange country hab'nt changed you a bit."

Chloe stood gazing with rapturous delight into Miss
Enola's face. All Birchwood rejoiced. Gene was
absent from home, but would soon return. He, too,
longed to see his sister, and extend a welcome to her.

After a moment's quiet from the clatter and confusion, incident upon their return, Col. Baring said:
" My daughter, here are the keys to your room, your

piano, your guitar-box and dressing-case. Everything
is at your command. You have many competent servants to wait upon you to do your bidding. I have
never entered your room since you left, only to have
it ventilated and renovated. I trust you will find all
your things just as you left them."

"Claude," he continued, "there are, in my stables,
my horses, which are at your command; my gun and
dogs, and everything to make you enjoy yourself."

"Thanks—oh, thanks, Col. Baring," Claude replied. "I can only remain a few weeks with you all,
as my urgent business demands my attention at home."

Col. Baring, although a wealthy but cautious man,
was not willing to entrust a large amount of money in
his son-in-law's hands until the future revealed to him
what kind of a business man he made.

Capt. Vernon (the father of Claude) was a noble old
sea captain, greatly beloved by all who knew him—a
warm-hearted and generous man. Enola had become
very fond of him, and often enjoyed short sea trips
with him. When reverses of fortune came like a rushing avalanche upon him, he bore up so manfully under
the calamity, that at the earnest solicitation of Claude
and Enola he accepted an invitation to come and live
with them, hoping to be able to engage in some lucrative business in the near future by which he could build
up his lost fortune.

Capt. Vernon loved his family, and his heavy losses
distressed him only on their account. Owing to the high
standing of the Vernon family, Claude procured a lucrative position in "Municipal Hall;" he became pop-

ular and led a gay life, mingling in the very best society, until his mind became dazed at the brilliancy of
the fashionable world. His hours were passed away
from home and his wife; her anxious and loving heart
yielded to his seeming neglect, and her isolation found
solace only in weeping. Each day brought its petty
little cares to her. One day Claude came in and announced to her that urgent business connected with his
father demanded his immediate presence down on the
southern coast of Florida.

"How it distresses me, Claude," she replied, "to see
you leave me, for it does appear to me that we are separated so many long hours each day."

"I will not remain away long, my dear wife. It is
my bounden duty to look after my father's interest
since his unfortunate failure."

Enola felt sad at his departure, but her own true womanly heart consented for him to go, and after fond
adieus he embarked on board a steamer bound for
Tampa Bay. After several weeks' absence, with no
tidings from her husband, Enola, sick at heart and anxious in mind over Claude's seeming neglect, she finally
sought his friends to know if they had any news from
him. Capt. Brown said he had learned through a sailor
just from the southern coast of Florida, that Claude
was very ill down at Tampa Bay. Enola no sooner
learned this sad intelligence than she determined to go
at once to her sick husband, despite the many earnest
protestations of her relatives not to do so rash an act;
but she knew her duty and commenced her necessary
preparations for the journey. "I know my duty to

TAMPA BAY.

my husband," she constantly replied to entreating
friends, " and as no regular steamer leaves port before
Tuesday morning, I will embark on board the schooner
' Ringgold' that leaves to-night." In those primitive
days, thoughts could not be expressed upon the flashing wires.   How earnestly Harry plead with her not to
go; not to venture upon so unpleasant as well as hazardous a voyage, for, said he, " those little crafts, borne
only along by the wind, are at the mercy of the breezes
when they can reach their destination, for sometimes
they are known to lie at rest for days without one
movement in any direction." At last, his reasoning
powers having no influence over his sister's determined
will, he gracefully yielded to her desire and saw her
safely on board the schooner " Ringgold."   Six other
passengers (with the necessary crew), two ladies and
four gentlemen, were all that had taken passage on
the desolate craft.   Once on the vessel her heart
bounded with joy at the prospect of so soon being with
her loved husband; she longed for the schooner to ride
the waves and rapidly bear her to Claude and her destination, for she had already pictured him upon his bed
of sickness among strangers, with no loving hand to
administer to his wants, or bathe his fevered brow.   It
was her first experience on board such a vessel.   She did
not know the danger or realize the discomfort.   It was
truly a trying time to the " Ringgold;" for fourteen
long, sultry days that little vessel rode the gulf waters
and, sad to relate, had only made about twenty miles
in that length of time.
  Capt. Johnson was greatly annoyed at what the

old sailors called "becalmed." He felt for his lady passengers, especially the young and deathly sea-sick Mrs. Vernon, who finally became so ill from ship-fever that she could not travel any further without periling her life ; so Capt. Johnson, a most kind and considerate man, deemed it best to run into St. Marks, and send Mrs. Vernon ashore. Always "a calm before a storm" is a true and old adage; not a flying cloud visible in the boundless azure sky. How well the bred and born sailor knows when a storm is approaching ; even days before it reaches them, they are perfect barometers. Enola, scarcely able to leave the vessel, was slowly led up to the hotel near by on the beach, where every comfort was given her; for a few days she was very ill from sea-fever, but the healthful winds, laden with the odor of turpentine, blended with the sweet-scented wild roses, soon restored her to such a condition of health that she began to watch out for a steamer to bear her yet on her journey. For two days a violent storm had been raging on the Gulf of Mexico ; hundreds of people had fallen victims to its angry waves, that washed and lashed the islands, until all perished who unfortunately resided on the lowlands or distant isles.

It was a dark and starless night. The heavy leaden sky was ominous of no good; the guests in "Hotel Pine" were silently (and as they supposed securely) slumbering, when the landlord was suddenly aroused by the most fearful and unearthly warning, resembling the sound just previous to an earthquake. It soon became appalling, this deep sullen cannonading

BAYOU NEAR ST. MARKS.

as it were. All in the house were aroused, and rapidly prepared to escape, for their lives were in jeopardy in a few moments, and with great power the surging, rushing waters of the briny Gulf came pouring into and over the roofs of the houses of the village. The people, all greatly alarmed, had to flee to the highlands to save their lives. Even the third stories of the buildings soon became submerged. In great fear and trepidation Enola plead to be saved : she rushed to Mr. Baird, an old resident of the Gulf coast, who boarded in "Hotel Pine," to protect her from this awful death that now wildly stared her in the face.

'Mrs. Vernon,'' he said, "do not be so alarmed. I have a life-boat at the window, I am a good oarsman, and it is my earnest desire and intention to save you, with my own wife and child. I admit that our situation is a precarious one, but I can row us safely out among the pine forest, away from the angry Gulf now threatening our lives. We can soon be beyond the high tide,'' he continued. The ladies bravely stepped into that little life-boat, placing their lives in the hands of the great Omnipotent, and invoking His mercy. The night was inky blackness, and not a sound to be heard but the angry billows rushing on and on to fill their purpose and do their deadly work ; destruction, destruction to everything that perchance should be in their way. In the fearful darkness of that awful night, never to be forgotten, Enola vowed to give herself to God, for surely He could not speak in grander tones of His mightiness, and at the same time His power to save, if we will but trust Him. Mr. Baird, with Mr.

Sands' assistance, groped their boat-way as best they could to the highland pine forests, where the terrified party would find a haven from the angry waves. The sealark shrieked its midnight cry at such a feast of water, when all domestic animals fled in wild dismay before the raging flood; some to find a watery grave and others to satiate the appetite of the dreaded shark. Such water-storms, though rare, were viewed with great horror in those days long ago; but in the present age cyclones more awful in their fury than my feeble pen can describe, are of such frequent occurrence that man's intellect and scientific knowledge are swallowed up in wonderment at the great electric display in the heavens during a modern cyclone.

As the light of the eastern sky slowly crept above the horizon to sufficiently warn Mr. Baird of the locality that he was in, he took advantage of the morning light, and rapidly steering toward the dry land, the various life-boats could be seen trying to wend their way through sand and debris. Soon he landed his little boat on a high cedar bluff, where the ladies lightly stepped on *terra firma* once more, with hearts full of thankfulness to God for having spared them from the perils of the past awful night.

The gentlemen started out to reconnoiter, and after a few hours' wading through ocean sand and among dying animals, they reported to the ladies that they could venture down to the Hotel Pine, as she had stood the test and braved the storm, but the furniture *all* swept away and ruined. It was indeed a ludicrous as well as doleful sight to notice the inhabitants of St. Marks pulling through the ocean sand to view their demolished homes, many of the less substantial houses having been swept into the sea. It was a sad sight to view the wrecks of once bright and sunny homes, now filled with the finny tribe and creeping reptiles. Many horses that had been overtaken by the angry billows were lying dead upon the beach, with innumerable reptiles crawling through the sand, until it appeared a moving mass. Rattlesnakes with twenty or more rattles, together with the alligators, were lying upon the debris, basking themselves in the morning sun. It was a strange sight and wonderful to Enola, long to be remembered by all who passed through the terrors of that fearful night—a night of horrors never to be forgotten.

Far out upon the waters of the placid Gulf, the blue smoke of a steamer could be seen moving in the direction of St. Marks. Enola immediately arranged her hat and gloves, and sought Mr. Baird, to learn if the vessel would stop at that place. He informed her that it would, and might probably remain until evening. At once Enola decided to engage passage upon her for Tampa Bay, and immediately prepared for her hasty departure. She had been anxiously watching for a steamer since the morning after that memorable and dreadful storm. Again her heart grew light at the thought of seeing Claude. She had not heard from him since his departure, as all communication had been obstructed or cut off. She felt anxious to know his true condition, for he was ill, according to accounts, when she left home. This Cuban steamer would soon

run into Tampa Bay. She moved steadily up to the
wharf, and Enola, with several others, stood waiting
for her to land.

After parting with her new-made acquaintances she
retired to her state-room. A few moments more
and the grand vessel was rapidly ploughing her way
through the briny waters. Enola amused herself by
watching the swarms of porpoises that followed the
ship. She had an infatuation for the sea and its monster inhabitants. She delighted to see the phosphores-
cent light, and compared it with the weird illumina-
tions she had observed in traveling through the depths
of the loamy forest that the rural people style "Jack o'
Lantern," or "Jack with Lantern." It was a calm,
bright morning, "a perfect bridal of earth and sky."
The sun seemed rising from the misty deep, shaking,
as it were, the glistening spray from its golden rays,
and ploughing its way through trackless space, shedding
its yellow sunbeams on all the surroundings. Far away
in the distance the fort could be seen, with a field-
glass : all the passengers were eagerly watching to near
the fort. Enola sat upon the upper deck, hoping to
catch a glimpse of Claude. The captain cried out,
"Round to and stop in front of the fort," now peeping through the live oaks. The gray-green moss, completely enveloping the trees with its twining tresses,
hung in heavy festoons from the burdened limbs, almost
concealing the entire tree from the admiring gaze.
The mellow light reflected from the dancing, sparkling
waves, shed a beautiful softness upon this romantic
picture. As the vessel neared the strongly built fort,

MOSS TREE AND FARM NEAR TAMPA.

that stood a short distance from the bay, filled with soldiers, ready at a moment's warning to " shoulder arms," the steamer fired her great gun, and a wave of handkerchiefs, amid shouts, went up from an hundred voices to welcome her to the fort. Even then, in silence, the war cloud was thickening, that was soon to burst in all its fury upon our glorious, prosperous land. Little did the officers and soldiers think that brethren of the same nationality would so soon be engaged in deadly conflict with each other.

Claude met his wife, and from his own lips she soon learned that he had not been ill. He said he had never enjoyed such perfect health. " We will remain here a few weeks," he said, " since you have passed through so many perils to reach me, and I will return with you to our home. One could spend days, weeks, ah ! years in this heavenly clime, and long to think they had not ten thousand lives to pass in such an ethereal spot."

Tampa Bay, whose banks are fringed with the trailing greenish-gray moss, interspersed with gorgeous tinted flowers that crowd their way through this labyrinth of silken chenille network, presented a scene beautiful in the extreme, for the day-god's golden rays, together with the sublime after-glow, shed its gold and crimson light upon all this, Nature's handiwork, presenting to the admiring gazer a picture never to be forgotten. The strong, rough limbs of the live oak, clothed in its dainty garb of Spanish moss, seemed to ask the curious to " admire me." The mangrove region, with its banks of palmetto and oak, awaken a feeling of interest in this lotus land, and each varying

scene presented new beauties. The background of the
tall, olive-green pine, with the dancing, quivering sun
rays leaping from water to tree, dashing over this, Nature's fairy picture—a weird light, resembling a gauzy
illumination that is frequently seen upon the stage.
Far up the bay gaily painted sail-boats glide through
the tinted and variegated waters ; arousing the eye from
the beautiful only to rest upon as pretty a view.   I can
only compare this tropical country to a fairy land all
the time.   The fish were more than delicious in flavor,
and oysters, though not large, were nice and dainty.
The balmy breezes wafted across the healthful waters
were considered cures for pulmonary diseases, and
many afflicted people had settled upon the bay, expecting to spend the remaining years of life *"right here."*
With the charming society at the fort, together with
the fine fishing and boating, so delightfully did time
pass away that it was with an effort that Claude could
tear himself away from this enchanted sea-girt town.
Pressing business, however, demanded his attention in
New Orleans, and he at last decided to go there forth-
with.

Ere the steamer had landed at the wharf, the news
was heralded that a civil war was imminent, that there
was no possible way of averting the calamity. All true-
blooded southerners would be compelled to defend their
native soil.   Great excitement prevailed among all
classes.

War! war! was the cry from land to land. It was
echoed and re-echoed until the sound was heard by the
storming of Fort Sumter. It is needless to attempt

to give a description of this bloody family quarrel, for able pens and gifted artists have painted it, with all its horrors, until it is stereotyped upon the heart of every true American. That it demoralized this country, none can deny. It estranged many families, and brought about various divorces that otherwise would never have occurred.

Claude Vernon, with his three brothers, anxious to avenge the wrongs of their native soil, as they supposed, joined the southern navy and army, leaving poor Enola, with her little infant daughter, Alcia, only a few weeks old, to battle with the terrible times that are surely coming upon the whole of the southern country. Harry Baring, too weak and feeble to enlist in the defence of his country, promised to stand by and protect his sister and little baby niece, Alcia. Long will the ladies of New Orleans remember the memorable morning when Gen. Butler marched through the streets of that beautiful city of flowers, sun and breezes, commanding everybody to take the oath of allegiance to the United States, and if they refused to obey his command to be banished to any point he chose to send them out into the Confederacy. Silver, gold, diamonds and valuables of every description melted before this moving mass of humanity like snow on Lammas day. Harry placed Enola's jewels and silver plate in a bank, but bank bolts, locks and safes yielded readily to the avaricious worker. Poor Enola, refusing to take the oath of allegiance, was banished from her home, with eleven hundred other southern ladies, each given so many hours to prepare for the life of a refugee.

8

Harry was sadly convinced that the dreaded disease consumption had selected him as its victim. He was deeply distressed at parting with his sister and dear little Alcia, who had become the idol of his heart. He longed to live to see her grown. It was on the broad pier that leads to the Mobile line of boats that Enola, with Alcia, kissed Harry farewell—herself and baby destined for Richmond, Virginia, and Harry Baring returning to his native place, Meadowville, Kentucky.

No one can fully appreciate the lonely, desolate feeling Enola experienced when she found herself a refugee from home, among strangers, with her baby, a delicate little frail teething infant, and not knowing when or where she would meet Claude made her condition more dreary. She quickly sought her state-room and gave way to bitter weeping, until baby's precious tiny fingers wiped away the scalding tears. "Blessed baby, you are the solace, the comfort of my devoted heart, and mamma," she thought, "can endure everything so her charge is comfortable and healthy." Closer and closer the fond mother pressed her little waif to her bosom. "Yes," mused Enola, "I know my darling will be spared to lighten her mother's sorrows, and in her declining years, when her hair, so raven now in color, when bleached with age, my loved daughter, with tender touch and loving heart, will say, 'Mamma, I will bear your trials and sorrows; cast them upon me, dear mamma.'" It is a strange fact that the mother as tenderly loves the homely infant as the beautiful. No mother will grant that her own babe is ugly. They are always beautiful in mother's eyes, but Alcia was

indeed a very, very unprepossessing child, with no redeeming feature save her large brown eyes. They
were expressive and winning. Her mouth, so expansive as to render it expressionless, a little pinched-up
nose, with a perfectly hairless head, she was certainly
a cadaverous-looking infant, *but very beautiful* in
Enola's eyes. It was a charming sight to watch the
devotion of this young mother, so tender, loving and
patient during all the wakeful nights she had passed
with her infant. "Naughty little girl," she said, "can
you ever repay your mother for so much love meted
out to you?"

CHAPTER VI.

WEARY and worn even to sheer exhaustion, Enola was compelled to tarry by the wayside to recuperate before going on her lonely journey to Richmond. Stoping at a small village on the western borders of Virginia, Enola learned that an aunt whom she had not seen for years was a refugee, living in the country a few miles out from the depot at the foot of the hill. Eager to see some kindred face and once more be with relatives, she procured a carriage, and with Alcia, drove into the country in search of Mrs. Randolph (an own sister of Mrs. Baring). Mrs. Randolph did not at first recognize her niece, but a moment more and they were clasped in each other's fond embrace. Enola felt that she was in the presence of one as dear to her as her mother. As the whole country was in a terribly un-unsettled condition, with vast armies of soldiers marching through the invaded land, devouring everything before them, Mrs. Judge Randolph persuaded Enola to remain with her until she heard from Claude. "Oh, aunt, I am so anxious to get a nice nurse girl to attend to Alcia before I continue on my journey," she said, " for I am completely worn out with the care of my babe so constantly." " Dear," said Mrs. Randolph, "I know of a very competent and trusty girl who is a slave belonging to old Gen. Grafton ; I will try and procure her for you, and if you can be so fortunate as to hire

(116)

Florence from Gen. Grafton, you can consider yourself lucky." "Oh, aunt, let me send or go at once for her. Alcia is so fretful that I cannot bear the annoyance of nursing much longer, and am not well myself." Mrs. Randolph jumped into her buggy and was soon on the way to Gen. Grafton's residence to hire Florence. Without much difficulty, the old gentleman consented that Mrs. Vernon should have her for a year, anyway, and exacted the pay for her hire in gold coin, as he contended that neither "greenbacks or confederate bills were any good : worthless, worthless paper stuff," he said, "I would not count it for it." Mrs. Randolph was delighted to turn Florence over to Enola. Little Alcia would have nothing to do with her upon first acquaintance, but in due time her kindness won her little heart, and she soon became warmly attached to her, which relieved her mother greatly.

Time sped on—no letter from Claude; he must be on the battle-field ; any hour he may be killed ; oh, that this cruel war were ended.

After weeks of anxious waiting Enola concluded to venture on to Richmond, the place to which she had been banished. Gen. Lee's army was fighting around the city and through the interior. Surely Claude Vernon must be in that locality. After a great effort Enola succeeded in learning just where he was stationed, and flattering herself that he would be overjoyed at again seeing his wife and infant, she hastily took her departure for Richmond, happy at the thought of so soon being with her husband. Imagine the young wife's pain and distress, at meeting her long-absent hus-

band, to notice his utter indifference to his family.
With a true wife's devotion she implored him to tell
her the cause of his coldness.   She begged him to have
no concealments.

"Oh, Claude," she bitterly cried, "how can you
treat me with such indifference?   Have I done anything
to cause you to cease to love me?   Speak, Claude, or I
shall go mad; my brain is on fire, and I feel that I cannot live and have you not love me as you once did.'

"Enola," he said in the most frigid manner, "why
did you follow me to this place?   What brought you
here, anyway?   Why did you not go to your old father,
instead of coming out here to watch my actions?   He
has plenty of money, and no doubt loves you more than
I do.   You thought to find me loving somebody else,
did you?   Well, I can gratify your womanly curiosity by
telling you that *you* are not the only woman that I
love."

At [this candid confession Enola fell fainting upon
the bed.   Her frail nature and sensitive heart could not
bear this crushing neglect from one she loved so dearly.
It would have melted a heart of stone to see that dutiful young wife, crushed and broken-hearted, with their
innocent little child clinging fondly to her.   Enola, wild
with despair, insisted upon leaving at once and returning to her kind and motherly aunt.

"Never mind about leaving," said Claude Vernon,
"as I am ordered in a few days to join my command,
and you can do as you please."

"Claude Vernon," said Enola, "think how you have
treated me; is this the outcome of your solemn vows

and 'undying love' for me! May God forgive you as freely as I do. I know *all*, now, Claude," she continued; "yes, the little Frenchwoman has won your affections; but the day will come, sooner or later, when you will spurn and despise her for wrecking your life and driving away from you your devoted wife."

It was too true. Claude Vernon had become a reckless man. Certainly he was greatly enamored of a petite Frenchwoman, Louise by name, lovely to behold—as beautiful as a fairy queen—but with a cruel, wicked heart. Truly her beauty proved a curse to her.

Enola, musing—"I am alone again; my name is truly appropriate."

Florence had been so attentive and obedient to Mrs. Vernon that her heart clung to her for sympathy. She grew so fond of her, prompted by her kindness, that Enola treated her more like a companion than a servant. She frequently found herself seeking consolation from her sympathetic heart, for her soul yearned to unbosom its sorrows to one so full of sympathy. Florence was so patient with little Alcia that she (Enola) could but love and appreciate her all the more.

"Miss Enola," said Florence, "I wish you would make up your mind and go back to Mrs. Randolph's. I cannot bear to see you cry all the time. It does make me feel so bad, Miss Enola."

"Florence, you are kind to me, and I love you an need your sympathies."

The strain upon Enola's system was more than she could endure, and she became dangerously ill from nervous prostration, followed by delirium. It was sad in the extreme to witness the intensity of emotional feeling portrayed in this young, neglected wife, and listen to her mournful pleadings. In *all* her illness no one attended her but faithful Florence and a strange physician that was called in to prescribe for the afflicted refugee. Alcia was too tender in years to realize the agony her mother was enduring; she clung to Florence and would not permit her to leave her presence.

After several weeks of extreme illness and suffering, Enola slowly became convalescent. Claude Vernon was with his command, enjoying his camp life and pretty little Frenchwoman. She followed him, doing all in her power to fascinate and estrange him from his wife. In the sight of the world, as yet, no suspicion had attached itself to the once fair name of "Louise." But Enola felt too keenly the wrongs that she was suffering at her hands. Beauty wields a mighty power. It has overthrown kingdoms, and brought to ruin and wretchedness many of the noblest families of earth. Still, where is the woman that would not accept the boon, were it within the gift of mortal to bestow? We love the beautiful, be it in woman, flower, tree or bird, but we love also the pure in heart. Enola felt that it was her duty to again try to reclaim her husband, and many a sleepless night she passed in devising the means best calculated to win his affections back to her. "Florence," she said, "hand me the pen, ink and paper; I am going to write to Claude," and leaning her face upon her small hands as if in deep thought she thus soliloquized: "I cannot believe that his love for me has entirely vanished; it is only this fearful war that has estranged us, for he once was kind and I am sure he loved me. I will try to entice him away from the influence of a most wicked woman. I will offer every inducement to render his life happy. Oh! that I possessed some talisman to draw him back to me. I can only recall that cold wintry night, when I turned away from my beautiful home. How keenly I realize now the truthfulness of my father's warnings. How truthfully *he* read the future. Yet I was blinded to all that was in store for me.'' Having learned his address, after serious reflection, she resolved to write to her husband:

ABINGDON, VA., 18—

MY DEAR CLAUDE:

After several weeks of dangerous illness—brain-fever—God has in His mysterious providence, spared me, for what purpose He alone knows. No letter from you, my absent husband. It cannot be that you have ceased to love me, or do not wish to hear from your wife and child any longer. God forbid. As soon as I am able to travel I desire to go to my aunt. She loves me with a mother's tenderness, and is devoted to our little Alcia, who is growing rapidly. You would scarcely know her. She is a bright, cunning child . I still have Florence, who has proved herself to be a faithful girl. With prayers to God to keep you from all temptation, I am as ever, your devoted wife,

ENOLA B. VERNON.

My address will be Scottville, Tenn., care Mrs. Randolph.

Enola being sufficiently strong, desired to return to her aunt, and there, amid the quiet, smoky mountains of

East Tennessee, and away from the battle-cry, she could regain her mental as well as physical strength. So, bidding adieu to the charming valleys of Virginia, where she had heard the roar of distant cannon, had viewed the battle-field, where many brave men had yielded up their lives in honor of their country's cause, where she had listened to the dying words of some gallant son, far away from home and loved ones, with sacred vows, to bear the last words of the noble soldier safely to his mother.

These sad scenes, necessarily connected with war, Enola was only too glad to be relieved from witnessing any longer, for her very soul craved a brighter, sunnier life. The scenes of suffering that she, with thousands of other refugee ladies, were daily thrown in contact with, almost unnerved her, for it is ever so with the sympathetic.

Learned physicians have described emotional sufferings to be almost as great as the physical pain of the afflicted body, where the latter more readily yields to medical treatment than the former. This only goes to prove the great influence the imagination has upon the disease of the body.

Enola, although religiously inclined, did not feel the great necessity of turning to God, and praying to Him for help to carry her burdens, and to restore to her the love of her wayward husband. Had she considered this momentous subject, and acted in firm faith, she could have been spared years of anguish. This is only a life of probation, to fit us for a higher and nobler existence.

" What a beautiful world this is, aunt," said Enola,

WESTERN BORDERS OF VIRGINIA.

as she sat upon the broad piazza of Judge Randolph's residence.

"Yes, it is, my dear girl; but sin has blighted it, and left its curse upon all living things."

Mrs. Randolph was a woman of sound common sense, and disliked the weak and frivolous. She continued:

"Enola, have you ever thought that had sin never entered into the world, all mankind would have been faultlessly beautiful, both in form, face and character?"

"No, aunt, I only look for the beautiful in rural scenery. How I admire those high, towering cliffs, covered with the wild rose and gracefully clinging vines, intermingling with the forest berries, where the lichen craves the rock. My mind wanders retrospective to this earth in all its Edenic purity and loveliness."

Judge Randolph's rustic house was situated at the foot of a sloping range of picturesque mountains, and reaching far away into the distance were rich pastoral views, with streams of water as clear as crystal, creeping and gurgling through the green valleys, over jagged rocks, forming cascades that swell and roll on and on to the great Mississippi, and thence into the broad ocean, there to be lost in its immensity.

"Strange that Claude has not replied to my letter," said Enola, turning to Mrs. Randolph, who sat a few steps from her, arranging a bunch of wild wood flowers. "I trust he is not ill," she continued. "The mails are so uncertain; I will wait a few days, and if I do not hear, will write again."

No response came, and a week has passed. She quietly seated herself under the spreading boughs of one of the grandest of forest trees—the majestic oak—hoping, perhaps, to receive some magic inspiration from its loftiness, and penned another letter to her absent husband. It ran as follows:

OAK VALLEY, 18—,

MY ABSENT HUSBAND:—Can it be possible that I find myself again writing to you, and still no response to my first letter from you? A strange something impels me to again write to you. I feel, Claude, that an evil influence has surrounded you, and driven away the sweet guardian angel that prompts us to acts of goodness. Oh, God forbid. Dear Claude, I do long to see you, and tell you with lips that have never deceived you (and pray never will), that you are forgiven, and all the past, with its sad memories, shall be buried in oblivion. Yes, I will forgive your follies.

I feel that away from all evil surroundings, with darling Alcia as your daily companion, with her tiny arms around your neck, and her dark brown eyes, so full of tenderness and love, gazing into yours, that with such an influence you will become a changed and better man. Desist from your present course, Claude, and see how happy you will be. You don't know how my heart yearns to see a reformation in you. You possess many noble traits of character, and with proper cultivation will ripen into a perfected state. All shall be done in our home to render your life happy and content, and when this wicked war is ended, God willing, we will select some lovely spot, away from the busy, bustling city, away from all temptation to do evil, and our lives will be fraught with many blessings. Oh, Claude, has my excited fancy pictured in too glowing colors our future? I trust not; and when our earthly days are finished, let us pass through the valley of the shadow of death together, and receive a glorious reward for the many good deeds done in the body. That I love you, Claude, none can doubt, and to forgive is divine, you know. With kisses from Alcia and true love from

Your devoted wife,
Enola Vernon.

Safely mailed, and speeding on its way to Claude, Enola felt this letter would be a sacred blessing to each, and be the means of restoring his love to his wretched wife. How anxiously she awaited a reply from him. Days and weeks were quietly spent at "Oak Valley," and no letter came to soothe her anxious heart. With her charitable disposition she framed many plausible excuses for Claude, and would not permit her aunt to think his silence was prompted by neglect. Her intuitive pride in vain tried to conceal the seeming or apparent neglect of her husband. It was not an unusual occurrence for letters to be weeks finding their destination, or sometimes entirely lost. The mail system then was very imperfect. All thoughts were centered on the last great battle fought, or to be fought.

One gloomy, dreary morn in the autumn, when all nature appeared in deep repose, the gray light casting

its leaden rays upon the barren, leafless wood, the
chirping linnet searching in vain for its leafy bower, so
ruthlessly torn from its place by autumn's chilling
winds; when the very forest, now stripped of its once
gorgeous foliage was indeed a sad reminder of the fate
of man, as Enola was quietly meditating upon the disappointments incident to her young life, and trying to
reconcile herself to the belief that "God doeth all
things well," Mrs. Randolph handed her a letter. She
instantly recognized the handwriting, and clasping it
eagerly and pressing it to her lips, with great, round,
beady tears falling from her lustrous eyes, she exclaimed, "Oh, aunt, this letter is from Claude."
Quickly breaking the seal, she read as follows:

CAMP LEE, October, 18—
MY DEAR WIFE:—Your last kind and noble letter
was gratefully received by your penitent husband. It
shall be a tie to bind the present and the past when you
fled from your home to be my wife. When you entrusted your fate, your happiness into my hands and I
made a vow, which I thought was registered in Heaven,
to love, to cherish and protect you. That vow shall
again be reiterated by your unfaithful husband. Do I
deserve such a wife as you, Enola? I answer no, no.
Since you have forgiven my youthful follies, I have resolved to be a better husband, to improve the future, and
henceforth to live so as make myself worthy of such love
as yours. Cheer up, my darling wife, I shall never,
no, never give you any cause to complain of me again.
I admit that in the army a man sometimes becomes ob-

livious to a sense of duty, but you must remember I am also young, and did not realize the true worth of the affection of my devoted wife until I tested her love, which is alone mine. I long to see you and kiss forgiveness from your lips. How is bright little Alcia? Kiss her many times for papa. How long we may remain at Camp Lee I cannot say, but may at any moment march. A soldier's movements are uncertain. If I possibly can, I will get a furlough and run over to see you for a short time. Remember me to your aunt, not forgetting faithful Florence.

Since writing the above I have just learned that the Federals are marching in great force upon our fortifications. So as all are in anxiety to know the next move, in haste I will be compelled to close. God bless you, my devoted wife.

Affectionately,

CLAUDE VERNON.

Ninth Louisiana Regiment, Camp Lee.

Enola's eyes, as well as heart, feasted upon this (to her) precious epistle. After carefully reading and re-reading it, she placed it near her heart. "Aunt," she said, can I ever cease to feel grateful to Divine Providence for leading me safely into a haven of rest, for my mind has not been so peaceful in many, many years."

Recent news from the seat of war bring tidings of a great and bloody battle. Many hearts were beating anxiously to know the result. Devoted wives, fond mothers and affectionate sisters longed to catch a glimpse of news, to learn if *their* loved ones had been spared in the last desperate conflict. Eager hearts grasp at chance, and hope on through the trying hour.

A brief time, and all the Confederate States are wailing over one of their fallen chiefs, the gallant Gen. Stonewall Jackson. A pall of gloom settled over this struggling land. "Shot by one of his own men," was heralded throughout the camp, and just at that particular moment to be invoking, from our Heavenly Father, blessings for all soldiers enlisted in the "lost cause."

Mrs. Judge Randolph had four brave sons in the Confederate service, and her anxiety was always great when she heard of a battle being fought.

As Enola stood pressing her face closely to the window glass, she saw a lonely horseman rapidly riding toward the house. Her first thought was, "Oh, I fear something dreadful has happened to Claude, or some of my cousins."

Mrs. Randolph said to Enola, "You must not look on the dark side of life so much."

A moment more, and a soldier, dressed in gray, stood before the nervous ladies. "I have a note for Mrs. Randolph, from her son, Col. James Randolph." With that, he handed her the note. It read as follows:

DEAR MOTHER:—Poor Roland, our favorite brother, fell mortally wounded on the field of battle. We buried him in his blanket, under a willow tree. We marked the spot, so when the war is ended, we can trace his grave. He died without a struggle, and as a brave soldier should. We fought a terrible fight. Bear up, mother; many a son is dead and dying to-day. This is a cruel war, but we must, and will, defend our homes. Dear mother, how I wish I could be with you, to add my mite of comfort to your distressed heart.

With love, your son,

JAMES RANDOLPH.

Camp Buckner, 12th Tenn. Reg., 186—.

It is needless to picture to the reader Mrs. Randolph's distress of mind. Roland was truly the favorite of the family; a brave, gallant young man. Let his ashes rest in peace.

In due course of time Claude Vernon procured a furlough of ten days to visit his family. It was a joyous meeting, so different from their last. Claude was a changed man, and now seemed to realize the true devotion of his wife. He was devoted to little Alcia, and fondled and caressed her constantly.

Many good resolutions were framed, and Claude seemed himself again. That *letter* written by Enola to her husband, whilst she sat under that noble tree, had inspired him to a new course; to put away all neglect towards his faithful wife. He could not, he thought, cast aside such devoted love as Enola, his own lawful wife, had given him, for such a woman as "Louise." She was too treacherous for him to mention her name in the same connection with his wife, he thought.

Enola's life *now* was full of sunshine and happiness, for she felt she possessed her husband's love again. Whilst Claude was with his family, letters came through

9

the lines from Col. Baring, to his daughter, announcing the painful fact of his serious decline in health,
and great desire to see her, if she could possibly pass
through the blockade.   Judge Randolph's house having
been raided by the marauding bands that infested the
mountains, and been rifled of all the valuables. of the
inmates, by the terrorizing party, Claude thought it
best to consent to his wife's return, as soon as possible,
to Kentucky ; more especially, since all the family had
come so near being murdered, on that eventful night
when a hundred armed men burst the front door open,
and with drawn bayonets rushed over Florence,
threatening death and destruction to all, and faithful
to her devotion and love for Mrs. Vernon, Florence
boldly defied them, and kept them at bay until rescue
came.   Enola ever afterwards felt that she really owed
her life to this faithful girl.

Early in the autumn it had been arranged that Enola
should try to pass through the strongly guarded
Federal lines.   Claude accompanied his wife to a
friend's, near the romantic little village of Leighville,
where Enola desired to remain for a while before
making any attempt to pass through the lines, as
it was considered quite a hazardous undertaking,
the country being in such a demoralized condition,
with many interruptions to impede travel.   They found
quarters in a quiet farm-house on the rushing Roanoke,
a stream well known for its deep and rapid running
waters.   In an autumn month, one holy sabbath
evening, a son was born to Claude Vernon and Enola
Beatrice Vernon, another link to bind their hearts to-

together. "Wickliffe" was a beautiful little cherub boy, with heavenly blue eyes, and complexion vieing with the alabaster vase that stood upon the mantel full of violets—such a wee picture of angelic beauty. He too must share the love of parents, nurse and friends. An invading foe soon drove this little family from their secluded retreat. Enola, with her two small children, fully decided to leave, and make an attempt to reach "Glenwood." Claude promised to join his family later, and see them safely on their journey. They would be compelled to take a gunboat. When once safely on board a Federal man-of-war, a feeling of security would necessarily follow. After few days of weary travel through the deep bogs of lower Mississippi, inhaling the rich perfume of the queen of all flowers, the magnolia, scattering for miles around, the fragance so sweet and yet so penetrating, they came in view of the great ironclad "Avenger," lying like a huge serpent upon the bosom of the broad Mississippi. Capt. Gould, the commander, welcomed Enola and her little family kindly, and made them feel at home., What perfect neatness and rigid discipline on board the "Avenger," with three hundred soldiers treading the deck, ready at any moment to open fire upon the "Rebels." The trip up the river was a dangerous one, and fraught with much risk to life and property. With what joy and delight the passengers hailed the gaslights, as they approached the city of Louisville.

Enola, nurse and children were soon registered at

one of the leading hotels, and she lost no time in making inquiry regarding her brother, Harry Baring, whom she had not heard from for months. The landlord, who was an acquaintance of his, sent his card to Mrs. Vernon, requesting to see her in the parlor.

"I have painful news for you, Mrs. Vernon," he said.

"Oh! speak, and tell me what it can be," she eagerly inquired.

Hesitatingly he said, "Your brother Harry is *dead!*"

"Dead!" Enola screamed, "that cannot be."

"Yes, madam, he died several months ago, at his old home, Meadowville, and was laid beside his mother in the cemetery near the village.

Words cannot express Enola's agony of heart, for she adored him; he was all that was noble and good in man. Such was her great distress of mind that she had not the heart to inquire further into anything connected with her family. In due course of time she ventured to ask after her father, Col. Baring. She was informed that he recently left Kentucky for some portion of the West. It was quite a while before she could ascertain his whereabouts, as recent letters from him had failed to reach their destination. The western country comprises a vast amount of land—many thousands, yea, millions of acres. Through mutual friends she discovered his change of residence. After recovering sufficiently from the great shock of her brother's death, she concluded to continue on her journey until she found her father, who she learned had

OX TEAM HAULING PRODUCE INTO "WYOMING."

emigrated to "Wyoming," an Indian town, perhaps settled by some fur traders.

Peace soon being proclaimed in our desolate land, Enola felt that she would make her visit brief, and return South to join her husband, whom she did not like longer to remain away from, as he was lonely

Wyoming is a romantic western city, lying on the slope of "seven hills," strongly reminding the tourist of that far-famed and historic city where to-day stands the grandest cathedral in the known world, whose magnificent altars, fountains, shrines, and highly polished pillars, made of the costliest stones, with golden bases and crowns, put to blush all other temples.

Col. Baring, though deeply grieved over the death of Harry, was overjoyed at once more seeing Enola and his grandchildren.

All hearts were gladdened by the restoration of peace. To feel that the hand of liberty was once more extended to a slave-cursed land, and that the Ethiopian could go forth a manumitted citizen of this glorious country. Freedom to them brought its cares and responsibilities, but "liberty is sweet."

After a few weeks more, delightfully passed with father and brother, Enola thought it best to respond to the urgent desire of her husband, and, as soon as possible, return home to their cozy little cottage, surrounded 'mid orange trees and trailing vines, concealing from view the golden fruit. Contentment must dwell within this home of love and sunshine.

In the long twilight of a southern clime, hours after the sun has grown weary of his daily cycle, and slowly

sinks behind the western hills, leaving the brilliant
after-glow, so gorgeous in its beauty, as a reminder of
his splendor, Claude turned to his loving wife and said:

"Enola, we are truly blessed, and certainly happy.
I owe my reformation to that treasured letter, and your
sincere devotion to me; but—," pausing a moment as
if in deep meditation, or fearing some impending evil,
or that some unforeseen demon might cross his pathway, he continued: "Will this happiness be permanent,
my precious wife? Is it intended that we should be
so blessed?"

"Oh, Claude," spoke Enola, with the tenderest
voice, "it is with *you* to decide our fate. I have resolved to do my duty and you must do yours: then
God will bless us."

"Have no fears, my darling wife, we have our precious children to live for, and we *must* heed the obligation and do our duty. We must be true to ourselves,
and God will help us to be true to each other."

"Yes, Claude, we must bear and forbear. We must
have full confidence in each other; let no *evil one* come
between us to dispel that confidence, and our love will
increase with our years. We shall then descend the
hill of life together, to rise to a higher sphere and receive our inheritance. Think of God entrusting us
with two children to have the training and the keeping of. I can picture Alcia to be a tall and stately
girl, possessed with all the attributes to make a noble
woman; and Wickliffe, our baby boy, now so beautiful
in his infant purity, a brave, strong and honorable man,
full of firmness and goodness."

"Stop, Enola, said Claude, do not picture too vividly these anticipated hopes, for there are many disappointments in life. Build no visionary castles, for God may call our loved ones to dwell with him."

Time passes on: With what feelings of maternal pride and interest Enola looked upon her infant children; she was all devotion to them. Was a feeling of jealousy creeping into their father's bosom? Was his wife devoting too much of her time and thoughts to those little dependents? God forbid; but certainly he was not the same man, or husband, that he was a short time ago. Was there ever in the domestic history of life a case known where a father became jealous of his offspring? Reason answers, no. Why, then, this moroseness—this coldness in the heart of this young husband? 'Tis a human being, bearing the semblance of a beautiful woman, stealing away his love from his wife, like the wily serpent strolling into the garden of Eden, coming to tempt and destroy. As soon as this Frenchwoman, of camp and war fame, learned Claude's whereabouts, she sought him again with all a wicked, fascinating influence a heartless woman could bring to bear upon a too yielding husband, and very soon, like the innocent, fluttering bird, charmed by an alluring reptile, he found himself within her dangerous influence; and all the sacred promises he had made to his wife on former occasions vanished from his mind like the pearly dewdrops before the noonday's sun.

That Claude Vernon was again madly and wildly infatuated with this beautiful and bewitching female,

none of his friends could deny. Each day brought its
anxious cares to Enola, with no fond and sympathizing
brother now, to flee to and unburden her aching
heart.

Florence knew her mistress' sorrows, and felt keenly
her wrongs. Little Alcia noticed her father's indifference, and in her childish fondness for him she was
frequently repulsed by him, and in wonderment would
steal away to cry. Wife and children's love at length
were cast aside, Claude often spending days away from
his family and home, many painful circumstances
occurring to widen the estrangement between them, and
at times almost frenzying her into despair. But
her guardian angel kept vigil over her acts. She
remembered her duty to her children, and a ray of
sunshine would peep through the curtain of misery,
and pressing each one of her dear ones more closely to
her bosom, she would say: "Never, never can Satan
tempt me to take my own life. God's wrath would
ever be upon me. No; I will go to my deeply wronged
father, if driven to it, and, after struggling with my
pride, will seek his protection. I know he loves me
still; he is my only comfort and support."

Whenever Claude was in the society of his family, a
strange guilty nervousness took possession of him.
His heart certainly prompted him to do right, but the
beautiful face of Louise haunted him, until he lost control of his better nature, and fluttered around her
charms like the dove yielding to the insidious fasci-
nation of a serpent. She came, like an evil spirit,
and stole away his honor, his pride, and his affection

for his family. Could the silent inhabitants of the city
of the dead speak, the suicide and broken heart would
tell their tale of misery and woe. But let us draw a
veil over this gloomy picture, and not recall from
memory's tablet the sad, sad scenes of long ago.

Friends began to notice the expression of wounded
pride and hope in the once bright, and still beautiful,
face of the neglected wife. Her large, sad, thoughtful
eyes told, too plainly, the terrible anguish of her bleeding heart. She guarded her secret closely, but the
busy world is ever ready to send, on wings of lightning,
an unhappy message. At length, a disguised friend
to Enola penned a letter to Col. Baring, stating the
cold and cruel facts of his daughter's misery and condition.

The aged mother-in-law, always so kind to her,
advised her, with an own parent's love and interest,
to return to her father, and perhaps the separation
from wife and children would bring her wayward son to
a sense of his duty, and might be the means of a reformation in him. Still, Enola lingered in the valley of
indecision, not knowing the better step to take in so
important a matter. Days and weeks brought no
change in this unhappy household, for even little Alcia
dreaded to see papa come home, he was so cross.

Where a gleam of sunshine would creep through the
leaden skies of sorrow, a dark cloud of despair would
quickly follow to overthrow the least ray of hope in
the lonely wife's heart. Enola in vain plead with her
husband to put away this hallucination. She pictured
to him a gloomy future if he persisted in such a course.

Peace and happiness gone, "a sad change must surely come at no distant day," she mournfully said.

"Enola," said Claude, as he drew something from his pocket, "I have a letter for you. I think it is from your old father."

In an excited manner Enola broke the seal. It read as follows:

WYOMING, 186—.

MY DEAR DAUGHTER:—Please find enclosed a check for five hundred dollars ($500). I am pained beyond expression to learn of your unhappy condition, and immediately send you relief, with the earnest desire that you *at once*, with your nurse and dear little children, return to me. I will meet you at St. Chelsea, and with a father's love I will welcome you to my heart and home. Let me hear from you upon receipt of this letter, and tell me what steamer you will come on, so I can arrange my movements accordingly.

With a sympathizing heart, I am,

Your affectionate father,

WILLIAM BARING.

Claude's eyes glistened at the prospect of getting money, for he knew if he approached his wife in a certain way that she would freely give him half the amount. She had parted with everything her father had given her, for him; why should she not do so yet? He knew her generous and weak points, and he at once assailed them. His whole manner toward her changed. He said to her:

"Enola, I have an obligation to meet; it is a debt

of honor, that if you knew its purport you would not hesitate to spare me three hundred dollars of the amount you have received. You have always been kind to me, and ever ready to assist me to the extent of your power, whenever I have been financially embarrassed. It will make me a happy man to pay this debt, for it has haunted me like a phantom."

Enola listened to his entreaties, when at last her ever-generous heart yielded to his importunities, and she counted him out the desired amount, with these words: " The remaining two hundred dollars I will keep to go to my father, as he so urged me in his letter to do so, saying he would meet me at St. Chelsea."

Claude Vernon longed to have Enola and his children go to Wyoming, but at the same time he feared the influence of her father over her. He could not support his family under the existing circumstances, but he did not desire a lasting separation.

" Enola, you have fully decided to *visit* your father, have you?" said Claude.

" Yes, I am anxious to see him. He is growing old, and the children will comfort him in his declining years," she kindly replied.

" Then you expect to remain away until the old gentleman dies, do you?"

" I did not express myself that way, Claude."

" You need not answer me so curtly," he said.

" I am only answering you as I feel, for I am sad at heart. Of course, Claude, it has always distressed me to be separated from you, and only since I have been through the school of neglect have I been able to bear even a few months' separation. You will never fully understand how I have suffered since ——, well, I will not finish my sentence, as it might harrow up your feelings."

"You need have no scruples about my feelings. I care very little about your opinion, hence it would not annoy me in the least," coldly answered Claude.

Enola replied, with the tears springing to her eyes, "I am pained at your total indifference, but the day may come, Claude, when all the past will be brought before you like a moving panorama. It will then be too late to repent of your painful conduct."

"I wish, if you intend to go to your father's, that you would hurry up and be off," he said sharply.

"I can be ready to leave to-morrow evening," she said; "May, her husband and children are going on the 'Silver Bell,' a fine, safe steamer, and I will accompany them as far as St. Chelsea. I will not trouble my father to come such a distance to meet me, for with the children and Florence, I can get along very well. I hope, Claude, when we again meet, that you will be a better man, and we will feel differently toward each other."

"I am sure that I will always feel the same; I can't answer for you," he said abruptly.

The last evening Enola spent at the little cottage among the roses was a sad, sad time, long to be remembered. Claude was absent with gay friends, and did not return to his family until the cold, gray dawn of the morning. He came noiselessly into the house, and retired immediately to his room. He did not make his appearance at the breakfast table, preferring sleep to hot rolls, beefsteak and coffee.

Everything is now in readiness for their departure. Trunks, baskets and satchels, all packed and strapped, and the carriage is at the door that is to carry the little family down to the boat. Claude accompanied his wife and children to the steamer, and after a sad adieu, on Enola's part, the husband and wife parted.

As Enola's eye followed his receding form, she felt that the last ray of sunshine had departed from her pathway of existence. She realized that her young life was not worth the effort of living. All, all, hope had fled from a future she had pictured so bright and happy.

Florence came into the state-room and found her bitterly weeping; a shudder convulsed her frame. "Oh! it is only you, Florence," she said.

"Yes, Miss Enola, I was afraid you was crying, and I thought I would come in and see if you wanted anything."

"No, Florence," she quietly said, at the same time drying her eyes, "I only desire to see my darling children; bring them to me. Florence, they never were so dear as at this moment;" and looking at them as only a fond mother can look, she kissed them over and over again.

Alcia said, "Mamma," in her lisping, childish way, "Won't we see papa any more? Has he *run* away from us? I saw him *running* up the hill."

"No, papa was only trying to avoid the crowd that surround steamboats when they are about to take their departure."

The bell rings, the wheels turn, roll, dash and splash the water like a great drowning monster. At last the mighty power of steam propels the boat to move, and with great volumes of smoke, and with myriads of falling crimson sparks reflecting upon a watery background, she is soon carried out into the deep stream, puffing and blowing like a powerful, huge animal.

Up the stream, against the tide, she travels, the pilot careful to keep her in the proper channel.

WYOMING RIVER AND FALLS.

CHAPTER VII.

A S the cars came gliding up to the depot at "Wyoming," a tall, dignified gentleman, with iron-gray hair, his age perhaps sixty years or more, stood anxiously waiting on the platform for the cars to stop; as each window passed him, of the the long train of coaches, he peered into them to catch a glimpse of his daughter and little grandchildren, whom he is looking for, and expecting on this particular train. A moment more, and father and daughter are clasped in each other's embrace, whilst Gene caught up Alcia and overwhelmed her with kisses. Florence stood by with little Wickliffe in her arms, who is not forgotten, but his time has not arrived for his share of caresses; his little pouting lips will receive many fond kisses from dear ones—for he is a lovely infant.

"Welcome, welcome home, my dear children. We will drive to my country seat some few miles up the road," said Col. Baring. Gene, you take the reins, as the horses are inclined to be a little unmanageable."

Dashing over the smooth road, away through the forest and plain, the party were soon in front of a commodious and substantial frame building. The interior was unadorned by woman's handiwork. It was only a home in the wild West in its crude state, though capable of great improvement, situated near a beau-

(143)

tiful lake, Ostoaso, named by the Indians. It is but
a few years since that the white man's foot pressed the
soil of Wyoming. The broad expanse of prairie inspires the same feeling of awe in him who is alone in its
solitude, as one would experience on the bosom of the
ocean. On sea or land, solitude inspires the same feeling of loneliness. This rich and fertile country was in
a high state of cultivation, at the same time affording
many pleasures for the hunter and sportsman.

Many of the old family slaves, formerly belonging to
Col. Baring, emigrated with him to the far West, but
their hearts still pine for the good old times they used
to have at Birchwood.

Around the large, old-fashioned hearth, with a crackling, blazing wood fire, sat Col. Baring, with his little
cozy family, the perfect picture of contented bliss.
The day was bleak, and the children were kept in doors,
playing with their toys upon the heavy-carpeted floor,
whilst Col. Baring and Enola sat near by, in earnest
conversation.

"Enola," he said, "I want you to promise me one
thing. Months have passed since you came to me for
protection, and not one line has Claude Vernon written
you. I do not ask him to furnish you or his children
with money now, but I deem that there are certain
duties devolving upon him that he must attend to, or
he cannot longer be your husband. He has never supported you as he should, and I say to you now, my
daughter, that if he does not write to you within a
year from this time, you will have to make your
choice between your father and him. You must give

him up, divorce yourself from such a man, or return
to him; to a home of wretchedness and misery. I will
give you a year to decide this question, but upon that
very day you must act firm and decided in the matter.
I always knew that Claude Vernon was not worthy
of you, but I will not reproach you for what has passed.
I only want you to show firmness in this affair when
the proper time shall come. I am willing, and intend to
educate your children—to be a father to each of them.
I will not permit your husband to neglect you when
you are under my protection. I know that you did
your duty as a wife, and you do not merit such treatment from one who stole your young heart away from
me, from home and all that love you; and now, to
desert you and his dependent, helpless offspring, is
more than I can submit to."

"Papa," Enola said, "I fully appreciate all that you
have said to me. I know you are my best friend on
earth, and I am willing to take your advice in all things.
Would to God I had listened to your counsel years ago;
I should have been spared much unhappiness; but it is
too late to repine over the past. I will strive to
improve the future, and live over my life in my darling
Alcia. I desire to do all in my power to make a good
husband of him, and if all my efforts should prove
futile, then I will consent to give him up *forever.* I
think, papa," she continued, "that it is the duty of
every true wife to exert all the influence she can to
keep her husband from wild and vicious associates; to
make home attractive, and with the spirit of religion
pervading their household, there are but few men who

10

would not make worthy husbands. I can't think, yet, that Claude does not intend to write to me; he may be sick. I pity his weakness, his lack of firmness to resist the wiles of such a woman. I will wait patiently for tidings from him, and if I am disappointed, *then* I will consent to all that you propose, papa.''

''I am glad to find you so hopeful. I trust you may not be disappointed,'' said Col. Baring.

Almost a year of anxious solicitude and waiting. The long-expected letter has not yet arrived. Enola, weary and careworn from waiting and watching, refusing to see anybody that called upon her, leading an isolated life, was almost prostrated with anxious suspense. Well she knew that at the very time appointed (and still no news from Claude) she would have to yield to her father's *just* and kind decision.

One dreary wintry morning, as the frozen rain patted upon the window-panes, and fell to the ground in icy beads, all nature outside cheerless and desolate, Enola was in the most gentle way reminded by her father that the year had expired. He kept the date when the Rubicon must be passed. The appointed hour had arrived when she must decide this matter.

'' I hope, Enola,'' he said, ''that you will show firmness in this undertaking. Let good common sense and reason come to your assistance. You must realize by this past year's experience that your love is not appreciated by one so unworthy of you, my poor daughter,'' said her father.

Enola affectionately approached him, and throwing

her head upon his shoulder wept bitterly. "I am not weeping because I love him, but for the disgrace he has brought upon me and my children, impelling me to seek a divorce from him. I shudder at taking such a step. I see my fatal mistake, alas! too late to remedy the wrong. Why did I marry Claude Vernon?"

"Oh! my child," said her father, "you are wasting your tears for an unworthy man; so think no more of him. By his heartless conduct he has alienated you from him. Woman's love is like the vine, often cling-ing to a worthless object. I will at once take legal proceedings to annul the marriage and forever divorce you from him. I will do all a father can, and there shall be no publicity to it. Cease weeping, my daughter."

"Oh! papa, I always looked with horror upon any-thing like a divorce. I shall feel so strangely not to be Claude Vernon's wife. Papa, shall I be committing a sin by applying for a divorce?" For she felt most keenly the pangs of wrong and injustice done her, and shrank from any publicity or notoriety connected with her unfortunate marriage relation.

Col. Baring replied, a little sharply: "By no means; sooner would I claim that you were transgressing by living with an unworthy husband. Well, you have con-sented for me to proceed at once, and have the petition drawn up, setting forth all the facts. Have you?"

"Yes, my dear father, I am wholly unable to attend to anything of this kind. It will all devolve upon you," she pitifully replied.

No sooner had Enola said these words than Col. Bar-

ing was seated in his buggy driving down to Wyoming
to consult a lawyer, and give the case to him to attend
to.

How checkered are the scenes of life! Had some
sibyl, in years passed by, imparted such a life to Enola
Baring, she would have doubted the skill or veracity of
the knowing one. There were not many girls that had
brighter worldly prospects than Enola Baring when she
stepped into the bark of life and entered the sea of
matrimony, drifting on into the gulf of despair and
misery. Surely there will be a bright and silvery lining
to the dark cloud that overshadows her pathway before
the journey of life is ended. As the refiner purifies the
gold, and the lapidary the precious stone, so affliction
moulds the heart and fits it for the heavenly kingdom.
Enola felt that her trials were working for her good in
the end. She now regarded every event in life with
serious meditation and as a kind dispensation of Providence. She had lived a very secluded life, with her
father, causing her to seek companionship within her
own little family circle. She watched the growth of
Alcia and Wickliffe with a mother's interest, and could
see beauties in plain little Alcia that no one else could
discover. Her bright yellow hair, too light to be
termed a poet's golden, hung in *strings* around her *puny*
neck. Her large brown eyes shone out from hollow
cheeks and expanding mouth, until she had the appearance of having a *face of eyes*. Her teeth were perfect,
and of pearly whiteness. 'Tis well they were, as the
mouth was so expansive. At a very early age Alcia

displayed many very commendable and redeeming traits of character. She never envied other children their dolls, toys or clothing; never envied really beautiful little girls; nor did she ever speak against any of her schoolmates—a commendable trait. She was always inclined to be an exceedingly haughty child. Her "grandpa" lavished many pleasures and gifts upon her. She had the benefit of the finest schools, and master teachers in music, painting and dancing. She was bright, though extremely ugly; and many who saw her exclaimed, "There is ample room for great improvement." She possessed the happy faculty of making people love her.

Time rolls on, encircling days, months and years—even centuries roll on until swallowed up in Time's immensity. The mighty thunders swell and roll from the East to the West—reminders of the antediluvian age. Time, the revealer of the future, has healed the wounded pride, soothed and bound up the bleeding heart, and put into Enola a fresh life. She imagines new beauties in the skies, the birds sing more sweetly, the flowers are more fragrant—all nature appears now smiling and happy, in consort with her own feelings. Mankind are apt to judge the world in accordance with their own experiences. "I am happy; I have my two children, my faithful Florence, and a kind father," she thought.

When Enola again entered into fashionable society, she made numerous friends, and was sought for by

many. Good and honorable men offered their hearts,
hand and fortunes to her in marriage, but she refused
to change her condition, being content and satisfied.

Col. Baring, feeling that the hand of age was pressing
upon him, his feebleness growing more apparent as
each year passed in quick succession, realized that a
separation from Enola and her children was in the near
future for him. His very soul, thoughts and feelings
were blended in their future happiness.

Years had passed, when, by chance, Enola was intro-
duced to Mr. Vivien Dale, a prominent citizen of Wyoming—indeed one of its founders, and closely identi-
fied with the interests of the village. He was a man of
noble impulses of heart; benevolence was beaming from
every feature of his face. Though not what one would
call handsome, yet, in looking upon such a man, one
feels most decidedly the impression of goodness stamped
upon his features. He was a man of fine form, and his
physiognomy was an introduction to his character.

It is useless to say that Enola was not deeply
impressed with the appearance of Mr. Dale ; and this
was augmented by the constant praises of mutual
friends in his behalf. She heeded, with an attentive
ear, all they had to say. One lovely friend, in whom
she had great confidence, and who was a real christian,
whose character shone through her life like the beacon-
light to the storm-tossed vessel, had made many
inquiries regarding the life of Mr. Dale (Enola's latest
admirer), and bore, to her *now* cautious ear, a good
report.

Mr. Dale frequently expressed to Mrs. Brantner (the

name of Enola's steadfast friend) his ardent admiration
of the handsome Mrs. Vernon, and they often held
counsel together regarding the surest way to win her
affection.

Mr. Dale was a man perhaps fifty years old, but bore
with dignity any traces of age, his iron-gray hair being
really an improvement to his healthy, ruddy complexion.

He was greatly respected in Wyoming, and held,
at times, many positions of trust. His visits became
very frequent to Mrs. Vernon, at the discomfort of
several other gentlemen who sought her hand and
heart; but none she smiled upon more favorably than
the noble Mr. Vivien Dale. He won her admiration by
his homage and devotion. It was only a short time
after making her acquaintance when he avowed, in
strongest terms, his love for her.

"I cannot give you an immediate answer upon a
subject of such vital importance to each of us," said
Enola. "I will consult my father. At the same time,
I am convinced a second marriage on my part would
pain him; not because he does not respect you highly,
Mr. Dale, but my early life having been wrecked and
blighted, my father can but feel great solicitude for my
future welfare, and I could not be separated from him,
at his advanced age, but would urge, and expect him
to pass his few remaining years with me and my children."

"Nothing could add more to my happiness than to
have Col. Baring make his home with us," said Mr. Dale.
"He would be happy, and we are congenial to each

other. I regard your father as a wonderful man; a good financier and scholar. I could sit entranced for hours and drink in his beautiful flow of language."

" Thanks," replied Enola, " for your high appreciation of my father. I am sure he merits all that you have said regarding him. He has been very kind to me and my children since I came to share his home, and it is the desire of my heart to have him glide down the declining pathway of life free from thorns and thistles; to pass on to the haven of rest amid sunshine and flowers, and to die in my arms when his appointed time shall come."

"Mrs. Vernon," said Mr. Dale, "I admire you all the more to hear you talk so feelingly and touchingly about your father. I hope, my dear friend, whom I love so much, will not delay long the most earnestly desired conversation (on my part) regarding our feelings, for I am assured that you, from your manner, esteem me above all others," continued Mr. Dale. " You have wealthy suitors, Mrs. Vernon, but none who will sacrifice as much for you, or cherish and love you as I do. If all my expected business arrangements should prove as I anticipate, I, too, can offer you wealth at no distant day. You know that I have such a high appreciation of your worth and character it is useless to say more. When shall I call again to see you and receive your answer?"

" I will advise you of my decision," said Mrs. Vernon.

They parted; Mr. Dale returning to his home in Wyoming, and Enola to her children, for Alcia was soon to commence going to school, consequently her mother

MEADOW LANDS.

had necessary arrangements to accomplish. The ousy gossips, that always infest a village, soon began to whisper among the ready listeners Mr. Dale and Mrs. Vernon's supposed engagement. One old lady even ventured so far as to proclaim that the very day for the marriage had been set, and on every side Enola heard her name blended with his.

Several years had passed since Mrs. Vernon had returned to claim her father's protection and support. Col. Baring's health failing him, his overtaxed mind, burdened with the great responsibility of looking after his large estate, had particularly rendered him less able to endure such a heavy drain upon his nervous system. He longed for that rest from the cares of life which the aged feel so necessary to their longevity.

"Papa," said Enola, "what would you say if I were to impart to you a little secret?"

It was a balmy spring morning. The sun's rays threw the long slanting shadows of the tall trees far across the level greensward, almost to the beautiful lake, over the meadow field. The birds flitted and chirped through the sweet-scented locust, till "Shelburn" (the name Enola gave her father's rural home) re-echoed back the sound of singing birds through the open casement. The very air, so richly laden with perfume from the surrounding meadows, seemed to add its soothing influence over Col. Baring, and he quietly said:

"Be seated, my daughter, and I will lend an attentive ear to your 'little secret.'"

"Papa," she replied, "there is one *now* that truly

loves me, and has asked me in all devotion to become his wife, and I immediately replied to him in this manner: 'Let me consult with my father first upon so important a subject.' Did I do right, papa?'' she continued.

"Yes, my dear child, you have shown great respect to my feelings, and we will discuss this all-important subject with judgment and plain common sense—the proper way, after all, to express one's mind. Don't you think so, Enola?''

"Yes, papa. All the romance I ever possessed has been drained from my nature by floods of tears — bitter, scalding tears, that would seem at times to almost separate soul and body. You understand *now* how important it is for me not to enter into marriage again rashly, but take a sensible view of all things.''

"I love to hear you talk with so much discretion, Enola,'' said her father. "Who is the person you wish to form a matrimonial alliance with?'' he asked.

"It is none other than the noble Mr. Dale,'' she answered.

For a few moments Col. Baring was silent, when, drawing his emaciated fingers through the few straggling gray locks that fell over his wrinkled brow, and as if in deep thought, he at length spoke:

"Enola, my daughter, I would prefer, could I always be spared to you, that you should never marry again; but I feel already the finger of death pointing toward me. I feel its icy touch upon my feeble body, and I desire to see you and Alcia, with dear little Wickliffe, happy. I have accumulated a fortune to bequeath to my heirs, and you will never be dependent upon the cold charities of a heartless world. But money does not alone bring happiness, although it is a good thing to have at all times; and I have devoted many, many years to its accumulation, only that you and yours, Enola, might enjoy it. You are confiding and trusting in your nature, and from a small child you always believed everything told you, entrusting the heart secrets to friends. Hence it is very important that you should, after I am dead and gone, have a good husband to look after your interest. There are so many wicked, bad men that live only to defraud the widow and the orphan. They call them, my daughter, ' sharks,' or, more expressively, ' ghouls.' You will need some interested person to guard you against *such*, and protect your interests. I regard Mr. Dale as an honorable man, kind-hearted and benevolent. I know of but one fault I can attribute to him. Shall I tell you freely what it is?''

"Yes, my father," answered Enola, a little nervously.

" Have you ever heard that Mr. Dale was fond of the flowing bowl, and at times indulged too freely ? "

" No, papa, I never did; but I am sure if such were the case, he would never touch another drop of anything of the kind if I marry him. No, never," she vehemently exclaimed. " I am, as you know, a great advocate of the ' temperance cause,' and it would be the aim of my life to convert him to my views on that subject. And I assure you, my father, it would not be a month after I married him, before he would become a worker in the Temperance Union. Oh, what a magnet he would be. No, Mr. Dale is a man of social habits, and only when with old friends does he ever permit himself to indulge in any spirituous beverage, and then not to excess."

She grew quite excited at such an accusation ever being made against him. Col. Baring, agreeing with his daughter on the subject after her convincing powers had been brought to bear upon him, said:

"Enola, since you have made up your mind to marry Mr. Dale, I would not object to such a union, if you think you possess sufficient influence over him to make a temperance man of him. I do not disapprove of taking a mint julep when one feels the need of it," said Col. Baring.

"I do, papa," said Enola, "for it is a habit that grows upon a person so rapidly that nothing can arrest it in its path of utter destruction to all that follow in its wake. "Touch not, taste not," must ever be the motto. Had I not worked in the temperance movement, and under my own observation seen the misery that alcohol brings upon families, I could not thus plainly speak of its evil influences; but our journals all over the land, north, south, east and west, are teeming with accounts of bloody murders, and crimes too revolting in their nature to describe. What causes this great increase of wickedness now sweeping over our land? *Whiskey! Whiskey!* Go into the homes of squalor and poverty; hear the wail of death from starvation and ask the cause. It is always *whiskey!* Oh, that intoxicating liquors could be cast into a pit so deep that it were bottomless; that not even the scent of whiskey could rise from its fathomless depths."

"You are very vehement in your condemnation of whiskey," said Col. Baring.

" Why should I not be papa, when I see every day from our reliable journals the injury and suffering it brings upon frail humanity? It truly goes stalking over the land seeking whom it may devour. Strike at its base, and soon the monster will be annihilated. I do not believe there was ever an instance where whiskey did any good to suffering man, or where it ever relieved any one from mental or bodily ailments, but on the contrary it has caused· a great many diseases that never would have been."

"I am sure, Enola," said Col. Baring, "that *my* life has been prolonged twenty years or more, by enjoying a whiskey toddy every morning. I always take the genuine article. It is the adulteration that frenzies the brain and hurries so many off, yes, prematurely to the grave."

"I would not ask you, papa, to desist at this advanced age, when you have never taken it to excess, still, if you had never tasted whiskey, I would not ask you to try it. *Never! Never! Never!*"

" I believe," Col. Baring said, " that this great temperance movement is extending over the entire world, and that there will be no whiskey to be found, but it will take·years to accomplish this end. You temperance people are fighting a mighty element in its opposition; and strong and firm influences must be brought to bear upon the present administration of the country in order to cause them to come to your decision."

CHAPTER VIII.

WHAT means this confusion at Shelburn? Mrs. Brantner is with Enola, and has been for several weeks, and to-day much excitement pervades the entire household. Through a blinding snow-storm, guests, some sixty or more, in gay livery and brightly painted cutters, are dashing over the snow-decked road to Shelburn, their destination. Alcia is arrayed in her new sea-shell pink silk, her golden tresses carelessly tied back, with dainty ribbons to match, pink silk hose and black kid slippers. She sits alone, with only Wickliffe standing beside her, looking the picture of despair, despite his heavenly expressive face, which usually beamed with smiles at the prospect of cake, cream and fruits, but to-day his little heart is full of trouble. His eyes glisten with tears as he watches for his mamma, robed in her pearl-colored satin, with handsome lace that adorned her mother's wedding dress forming the draperies that fell in graceful folds about her girlish figure. Enola looked the picture of youthful dignity, as she hung upon the arm of Mr. Dale, taking their stand in the center of the large old-fashioned drawing-room, where a few words pronounced by Rev. Mr. Harden made them man and wife. The ceremony being over, many congratulations were offered, and the party adjourned to the dining-room to enjoy the viands that weighed the tables down.

After partaking of the wedding *dejeuner*, the bridal
party returned to Wyoming, merry and joyous. Though
the drifting snow played hide-and-seek with their cutters, they dashed on, passing and repassing each other
in the gleeful ride.

Enola had cast her fate into the hands of one she
knew would not in any way deceive her. She respected
Mr. Dale above all men she had ever met, and she felt
that the love she bore him was a wiser and calmer love
than she had experienced for Claude Vernon. With
firm and christian resolutions, she entered the home of
Mr. Dale a wiser woman.

The following spring Col. Baring left Shelburn and
came to Dalewood to reside with his daughter. Their
numerous friends commented upon the happiness of
this household. Again the sunbeams of life were casting their peaceful rays over the heart of Enola Dale,
and seemingly the very trees and flowers responded to
her cheerful, happy smile. Col. Baring was growing
more feeble, and the family, with great solicitude,
noticed the decline in his once vigorous constitution.

After the birth of his little namesake, "William Baring
Dale," he seemed to have taken a new lease of life, and
every morning his devotion for Baring was displayed
by the rides they took together through the deeply
shaded streets and by-roads around Wyoming. "A
beautiful boy," was the universal exclamation of all
strangers that perchance got a glimpse of him.

Alcia was placed in a famous school, and Wickliffe,
though inclined to be delicate, attended one near by.

The former was developing into womanhood so rapidly that she had really outgrown her years ; as if by magic touch, she had commenced a perfect transformation, her features and face filling out, with a complexion brilliant and as fair as a lily, with teeth that rivaled the rarest pearls, golden hair that fell in its silky masses to her fragile waist.

She was indeed developing into a beautiful girl, in face, form and disposition. Although envied by many less fortunate misses, she was unconscious of any especial attraction she possessed over them, and had a kind word for all. Enola watched her daughter with growing admiration, and often would exclaim : " How exquisitely lovely !'' and "With such beauty of face, combining such a perfect character, I can but feel exultant.''

Col. Baring would frequently remark : "With such eyes as Alcia possessed, she could not but be beautiful when fully matured, for her nose was fine, and those two features would ensure beauty in any one.''

Across the broad, blue ocean, in a strange land, under the azure of an Italian sky, far away from home, was a stranger languishing upon a bed of illness—a stroke of paralysis had overcome him. His brain, too, was on fire, and in his wild delirium he tossed upon his bed of remorse, and continually cried, in low, sad tones : " It cannot, cannot be possible that Enola is married and loves another. O my Enola, how could you treat me so cruelly ? Why did you ever give your heart and love to another ? Remorse haunts me day and night. And am I to die alone or among strangers, away from my once true and devoted wife? What a fool Claude Vernon has been. Could I recall the past, and bury, deep in the stream of oblivion, all, all my follies; oh, could I call Enola back to me: yes, as she was years ago—my fond and loving wife, whom I so cruelly drove from me—I might have hope. Now, I am left alone to die."

He had paroxysms of weeping that seemed to completely overwhelm him, and excite and aggravate his disease. He asked his nurse if he would recover; only long enough to see Enola.

"Yes, Mr. Vernon, you will soon be strong enough to continue on your journey, and the change will benefit you, and you will soon be convalescent."

"But," he said in a distressed tone, "even should I recover, Enola is lost—lost to me, *now*."

The nurse did not comprehend his meaning, but thought it the raving of a distorted mind. He tried to say soothing words to Claude Vernon, but it was like pouring oil upon the burning flame.

Time wore on, and with its sunny days and silvery nights, Claude Vernon slowly recovered from the shock of Enola's marriage. He would go forth again into the busy world and drink, to the dregs, the cup of forgetfulness. Oh, delightful thought! that time may obliterate from memory's tablet the unhappy past, and fill the aching void with dreams of peace.

How strange, yet nevertheless true, that "coming

11

events cast their shadows before them," as the sun reflects the shadow upon the wall.

Mr. Dale was a man possessed of unusually good health; robust as a boy, and seldom sick. Did he realize that such perfect health could not always be the lot of man? Enola was his *vade mecum*, and often they would sit for hours under the cherry trees, alone in the garden, and exchange thoughts. They were happy and content with life.

They pictured years of happiness together, basking in each other's smiles. They walked, drove and chatted together constantly, and upon one occasion, in passing through a favorite hunting-field, he remarked to his wife:

" I shall never again hunt in these fields, Enola. A weight of sadness has overcome me so completely, that I must rest my head upon your shoulder, my dear wife. This peculiar feeling has almost prostrated me," he continued. " Drive home, John, and I may feel differently when we leave this ill-omened field."

Enola pressed his temples tenderly and laughed at his superstition. They soon arrived at their destination, both feeling much improved from having enjoyed the cooling breezes that the autumn months bring with them.

Although not believing in the supernatural, a strange hallucination seemed to take possession of him, which was shared by Col. Baring also, but by no other members of the family.

Shall I relate it here? *"Nemine contradicent."* Then I will proceed, trusting it may interest but not over-excite any of my readers.

It was upon one of those sublime and balmy autumn evenings, at about ten o'clock, when the silvery moving clouds passed and repassed the brilliant moon (for it was a gorgeous night), casting a peculiar weird light over the sleeping earth, Mr. and Mrs. Dale sat upon the broad front porch, enjoying the lovely scene; and, seated upon the lower porch, was Col. Baring in his easy chair. He too was silently contemplating the scene, when suddenly a tall female form clothed in spotless raiment, bearing what seemed to be a wand in her hand, was observed by Mr. Dale. With noiseless tread she approached the house. The rays of the moon flitted over her pallid face. Mr. Dale exclaimed:

"Enola, do you see that tall female figure coming toward the porch? See! she is approaching your father!"

"No," replied Enola; "I see nothing but the tall, waving cottonwoods, and their shadows playing between the evergreens bending over the walk. Your imagination is so vivid to-night."

Just then Col. Baring called up to his daughter, saying: "Enola, hurry down. A female has entered my room, clothed in white, and she looked at me so strangely that it sent a shudder through my very soul. Come quickly, for my gold watch is lying upon my bureau."

Enola sprang to her feet and in a moment was in her father's room, but the spectre had vanished. Had she come from another sphere, to bear to them a message of impending ill?

"I don't know," said Col. Baring, "what it means

for a lady to intrude upon my privacy, and not be seen by anybody but you and me."

" I am convinced," chimed in Mr. Dale, " that this being is not of earth. Has she come only to us, Col. Baring, as a warning that you and I are soon to leave this world and enter that spirit life where she belongs ?" asked Mr. Dale, a little agitated.

" I do not understand this woman's mission," replied Col. Baring, mournfully. " I only know that no apparition is necessary to warn *me* that my earthly race is nearly run. The finger of Time points too correctly upon this life chronometer of mine, for me to be deceived. Still, I believe that mysterious warnings do come to many of us, and when they do we should take heed to them. I shall never forget the weird face of this woman. But let us not dwell upon the supernatural, since so many would ridicule our harboring such an idea."

Enola laughed at them both, heartily, for their superstition.

Search was vigorously made, but she could not be found upon the premises.

A fortnight from the time Mr. Dale and Col. Baring saw the peculiar " woman in white," Mr. Dale was stricken down " *articulo motis* " with a sudden illness. Gloom filled the entire household. The gravest apprehension followed his extreme illness, and skilful physicians administered to the dying man; but in vain. Death had claimed him; science could do nothing to relieve him. The husband, so kind and considerate, was passing away. Enola, in great agony of mind, stood beside his bed, and she watched his pulse beat more and more slowly, until all outward signs of life were gone. Mr. Dale was *dead*. His spirit had ascended to the God who gave it.

No one can picture the agony of the wife. She had looked upon her husband for the last time on earth, who had been cut down in the vigor of manhood. Consoling friends told her the oft-repeated story, "God doeth all things well." Col. Baring was completely overcome by this sudden affliction, for he was greatly attached to Mr. Dale.

The obsequies were very imposing. He was laid to rest in "Moreland Cemetery," a quiet, beautiful spot, where the weeping elm shades his grave.

After the death of Vivien Dale, the universal exclamation was, "A good and noble man has passed down to the grave, beloved and lamented." He was never known to refuse assistance to the oppressed and needy. He was especially kind to the fatherless and widow. He was a grand type of the Brotherhood of Masons and Knights Templar, of which he was a faithful member. As these benevolent organizations escorted their brother member to the quiet city of the dead, they could but realize that a shining light had passed from them, leaving only the remembrance of his many acts of kindness to be cherished as a souvenir. He had frequently expressed to his devoted wife the benevolence characteristic of the Masonic fraternity. He said that the outside world were not cognizant of the amount of good emanating from such benevolent societies. Men of a high order of appreciation, spurning any semblance of wickedness, seeking objects deserving their christian attention, usually connected themselves with the order. They guarded the interest of the families of their departed brotherhood.

Col. Baring stood beside the new-made mound until all friends had departed from the cemetery. He was motionless and abstracted, his mind no doubt wandering away back to the years of long ago, when he laid his sainted wife away beneath the trailing vines and under the churchyard window. He lingered in this quiet city, from whence no one ever returns until the resurrection morn, standing upon the long matted grass, full of the dampness of earth. He scarcely knew how long he stood chained to that sacred spot; he only knew that he was waiting. At length friends conducted him to the carriage, and he was rapidly driven home. Col. Baring grew more feeble as each day passed, and Enola, though bowed with the keenest affliction, tended her father through months of great suffering. One morning Alcia was dispatched for to return home as quickly as possible from her school to see the last of her devoted grandfather. Col. Baring died in the arms of his faithful daughter. He sleeps beside the wife he loved so tenderly.

Enola received many expressions of sympathy from kind, true friends, and Alcia, so thoughtful and obedient to her mother's wishes, did all she could to cheer her desolate heart.

"Alone in the world! Yes, my precious daughter,

I feel that all I had to look to for counsel and support have been taken from me by the chilling blasts of death. Mother, brother, husband, father, all gone, and *I* left. What am I spared for," she said, "to drink again and again from the cup of affliction?'

"Mamma, you must brighten up, for *we* will be a comfort to you."

"My angel daughter," said Mrs. Dale, "it is for you and your brothers that I care to live *now*."

She felt that great responsibilities now rested upon her, and she frequently expressed to Mrs. Yandall, a sweet friend of hers, who was a bride of only a few moons, her ardent desire to become less confiding. Her kind sympathies soothed the heart of Mrs. Dale, and her attachment for her has long since ripened into perfection. As the rose is matured in its beauty by the tears of April, so Enola's faith was strengthened by the tears of bereavement.

"Mrs. Yandall," said Mrs. Dale, "I feel a strange foreboding that there is still more sorrow in store for me. I wish I could keep Alcia with me, but she must return to school so as to complete her education. Sh᠆ is so fully developed that she appears to be older than she is. I shall visit my brother Gene, at Shelburn, and ask his advice as to what I had **better** do, for it does seem that I am beseiged."

Col. Baring having left, by a *will*, a large fortune to his daughter and her children, scheming men soon came forward, each to claim a share in this rich harvest. Not infrequently some of the legal fraternity, being anxious to accumulate money more rapidly than the mill of fortune grinds it out, suggest many new ideas to the credulous and trusting. Men of sharp wit and keen discernment know just *whom* to attack, and how to proceed in their avaricious undertakings. Sorrowful day when Mrs. Dale and Gene Baring listened to evil and selfish counsel, and yielded to an influence that was ruinous to everything connected with them. It were better to adjust all claims amicably if possible, than to be drawn into the meshes of the law. Though very many courts of justice guard well the minor's and widow's interest, and regarding the law of justice and right, protect them from *fraud* and *ghouls*, as Col. Baring termed the robbers of estates, the Baring estate once thrown into the hands of an administrator, God alone could tell where the money would drift; and finally sink, perhaps, so deeply that no court of equity, with all its justice and purity of law, could draw from dishonesty's fiendish grasp the spoils to restore them to the devisee. "*Dum vivimus vivamus*" is the cry and watchword of the man in search of spoil.

"Oh! Gene," said Enola, "do you think there can be any just cause to suspect that Mr. Albert Cheatem would mismanage the estate my father bequeathed to me? I have received so many warnings to watch him in all his transactions that I am really annoyed and unhappy over these accusations. I regard him as the soul of honor, Gene, and it pains me to hear him traduced by many professing to be his friends. I will not deny that he has ingratiated himself into my favor, and has my confidence; for I believe him to be an honest man, notwithstanding many proclaim publicly to the con-, trary; but *I* am not going to believe one word against Mr. Cheatem (for what is in a name?) until he robs me and my children. Then it will be time enough to send the message into the world. Don't you think so, Gene?"

" My credulous sister (for your credulity knows no bounds), I wish you would take heed to others, those that really have your interest at heart; and trust no man before he proves by all his acts that he deserves and commands your confidence; but until then, look upon all men with a suspicious eye, especially those entrusted with your fortune. As I am talking for your own good," continued Gene; let me gently whisper in your confiding ear, that it is gravely said that Mr. Cheatem does full justice to his *name*. Now, sister dear, you can take that for what it is worth; and in the future let me have your experience with Mr. Cheatem."

"Gene," said Enola, "your words have put me to thinking, but as a christian I will not wrongfully judge Mr. Cheatem, for I hope to find him honest. You know that would be going contrary to the principles of the Holy *Word*."

"Well, Enola," said Gene, "remember to inscribe on memory's tablet *all* that I have said to you this morning. We will meet again soon. Good morning."

Enola sat some time, silently meditating over what her kind, good brother had said to her. Musingly she thought; I will go at once and let Mr. Cheatem know just how the community regard him and his integrity. It is so hard for me to believe a wrong against any one, more especially those who have possessed my entire con-

fidence. I will go at once." Arising, she soon adjusted
her heavy mourning shawl and veil, and quickly walked
into his office.

"Good afternoon, Mrs. Dale," he politely said. "Be
seated, Mrs. Dale. A charming afternoon. Can I serve
you to-day, madam?"

He thought she had only called for a little money to
pay her necessary expenses. "Mrs. Dale," he continued, "you seem quite annoyed; has anything gone
wrong with you?"

Enola thought now was the proper time to perform
the disagreeable duty devolving upon her. With a firm
voice she said (at the same time handing him a letter):
"Mr. Cheatem, lately I have felt quite indignant on
account of being constantly taunted by various persons,
regarding your reported dishonesty, and unfaithfulness
to the trusts the Court has conferred upon you. It
distressed me no little," she continued, "to be compelled
to listen to such slanders upon your good name, Mr.
Cheatem."

Straightening his heavy, broad shoulders back, he
prepared himself for an eloquent appeal in his own behalf. Mr. Cheatem was anything but a handsome man;
tall and heavy set, with quite an animal face, and from
underneath his frowning brow could be seen keen blue
eyes, directed to the floor, as it was one of his charac-
teristics never to look into the eye of any one in conversation with him.

"Mrs. Dale, my esteemed friend," he said, "I am
glad that you have had confidence in me sufficient to
justify you in coming and making known to me the

wicked envy of the worid. Madame, I would sooner
rob this body of this arm than rob *you* and *your* children, my kind friend. Were I the monster that the
world makes me to be, even then I could not defraud
the widow of the truest friend I ever had, *Vivien Dale*,
and could he arise from his dusty shroud to-day and
speak the language of his noble heart, he would defy
these men and call it a foul calumny upon my good
name. O, that Vivien Dale could speak to you, Mrs.
Dale, and convince you of my true character. You
are, I fear, *now* in doubt of my doing justice to your
estate. Let me say, sooner would I sink forever into
H—l or become ashes under the soles of your feet, than
take one dollar from you, my confiding friend. I feel
that in robbing you, I would be robbing the dead. *I*
rob the *child* of Vivien Dale. *Never, never, never!* Return to your home, Mrs. Dale, with the same confidence
that you could bestow upon a brother. Trust me, and
you shall never have cause to complain of any violation
of said trust."

"Mr. Cheatem," Mrs. Dale replied, "your noble
protestations of friendship have relieved my mind, and
set at ease any apprehensions I ever may have allowed
to enter my heart. I will banish all anxiety from my
mind, and henceforth trust you implicitly. I am now
fully convinced of your nobleness and honesty, and no
one shall ever again dare to insinuate aught against you,
Mr. Cheatem. I shall defend you from those envious
people, and when you refund to me the full amount due
to me and mine, the world will then give you credit for
your honorable settlement. God will bless those that

deal justly with the widow and the orphan. I can then refute all wicked charges ever made against you, and I am sure that it will give me unbounded pleasure to herald to the world your just encomiums.''

Another evidence of Enola's confiding disposition.

Two years have passed since Mr. Dale was laid to rest in his lonely bed. The grass grows green and roses bloom around his grave as the seasons come and go, with none to molest his quiet repose.

Florence came in and handed Mrs. Dale a letter the postman had just left for her. With a look of surprise she broke the seal ; too well she recognized the writing. Thus ran the letter :

SUNNY VALLEY, 187—.

MRS. ENOLA B. DALE :

MY DEAR MADAM :—It is with the hand of a confirmed invalid that I pen you these lines. I wish to make a last, dying request of you. With a longing heart I crave to see my children once more before I die. No doubt they are nearly grown. Oh, Alcia ! Oh, Wickliffe ! Your father longs to press upon your fair young brows the paternal kiss again. Many, many years have passed since I gazed upon your innocent baby faces. Enola, my health is gone, and it is only a question of time when I shall be called to the great hereafter. I am only here, for a season, to enjoy a change of air. Will you not let me see my children before I die? I know you will grant me this request.

Yours, ever,

CLAUDE VERNON.

Address, Sunny Valley, Ark.

Ever impulsive, and full of tender sympathies, Enola laid the letter in her escretoire, resolving in her own mind to let the children see their father as soon as their school ended. "I cannot," she thought, "deny a dying man's request. Oh, how reminiscences of my past life come rushing upon my sad memory as I read this letter from Claude Vernon." She seemed dazed for a while, and, brushing the tears from her eyes, thought of the time when she was a happy young wife, full of hope. She had, alas, lived long enough to realize that all pertaining to this life is uncertain, and with a desire to do her duty, with no reproaches resting upon her, she answered Claude Vernon's letter as follows :

WYOMING, 187—.

MY DEAR MR. VERNON :—Your very unexpected letter was duly received, and contents carefully noted. I would be unwilling to send Alcia and Wickliffe to a southern climate at this season of the year, but shall not refuse you an interview with them. If you will appoint some suitable, healthful place, I will most cheerfully send them to meet you.

Very truly, etc.,

MRS. ENOLA B. DALE.

By the return mail the following answer came :

SUNNY VALLEY, 187—.

MY DEAR ENOLA :—With joy your kind letter was received. I agree with you in regard to our children coming to a tropical clime at this season of the year, consequently I will meet them anywhere you may suggest. I am more anxious to see you, dear Enola, than all else on earth, and desire most earnestly that you will accompany them. Please answer promptly, stating location and time. Anxiously waiting your reply, I am, faithfully your devoted

CLAUDE VERNON.

WYOMING, 187—.

MY DEAR CLAUDE :—Alcia and Wickliffe have just returned home from school, and fearing that you may grow weaker, I hasten to inform you that I will accompany the two children (with my own baby Baring) to " Hazel Hurst," an eastern watering place, where the mineral waters are pronounced wonderfully beneficial. You can meet us at the appointed time.

I am, as ever, faithfully,

ENOLA B. DALE.

In a few days this little family, consisting of Mrs. Dale and her children, with faithful Florence as nurse, took their departure for " Hazel Hurst Springs." It was one of those dreamy sultry days in August, that the old stage-coach rattled over the dusty road, and through the shaded forest, till at last drawing to a large swinging gate which opened as if by magic into a spacious lawn, the freighted vehicle soon unloaded its passengers; and among them was the family of Mrs. Dale, who were soon conducted to their rooms.

This was a rural watering place, with beautiful sloping hills creeping to the river banks, and long grassy lawns, reaching to healthful gushing springs, whose waters were medicinal, and clear as crystal. Around these springs were nice rustic cottages, and a hotel large enough to accommodate a thousand guests.

Primitive seats were constructed upon the grounds everywhere, with wild-wood flowers growing beneath your feet. Off in the distance could be seen snow-white tents, for those preferring camp life at a watering place to the low thatched-roof cottages that dotted the woods around. Trailing vines climbed gracefully over tree and shrub, till even many of the cottages were almost hidden from view. The sweet honeysuckle and English ivy coalesced until they seemed a network of leaves and flowers. The rooms in the cottages were plainly furnished, but as neat as possible. The table was delightfully kept with nice, dainty fruit, and fresh, ripe vegetables just plucked from the garden. The fat, tender chickens, deliciously prepared, were fit to set before a king. Indeed, Hazel Hurst Springs was a charming summer retreat. Away from the busy, noisy world, one could spend a couple of months delightfully there.

A card was brought by the waiter to Mrs. Dale's room and handed to her. Upon it was written:

" I would like to see you and the children in the parlor, whenever convenient to you.

CLAUDE VERNON.''

Enola, leading dear little Baring by the hand, accompanied by Alcia and Wickliffe, repaired to the drawing-room to meet Claude Vernon, the man who had once

been her husband, who had blighted her young life,
and cast her devotion and love aside for others. But
whenever duty called, she was ready to obey the command.

"And this is Enola," said Claude Vernon, Alcia and
Wickliffe advancing to shake hands with and kiss their
father at the same time.

"My darling children, how much happiness this
meeting affords your sick father. And who is this
beautiful boy by your side, Enola?"

"This is little Baring Dale, my baby boy," said
Enola, pressing him tenderly to her heart.

Enola, true to her womanly principles, taught Alcia
and Wickliffe to treat Claude Vernon with the respect
due to a father. Claude was perfectly enraptured over
meeting Mrs. Dale's family, and could not keep his eyes
from gazing upon his beautiful daughter.

"Enola," one day Claude ventured to say, "This is
the happiest moment of my life, to know that you have
forgiven me, to hear from your own lips that sweet
word *forgiven*; it thrills my very soul. And oh,
Enola, if you only knew how I have suffered, these long,
weary years, from remorse of conscience, you would
really pity me. I have been wild in my younger days,
but am now a changed man, and I can say in all truthfulness, that you are the only woman I ever loved.
Years ago you thought I did not love you, Enola, but
God knows my heart. I was fond of the world and
carried away by its allurements and pleasures, but I now
fully realize there is nothing certain in this life, that all
is vanity. Now, what I most desire is, to get me a

nice little home, with you, Enola, as my wife, again to preside over that household.''

For a moment Enola was spell-bound, and in panoramic view all her young life passed before her, with its blighting sorrows as well as joys. She could not utter a word.

'' Enola,'' Claude continued, '' I know you have lost confidence in me, but I will now try to prove to you that I am a changed man, and will make amends for all my past wrongs. For our children's sake you should remarry me, Enola; but I fear all love for me has vanished. Am I right, dear Enola? Answer me, for my heart is sad and desolate.''

She listened with indifference to Claude's second protestations of love. But she replied feelingly, for her heart felt pity creeping into it: '' Claude,'' she said, ''I should neither be doing you nor myself justice to think for a moment of a second marriage with you. All the wrongs you ever did me are freely forgiven. I pity you in your delicate situation, and sympathize with you in your sufferings, both in mind and body. I trust your physical condition will soon improve, and with robust health you will mentally grow stronger; but, Claude, you must banish all thoughts of remarriage with me.''

'' Why do you talk so cruelly, Enola?''

'' Do you wish me to be frank with you?'' she replied.

''I most assuredly do,'' he responded.

'' Well, Claude, with me lost confidence can never be restored. That I *once* loved you, no one can doubt. I adored you, Claude, and perhaps my intensity of feel-

12

ing caused me to be exacting with you, more so than if
I had not loved you so wildly. When I gained the
victory over my better judgment, and consented to
leave my paternal roof to become your wife, regardless
of a parent's advice, I thought you the noblest and
best of men. I was blind to any faults you might have
had. I only knew that I loved you, trusted you; and
oh, Claude, how cruelly you have betrayed that confidence, and crushed out all my love by years of cold
neglect! It took years, Claude, to overcome my affection that you so cruelly spurned, and now I can never,
no never, trust you again. In despair, when my heart
was lacerated and bleeding from your cold neglect, I
begged you to love me, and not forsake me for unworthy objects, and you coldly sent me to a father
whom I had so fearfully wronged. I was driven to
seek his protection and support, for I knew his tender
love for me would not permit him to refuse me and my
two little children an asylum from destitution and want,
to say nothing of your unfaithfulness to me, Claude.
It pains me no little to recall and repeat my past sorrows, but you desired that I should be candid, and have
no concealments from you, hence this painful conversation is forced upon me. I hope you are a changed
man. I believe in my heart that you are now thoroughly reformed. Admitting all that to be true, I
could never be happy with you again, Claude, so it
were better that we should never meet again in this
sinful world; but let us strive to live in such a manner
that on that beautiful shore of the better land we shall
meet and know each other as purified saints that have

gained the victory and reward through great tribulations.''

''Oh! how ·hard-hearted you are to say it were better we should never see each other again. Absence cannot obliterate my love for you. I care not to live if you banish me forever from your presence. I see that you have grown cold and suspicious of mankind, Enola,'' he said.

''No, Claude, I am not cold; but the world is not what I expected to find it years ago when I first met you. I long to dwell with you in that beautiful new earth, Claude, so graphically described in God's Holy Book,'' she said.

'' But, Enola,'' Claude answered, ''you know that I am an infidel; that I doubt the inspiration of your Bible. Christ was a good man, but not divine, as you would have me think.''

''Claude Vernon, with my present light upon facts and prophecies contained in God's sacred Word, it would be utterly impossible for me to respect a person who indulged in such views as yours. God is a being capable of great mercy toward those who believe in and love Him, also of great wrath toward those who deny His existence,'' she said.

'' Enola,'' said Claude, ''you have touched a chord in my heart that has stirred the very depths of my soul. It has often been a mooted question with me—is God a real being, or is Nature God?''

After serious meditation and silence for a few moments, Enola seemed to invoke the inspiration of the holy prophets to impart to her wisdom to answer

Claude's question, that from her answer some good seed might be sown in his heart and eventually bring forth fruits unto eternal life.

"Claude," she said, "I am now going to try to bring all my convincing powers to bear upon your mind, so you must listen attentively. The wonderful harmony of the universe (aside from the testimony of the sacred Scriptures) ought to convince any candid mind of the existence of a Supreme Being, an all-wise Maker, Director, and Ruler, not only of our mundane system, but of all things visible and invisible.

"But we have a more sure word of prophecy (Second Peter, first chapter and nineteenth verse), unto which you would do well to take heed, as unto a light that shineth in a dark place. For the last two thousand three hundred years the history of our world has been written in advance, as we believe, by the direct inspiration of the Almighty, as you will find in Daniel, second and seventh chapters; also in the Apocalypse, or last book in the Bible, and has been fulfilling, up to the present time.

"The image of Daniel (second chapter) represents to us four universal governments that were to obtain in the earth previous to the consummation, viz., the Babylonian, Medo-Persian, Grecian and the Roman. The last of these governments was to be broken up into eastern and western divisions, and afterward into ten kingdoms, all of which was accomplished between the third and sixth centuries of the Christian era. The stone that smites the image on the feet is a symbol of Christ's kingdom, which is to ' fill the whole earth.' "

" Whew ! " replied Claude, sardonically; " you have turned commentator, have you ? "

" Well, Claude, call me what you please, *but let me tell you* that if all the prophecies in the Bible are to be as literally fulfilled as those to which I have referred you, we must be living very near to the close of the world's history, and the ushering in of a new and more glorious era that has ever dawned upon mortal man. New heavens and a new earth, wherein dwelleth righteousness."

" If you can make me believe all this," said Claude, " I will acknowledge the existence of the God you worship; but I tell you that this will be no easy task for you. 'Prophecy' may have been written after most of it had been fulfilled."

" No, no, Claude ; you ought to know better than that. Much of it is being fulfilled now, before our eyes. The image is standing to-day awaiting the smiting of the stone upon its feet, representing to us what remain of the ten kingdoms, three of which, according to the predictions of Daniel, have long since ' been plucked up by the roots.' (Daniel, seventh chapter, eighth verse.) Then all the governments represented by the image of the second chapter, and the four beasts of the seventh, will ' be broken to pieces together,' and become ' like the chaff of the summer threshing-floor,' and ' no place ' shall be ' found for them.' Christ's kingdom, symbolized by the stone, shall then ' fill the whole earth.' "

" What then ? " replied Claude, earnestly.

" Why, Christ and his saints will take the kingdom

and the dominion *under* the whole heaven, and possess them ' forever, even forever and ever.' (See Daniel, seventh chapter and twenty-seventh verse.) You must look up and diligently study these prophecies, Claude."

" Those are beautiful ideas. Why do not the ministers preach upon this subject?" said Claude.

" Very many of them do," she replied.

" Enola, you have set my brain to thinking. You speak like one who knows and thoroughly understands the Bible."

She continued : " Claude, my earnest prayer is, that more light may be given me in regard to our blessed Saviour, soon to return to earth, to reign as King of kings and Lord of Lords. As he ascended up in a cloud, so will he return in like manner, to renew the face of the earth, and eradicate the last vestige of sin and death."

" Enola, you have almost persuaded me to become a believer," he answered.

" Would to God I had the power to convince you where we stand upon the great chart of prophecy."

" Who knows but what you may?" said Claude, wistfully.

" We have had all the signs predicted, in connection with the end, and we are now in the waiting time referred to so graphically in the twelfth chapter of Daniel."

" But," said Claude, " Christ will come like a thief in the night, according to the Bible."

" So he will. ' Of *that day* and *hour* knoweth no

man; ' but we are to know when He is nigh, even at the
door. Listen, Claude, what St. Paul says: ' But, beloved, ye are not in darkness, that that day should overtake you as a thief.' Read the twenty-fourth chapter
of St. Matthew, and you will find many of the signs
which were given to us by our Saviour, to show *when* he
was near."

" I think I will make a study of this Book, that you
revere so much. Who knows but I might become a
convert to its teachings?" he said.

Taking up the thread of conversation, Enola continued. " I laid my pride aside, and returned to my
parent and did my duty toward him, until he passed
away to a better world. No, Claude, I could never
again bear the sacred name of wife. I shall live in the
future for my children, and try to do my duty toward
them. Alcia is the joy of my life; she is a girl among a
thousand; few persons, in looking upon her beautiful face,
know her perfection of character. She is so free from
envy, malice and what is called meanness, that she can
but command respect. At home she proves her amiable
disposition, and is unconscious of her many attractions.
I shall send her to the best schools and have her cultivated and refined, and with such marvelous beauty as
she possesses, she can adorn a court."

" Yes, Enola," replied Claude, " I agree with you, in
all you have said about her; she is indeed a sweet and
lovely child, most deserving encomium. I had no idea
before I met her what a magnificent girl she was, and
our daughter's beauty and graces prompt me to ex-

press myself in warmest praise in her behalf. She is
of that

> Type of beauty rich and rare,
> Dusky eyes and golden hair,
> To the charms of form and face
> Adding woman's every grace—
> Bright of wit, of manners mild,
> In simplicity a child,
> Dutiful—thy mother's pride,
> Of her life the sunny side;
> Fortune might or smile or frown,
> Thou wert still our home's bright crown
> Could a perfect woman be—
> Dowered, and moulded, thou wert she.

I wish I could be with her always, Enola.''

"One word, Claude, then,'' she said, "before we separate. As I intend to send her one year to some cele-
brated school in Europe, and as you speak of going
abroad, and are so desirous that she should accompany
you, I am willing that you should take charge of her
and be her *chaperone*. Now, that ought to satisfy
you.''

"I am more than anxious to go with her, Claude
answered, "and whenever you are ready to make a
change in her school I will be prepared to accompany
her. I have been ill so long, Enola, having doctors'
bills and heavy expenses to bear, that my finances are
a little short. I only ask you to pay for Alcia.

"Certainly,'' said Enola, a little sharply; "my
father has always supported the children since the hour
they were born, and I can do so yet.''

"There is much in Alcia,'' Claude replied, "to make
a brilliant woman, and money spent on her you can
surely never regret. Beside, Enola, your father has

left you a handsome fortune, and you can afford to expend a good deal upon her education.''

"Certainly," answered Enola, "for I know when Mr. Cheatem makes his final settlement he will not only have all the money belonging to me and my children securely invested for our benefit, but he is such a thorough business man that no doubt he will have made and added to the trust-fund several thousand dollars over and above the principal received.''

"I am glad you have such an exalted opinion of Mr. Cheatem's honesty and business qualifications. I hope your fondest anticipations may be realized. But, Enola, I have heard some things I do not like about your friend Mr. Cheatem; yet, as Col. Baring's estate was so free from indebtedness, and *you* the widow of his old friend Vivien Dale, he will no doubt act honestly in all matters connected with the business entrusted to him. I have heard that he is a man of bright intellect, and quite an orator in his way.''

"Yes," Enola replied, "Mr. Cheatem is a gifted man, and I think a perfectly honest individual, although many persons say to the contrary; but I am not going to listen to anything prejudicial to his honesty, nor will I believe any calumny against him, until I myself find him unworthy of my esteem.''

"I admire your constancy in your attachment, and your vindication of your friends, but I am afraid that you are a little too confiding; you always were so. But we will see how all things end, Enola.''

CHAPTER IX.

"AND we are out upon the broad blue ocean. How the steamer rides the great swelling waves, each heavy roll of water bearing me farther and farther away from my native land and my dear mamma," said Alcia to her father. "Constantly I am thinking of my absent mother, and only wish that she were with us."

"Yes, my daughter, replied Mr. Vernon, "it would have been the joy of my life could she have accompanied us; but you must not get homesick. After your schooldays are ended we shall travel over the continent, and you shall feast your eyes upon the beauties of nature combined with art. I am improving so rapidly in health," continued her father, "that very soon I can be of great assistance by instructing you in German and French. Your mother has entrusted me with ample means to afford you all the advantages of a foreign education. What an accomplished girl my daughter will be when she returns home."

"I trust so. I shall certainly try to do justice to the many advantages offered me, and try to fill to perfection my dear mother's fondest hopes," she replied.

Enola felt quite relieved in mind when she received the expected cablegram from Alcia announcing their safe arrival across the broad Atlantic, ever fraught with peril and dangers, for upon water the traveler has cer-

(186)

tainly the two most powerful elements to contend with. The telegram read as follows: "Arrived safely at Queenstown."

Enola felt that now, her mind being relieved, she could turn her attention to the expected change in her residence. After many vain efforts to overcome, to a certain extent, the heavy afflictions that she had experienced in the death of loved ones, she had determined to remove her home to a city on the borders of a large stream, accessible to Wyoming, where most of her interest and property were located. She desired to be nicely situated in her own home before the return of Alcia, as she would then have finished her education and be ready to enter into society, a gay and accomplished young lady.

How many bright pictures a true mother's heart can paint for the absent child in whom her fondest hopes are centered. Duly located in the suburbs of a charming southern city, Enola felt that her mind, to some extent, was relieved. Still she had many cares devolving upon her, and claiming her earnest attention — responsibilities that her too confiding disposition had, to some extent, subjected her to.

The time had arrived when Mr. Cheatem was expected to make his final settlement, and turn over to the lawful heirs their dues in the late Col. Baring's estate. Enola, still trusting him as implicitly as she would a brother, expected her fortune to be largely increased under his wise and judicious management, and with a hopeful

heart and abiding faith she approved the settlement,
until she discovered that the money had, alas! been
consigned to the capacious coffers of Mr. Cheatem,
evidently for his own use, not to be reached unless a
high court of justice demanded its payment. Words
are inadequate to express the disappointment that filled
poor Enola's too confiding heart, only receiving a few
thousand dollars out of her large fortune bequeathed
by her father. She was to go forth into the world
with her children to educate and support. She knew
not what to do. She sought Mr. Cheatem and vainly
plead with him to satisfy her anxious heart, and reveal
to her the cause of this immense shrinkage of the
money he had accepted to keep as a *trust*. Feeling assured that there were no debts to be paid, it became a
very mysterious question to her, and one she could not
fathom. She sought him, and her trusting heart not
yet doubting his fidelity, whom she had believed could
not be guilty of a dishonorable act, much less rob the
widow and orphan child of Vivien Dale, she plead for
an explanation.

"Mr. Cheatem," she said, "I appeal to you as a
friend, and wish to have a confidential interview with
you regarding my business, over which you have so
many years had entire control and management. I still
feel that you would not wilfully wrong me or mine out
of one dollar. I simply desired a statement from your
own lips, to know what became of a greater portion
of the money you received as administrator. I am
sure you would not wrong any one."

"Madam, I can very soon answer that question, and

put your mind at ease." Arising from his seat, he continued : " Will you walk with me to the probate court, where no more honorable judge ever sat on the bench of justice, and there I will explain to you, through that venerable body, where the wealth disappeared."

Soon they were within the solid, cold walls of a massive building, full of vaults and heavy bolts, where earthly wrongs are expected to be honestly and justly righted ; where the widow and the orphan seek protection from dishonest men ; where fidelity in all its purity is supposed to exist. There, the interested parties were searching through those musty ledgers. Oh, that they could speak the truth to this wronged woman. But, alas ! in their silence they sleep on and on, closely guarding their secret.

After many strained efforts to convince her where the money had disappeared, with all traces of fraud being wisely enveloped in mystery, Enola, beginning to doubt everything, at length spoke :

" Mr. Cheatem, your explanations are beyond my comprehension. Why did you render your settlements so intricate ? I must say, sir, that a suspicion of fraud is creeping into my bewildered mind, causing me to exclaim, that, with the garb of honesty, your tracks are most beautifully covered up. The money is gone, gone, and what redress have I ? Oh ! Mr. Cheatem, you are a man of vast wealth, with high business attainments, and I, a lone widow in the world, with my children entirely dependent upon me, could I contend with you and recover my just rights, Mr. Cheatem ? Never ! never ! Are you the man that I so fiercely defended against your enemies, forfeiting their friendship in your defence? Are you the man that has thus cruelly robbed me, the widow of Vivien Dale? It cannot, cannot be !''

"Madam,'' Mr. Cheatham replied in the kindest manner, "you have yet an abundance to live upon, if judiciously managed. Do not seem so distressed over the loss of money; it is only filthy lucre at best. If the worst come, you can dispose of your real estate and live upon that, madam.''

Mrs. Dale replied indignantly to him, saying : "But, Mr. Cheatham, you have robbed my children, you have violated the trust imposed upon you ; beside, I am penniless, unless I——sell——my homestead.''

"Oh, no, madam,'' interrupted Mr. Cheatem, "I have left you plenty to live upon, if judiciously managed. You will have to live economically, though, Mrs. Dale. You should not care for money, madam, it is only filthy lucre.''

"Mr. Cheatem, as deeply as I now feel the wrong, I believe the day will come when you will regret this betrayal of that trust. Good morning, Mr. Cheatem.''

"Good morning, Mrs. Dale. If there is any way in which I can serve you, please call upon me, madam,'' politely answered Mr. Cheatem, who was universally known to be the most fastidiously polite gentleman in Wyoming.

"With a sorrowful heart poor Enola left for her home by the flowing waters, feeling most keenly that again her too confiding disposition had been deceived. She truly realized that there was but little in store for her but bitter disappointment. "Can it be," she thought, "that my poor lamented father's vow is following me on through my life, saying, 'If you marry Claude Vernon my curses will rest upon you!' Oh! no, I will not allow myself to indulge in such a thought." Ever cheerful through her deepest trials, Enola sought comfort in reading the witty, sparkling letters that Alcia had written to her, so intensely interesting to a mother's heart. Just then Florence came in with a letter from across the dark blue ocean. It was from her daughter who shortly was to take her departure for home, having spent a year at school in a foreign country. Enola had fitted up a beautiful house in the city of St. Chelsea, and everything was in perfect readiness to receive her daughter royally on her return from her foreign school.

Her mother was so anxious to greet her once more, that she kept pace with the hours, days and weeks, until the expected time for her arrival. Her room, styled the " blue room," was exquisitely tinted and frescoed ; bluebells and lilies of the valley decorated the deep frieze, so much resembling the natural flowers in all their freshness, that one felt tempted to pluck them from the wall. The heavy velvet carpet, with blue background and daisies carelessly dashed over it, appeared to vie with the drooping, graceful flowers, that formed the decorations on the ceiling. Rich antique lace curtains fell in massive folds from the broad, tall windows, permitting now and then a ray of golden sunlight to peep through their artistic meshes, playing and dancing upon the gilded mirrors, until this exquisite room was dainty enough to be the chamber of the "goddess of love and beauty." Alcia's chair, a large easy one, was placed beside a handsomely carved ebony table, upon which stood a Dresden china vase, filled with half-blown tea-rosebuds, blending with the daintiest of flowers—the azalia—whilst a bunch of acacias ornamented the mantel. The heavy, antique blue satin and lace spread was thrown over the downy bed, tempting the very nymphs to rest from their wild-wood ramblings. Many bright-colored pieces of handiwork, too, added their charms to Alcia's room.

The time having arrived for her return, mother and child were soon in each other's fond embrace. Kiss after kiss was impressed upon her lovely brow. Baring was wild over his sister's arrival. He had never, in his boyish fancy, looked upon so pretty a face. Cautiously approaching her, he said :

" And this is my sister Alcia."

" Yes, my darling little brother, this is your sister," she smilingly answered ; " look at me."

In his boyish enthusiasm he continued : " We are going to have a fair this fall, and all the beaux of St. Chelsea are going to have a tournament. You know, sister, what I mean, don't you ?"

" Oh, yes, Baring," she said ; " go on."

" Well, then, sister, they are going to have a large crown—of flowers, I mean ; live flowers—and the victorious knight is to place that crown of roses upon the brow of the most beautiful girl on the ground ; and, sister Alcia, I want you to be there upon that day, for I know you will get the crown," he said enthusiastically.

" Baring, my sweet little brother, you are too complimentary to me. Because you think your sister the prettiest girl in the city, is no reason that all others should think so. I would not attempt to compete with any for such a rare crown as that, my little brother, when the city of St. Chelsea is so famous for its beautiful women."

" Yes, sister," he continued, climbing up in a chair beside her, and stroking her golden hair, "you must go, sister. It will be a grand day. I am going, and mamma, too."

"I would like to go, because you desire me," said Alcia, but would greatly prefer to remain at home with mamma and yourself, my darling little brother."

" Oh no, sister," Baring persistently said ; " *you must go.* They are going to have fine horses, too. Don't you like a pretty horse, sister?"

" Indeed I do, Baring," she affectionately answered.

" Then, sister, I have settled the problem ; you are to go."

Alcia was indeed an elegant girl. Nature had done everything for her. She did not consult art, or resort to it, to add anything more to her exquisitely beautiful face. Her form was round and fully developed. Baring, though a small child, was an ardent admirer and a good judge of the beautiful. He certainly looked upon his sister as a grand and handsome girl, and wanted all others to agree with him in his admiration for her, and readily became offended with those differing from him.

Alcia soon became one of the leading belles of the

13

city of St. Chelsea. She was greatly admired, and shared equally with them in admiration and attention. Her manner was rather imperious, though possessing grace and ease, blended with a great deal of charity for her own sex, or those less fortunate than herself. She was never known to comment upon the faults of others, especially the society in which she moved. Great beauty frequently engenders envy and jealousy among the fair sex, and prompts some wicked hearts to say the most cruel things against their rivals; but such is life.

A crown of withered roses lies upon the stand in Alcia's chamber. She listened attentively to her little brother's friendly chat.

"I told you, sister, that you would get the *crown* if you would go to the tournament; and see (holding up the crown of wilted roses), you did get it."

"Yes, Baring, you little inquisitive, I had no idea of going, but I was out horseback riding with a friend, and he proposed stopping a few moments to look at the gallant knights, when, Baring, to my great surprise, a tall and handsome victorious knight, Mr. Cushing, crowned me the ' goddess of love and beauty.' There were very many beautiful girls on the ground, Baring, fully matured belles, renowned for their beauty, but somebody had to be crowned, to complete the order of the tournament."

"Oh no, sister, not that way at all. It was because you were the prettiest girl in St. Chelsea. Some of the old, ugly girls don't like you, sister, because you are so pretty," said little innocent Baring.

" Now, there, my little brother, you have talked enough ; let that tongue of yours rest a short time,' she said, playfully and affectionately.

" All right, sister," he said ; " I am tired, anyway, so I will lie down on the sofa a little while."

Throwing himself carelessly upon the lounge, he was soon soundly sleeping. The ringing of the front door-bell aroused him, and, springing to his feet, he came running to his mother, greatly amused. Just then, Florence entered the room, and said:

"There is a man in the back parlor who wishes to see you, Miss Enola."

Baring, still laughing immoderately, " What is the matter with you, Baring?" said his mother. " Be quiet."

" Why, mamma," said the little fellow, " I am laughing at that funny-looking man down stairs; and he wishes to see you, mamma."

Florence said, " Hush, Baring, the man will hear you."

" Florence," said Mrs. Dale, " you ask the gentleman to please excuse me, as I am quite indisposed to-day."

" Yes, ma'am," said Florence.

Soon she returned, and said, " the man would call in the morning, as he had very important business with you."

" What can be the object of his mission?" thought Enola.

" Florence," said Mrs. Dale, " what kind of looking gentleman was he?"

"Why, Miss Enola, he reminds me of the D——l."

"Well, well, Florence, did you ever see his Satanic Majesty?"

"Yes, Miss Enola, I saw him once in my dreams, and this man, if man he is, looks like the image I saw that night."

"He is coming back in the morning," said Florence, "then, Miss Enola, you can judge for yourself what he resembles."

"Strange," thought Enola, "that such a personage should have any business with me."

The following morning, at the appointed time, the stranger was again admitted into the house, and as Mrs. Dale entered the parlor, a look of surprise suffused her face. "Did you desire to see me, sir?" she politely enquired.

Advancing, he said, "I am Mr. Peccavi."

"Be seated, sir," said Mrs. Dale.

"Yes, madame, I came upon a business mission. I understand that you have an interest in a large body of land—a wife's dower—and, madame, there can be no title procured to the land without your deed." Mrs. Dale was all attention to this peculiar-looking personage, for she at first thought him to be deranged; indeed, she scarcely knew where to place him, he was such an odd-appearing individual. "Madame," Mr. Peccavi continued, "I am the attorney for the parties that wish to purchase this land." Mrs. Dale could not understand what his peculiar mission meant, as she was not aware of any landed interest she had in that portion of the State; although Mr. Dale had been a large land speculator, and she would not be surprised at any thing she might learn about his real estate investments. Still, she was bewildered. "Mrs. Dale," continued Mr. Peccavi, "if you will let me have a small amount of money to pay some back-taxes that are now due upon this land, I will send you a receipt, and also the papers that will show you your claim to your dower interest."

Mrs. Dale felt that a streak of good luck had overtaken her, and the story of this wonderful-looking specimen of humanity was apparently a straight and plausible piece of information, although his appearance was greatly against him. His height was over six feet, with narrow, contracted shoulders; a face most repulsive to look upon; a wiry, awkward individual, with no redeeming feature to recommend him to a stranger. A very peculiar combination.

He left, telling her that he would call again in a few days. She at once gave him the requested amount of money to pay the taxes upon her newly discovered land, and felt that she was the fortunate owner of soil she had known nothing of. In a few days this wily individual called again to see her. He was all excitement, having, he said, just received a telegram from an old friend requesting him to come out at once to Wyoming.

"I leave to-night, Mrs. Dale, and as it is upon your business that I am going, I will have to make another demand upon you for sufficient money to defray my necessary expenses. I will call and see you upon my return," said Mr. Peccavi."

One cold, disagreeable morning, who again should be announced but Mr. Peccavi. Mrs. Dale was quite anxious to know his business, as he had just returned from Wyoming.

"Good morning, Mrs. Dale, I have had a very eventful time since I last saw you," he said.

"Indeed," she replied.

"Yes, ma'am. Your old attorney, Mr. Holdum, sent for me, to express to me his dying wishes, and as the entire interview is closely connected with your interest, I will relate it to you: Mr. Holdum is now dead, poor fellow. Well, madam, he made me promise that I would attend to recovering back for you all the money that Mr. Cheatem had so cruelly purloined from you and your children. I made him the sacred promise," he continued, "that I would as soon as possible obtain an interview with you, and you could act upon your own good judgment in the premises."

Enola, feeling deeply annoyed at the possibility of being drawn into the meshes of the law, said, in a very subdued tone of voice, at the same time trying to read every expression of Mr. Peccavi's cold, hard face, "Mr. Peccavi, did you make an investigation of all the settlements Mr. Cheatem ever made?"

"I did, madame," he promptly answered. "You perhaps do not know, Mrs. Dale, that I have attended to a great deal of business for Mr. Cheatem, for which services he owes me to-day—heavy lawsuit, involving large amounts of money—and I am fully up to him in all his tricks and shrewdness, and having been associated with him in various ways, no one knows him more thoroughly than myself. He owes me to-day, madame, many thousands of dollars. He is fully able to pay me, but I cannot get it."

Mrs. Dale, after listening most attentively to all he said, replied, "You did not explain to me fully what Mr. Holdum told you."

"Yes, madame, I have digressed a little. Well, I went with Mr. Holdum to the vault that contained all the papers necessary to ascertain the facts regarding your business, and there my keen eye, together with Mr. Holdum's clearly defined explanations, soon convinced me of all the wrongs you have suffered.

"When Mr. Holdum expected every day to be his last, and when I sat beside his dying bed, he explained to me all your wrongs, saying : ' Mr. Peccavi, I cannot pass away peacefully until you promise me that you will see this good woman (Mrs. Dale) righted, and all her money restored to her and her children which is now in the possession of Mr. Cheatem. I sat quietly and saw Mrs. Dale robbed of her money, and now, I am soon to stand before my maker, Mr. Peccavi; and oh, I cannot die with this foul blot upon my soul. You can come to my relief, Mr. Peccavi. I have known you a long time, my old friend, and there is no other living man I would entrust with this, my death-bed secret. You know just how to proceed to recover it back for this helpless woman, and promise me now that you will attend to it—all, everything. Could I be spared a little longer, she and her children should not suffer this great wrong. Mr. Peccavi, all is growing dark around me. Spare and forgive me, oh my merci-

ful Father, for this, the darkest stain upon the pages of
my life's history! Wipe out the blot, and let me
appear before my great Creator free from the awful
crime of assisting in defrauding the widow and the
orphan! Clasp my trembling hand, Mr. Peccavi, and
give me the desired promise, for all is darkness before
me! Kiss me, my darling wife; press my cold, damp
brow. And is this death? Can this be death?' So
passed away Mr. Holdum."

"Now," continued Mr. Peccavi, "I will leave you
to decide what you will do in regard to what I have related to you, and I will call in a few days and learn
your decision."

"Remain a moment," said Mrs. Dale, "I wish to
converse with you a little longer upon a subject that is
of such vital importance to me and mine. Do you
think, Mr. Peccavi, that you could recover for me and
my children this money, so cruelly taken from us?"

"Most assuredly, madame; without any trouble in
the world," he earnestly replied.

"Would it be a very expensive litigation, Mr. Peccavi? I have only my home, here in St. Chelsea, and
some real estate in Wyoming, so you discover, Mr.
Peccavi, that Mr. Cheatem did not leave me much to
litigate with."

"Mrs. Dale," replied Mr. Peccavi, his eyes fairly
dancing in his small round head at the thought of a
shadow of a lawsuit, especially against Mr. Cheatem;
"Madame, I will promise you that if you will let me
manage this business, that you will not be out one dol-

lar, until I recover all your money, and when once in your possession, I will charge you fifteen per cent, or fifteen dollars on the hundred; but,'' he continued, ''I will have to make demands upon you for my expenses during the suit, but they will not be very heavy.''

After serious thought Mrs. Dale replied :

'' Mr. Peccavi, I will agree to your proposition, and will entrust the entire business to your judgment.''

CHAPTER X.

FOR several long years Mr. Peccavi carried Mrs. Dale through all the intricacies known to the legal fraternity, and ofttimes she had a feeling of despair creeping over her. His heavy demands upon her for money became intolerable; but he always had a plausible story to tell, and invariably closed by saying: "Do you grudge a few thousand dollars when you will most surely recover so large an amount, madame? This is a 'mammoth' suit, and requires a larger amount of money than I thought. Besides, Mrs. Dale, any means you advance to me will be allowed in my settlement."

"But, Mr. Peccavi," Mrs. Dale would frequently expostulate, "suppose you should not win this gigantic lawsuit, as you term it; where will I then be?"

"Oh, madame," he replied, most excitedly, "but you are bound to win it. I have brought this suit in a *just* court—yes, a court of equity; and if there is any justice in law and courts, *you* will be victorious, madam. Why should our wise constitution have such institutions as *courts*, if not to defend and protect the interest of the people that are driven to them to seek for redress from the honorable chancery? Are they simply cloaks to conceal the dishonest acts of men? No, madame, far from it."

"I believe, Mr. Peccavi," said Mrs. Dale, "that there is still goodness among men. Lawyers can be

(202)

honest and just; bankers can prove true to their trusts. So it is in every department of business. I think I have discovered in my experience through life, that all persons have some redeeming trait of character, from the lofty monarch that sits upon his gilded throne, to the lowly, humble child of squalid poverty. God has implanted within the bosom of each one of his creatures some tender germ of good, that, if properly nourished, will develop or ripen into purity and nobility of character. Man was not made for selfish purposes alone."

"I agree with you in all you have said, Mrs. Dale; and I trust when I redeem my pledge to poor Mr. Holdum, and place you and your children into possession of your rights, he will rest more quietly in his lowly bed, and you will then have faith in chancery courts."

"Mr. Peccavi, I have expended a very large amount of money upon this controversy, and oh, if you are alluring me on to unfounded hopes, only to be dashed to pieces by some inexorable judge's decision, I am sure nature will certainly yield to the heavy disappointment, and all will be over with me. I cannot now bear the trials I did in former years, Mr. Peccavi."

"Madame, let me assure you: never fear; I am going to win your suit; for where justice dwells, law knows no contradiction."

Mr. Peccavi seemed full of hope.

"I feel quite comforted, Mr. Peccavi, to find you so sanguine in the matter," politely replied Mrs. Dale, "but law is uncertain and very expensive to those who are drawn into its mazes."

"You will express yourself very differently, Mrs. Dale, when I call upon you to count over one hundred thousand dollars," pleasingly responded the artful Mr. Peccavi.

"Yes," Mrs. Dale musingly replied, "I suppose I will then look at life a little differently. I have been treated very badly by those that should have had my interest at heart."

"You are a good and noble woman, Mrs. Dale, and God knows that all the money that you have advanced to me shall be paid to you. *I would not defraud you, madame,* for you have already suffered too great a loss by Mr. Cheatem. You have my sympathies, madame. If anything new should be developed in the case, I will keep you advised. Good afternoon, Mrs. Dale," said Mr. Peccavi.

"I wish, my dear Alcia, that I was free from these everlasting lawsuits," said her mother, "for they almost drive me wild."

"Mamma," said Alcia, "I wish you were through with this horrid old wretch, Mr. Peccavi; I have a contempt for him, and I am sure no such looking specimen of humanity could ever win a lawsuit, especially against such a man as Mr. Cheatem."

"My daughter," gently replied Mrs. Dale, "Mr. Peccavi is disagreeable looking, I admit, but every-body has spoken to me about his fine legal attainments, and what do I care for his appearance, if he is only successful with my law case."

"But, mamma, that old creature will never, never win your suit. Listen to me, mamma, for you are so confiding, and always did believe everything anybody told you. Now, I know what I am saying; you must not build your hopes upon success, for they will only be dashed to pieces, as the autumn leaves fall from their withered boughs to mingle with the past.''

"My sweet child is not at all comforting to her poor mamma," said Enola.

"Not in this suit, for I plainly see that this man Peccavi is only extracting money from you, as the vampire draws the blood from his victim," continued Alcia.

"I very much fear your words are too true, my precious child," sobbed Enola.

"Mamma," she said, "you should know that a man like old Peccavi could not command the respect of any court, besides he does not possess the attributes that constitute a gentleman, and I think if he is not deranged, that he is a bad and wicked man. I know that I judge him correctly, although I have never exchanged twenty words with him, mamma. His face and his whole appearance give the man's true character away."

"Well, Alcia, we will soon have our most anxious fears relieved. The day is fast approaching when Mr. Peccavi will be permitted to show to the court his ability as a successful lawyer. I am almost financially ruined now, by his insatiable demand for money, but I am still confident of his success, for he seems to have put all his talent into this case."

Alcia, possessed of an unusual degree of good common sense, endowed with keen perceptive powers, read the true character of this designing old man, which impressed her with such repugnance for him, that each time she saw him she only heaped contempt upon his head, and added fuel to her well-founded ideas of his belonging to that long list of "dead-beats" that are now flooding our land. Her mother would freely expostulate with her.

"Alcia, it is not displaying a christian spirit to show such perfect contempt for any one. The poor old man is doing the best he can to wrest our money from the possession of Mr. Cheatem, and you should not be so severe upon him, my sweet daughter."

"Mamma, not wishing to wound your feelings by reminding you of your greatest fault, *credulity*, and trusting that you will pardon me the expression, I must say that old Mr. Peccavi has completely duped you by his professions of truthfulness, when those that know him best universally proclaim that truth is foreign to his nature. Only the other day, I heard a gentleman say that he had known Mr. Peccavi for years, and in that length of time never heard him tell the truth but once, and that was when he said his child was dead, which was true, for the physicians pronounced it so."

"Alcia, my darling, I trust you will never allow the confidence you repose in people to carry you away from reason and your better judgment. I very rarely doubt the veracity of anybody that chance may throw me with. I wish, Alcia, I could look upon the world with more suspicion, but I have always detested a man or woman whom I suspected would or could be guilty of doing a wrong act; and frequently I am reminded of the golden rule: 'Do unto others as you would have them do unto you,' and we are to 'iudge not, lest ye be judged.'"

"Good maxims, very good," replied Alcia, "but everyone should let reason be their guide. Think, mamma, of Mr. Cheatem and his wholesale robbery, and I consider him a perfect gentleman in comparison with Mr. Peccavi, but both sharp, designing men, where they can play in a grab game, each lost to all sense of honor. But, mamma, let us drift into a more pleasant conversation, for it makes my heart sick to speak of men so unfaithful to all trust, and so lost to all that constitutes the good and honorable in man."

"You talk well, my child," said her mother, "and your views and ideas of what mankind should be are correct, and for one of your years it is wonderful, wonderful."

Alcia, the ever-winning and charming girl, delighting the society in which she moved by her sparkling wit and repartee, was admired and sought by many of the best marriageable men of our country. Men of the highest social, political and financial standing knelt àt beauty's shrine, longing for one encouraging smile from Alcia's young, fresh face, but all shared equally alike her friendship and regard.

"Cousin Alcia," said Bentley Cushing (a favorite cousin of hers), "I have a friend who greatly desires an introduction to you, my charming cousin, and I have

called to ascertain from you what time (if agreeable)
can we come?''

" Cousin Bentley, I have many engagements ahead,
as, no doubt, all society girls have, but if it will suit
your convenience, also that of your friend, I will
appoint next Wednesday evening for this anticipated
pleasure—on my part must I say, Cousin Bentley?''

" By no means, my angelic cousin," replied Bentley,
for he had been in love with her since her debut into
society, or her return from abroad.   " It is a freak of
mischief prompts you to taunt me thus ; you know too
well, sweet cousin, my heart toward you, and the wild
admiration I have for my Cousin Alcia. You have
taught me, by your gentle manner and sweet graces,
fearing to wound my sensitive feelings, just what I
can hope for from my idolized cousin; haven't you,
my lovely Alcia?''

"Bentley," said she, " let us change this subject,
for I dislike the sentimental."

"Oh, cousin," replied Bentley a little coolly, "when
the man of your choice offers his heart and hand to
you, then you will lend a listening ear to all his protestations of esteem, won't you?''

" As I have not had that experience yet, Bentley, I
am not in a condition to answer that question. My
heart is as free as the mountain bird that flies from tree
to tree, chirping all day long his merry song of freedom ;
love's thraldom has never placed its silken shackles
upon my heart, Bentley. I am as cold to that passion
you young sentimentalist call love, as the snow-capped
peaks of the Andes; as free from being pierced by

Cupid's darts as the lofty eagle that builds its nest amid craggy rocks, beyond the reach of mortal man."

"Stop!" said Bentley; "you are soaring so far away from our conversation, let me bring my beautiful cousin back to earth."

"Bentley, you are such a tease. What is it, now that you have bid me return to plain mother earth?"

"Well," Bentley Cushing said, "my friend, Mr. Manwell, and 'your cousin,' will call at the appointed time. So relentless, wicked, cruel, and desperate fate commands me, in its thundering tones to tear myself away from you, and puts into my desolate heart, causing my lips to speak and utter the painful words, ' good night.' "

"Ha! ha! What a boy my Cousin Bentley Cushing is. I like him, always so blithe and free from moroseness, like many of our men of the present age. The world is rushing on in its dizzy maze. Parties, balls, theatres, pleasure seekers, amusements of all kind to please the young as well as the aged. Alas! when is this microcosm of ours to end?" thoughtfully mused Alcia, always so versatile.

"I will seek mamma and draw her out upon this theme. She loves to talk Bible to me, and I sometimes like to hear her converse upon religious matters; for, if I am fond of society, I also love the plain, sacred truths taught in God's own Book."

Callers interrupted the desired conversation between mother and daughter. There are times when every heart requires *rest*. The wealthy and pampered, surrounded with all that endears them to life, have need

14

to withdraw from the allurements of the world for a
time; and the society man or woman frequently longs
to steal away to some quiet chamber to find *rest*.   How
sweet the word to the wayworn pilgrim.   "*Rest* is
what I most desire."   Visit the poor working woman,
that burns the midnight oil, toiling to procure subsist-
ence to meet the daily wants of herself and children.
Ask that pale-faced, careworn woman what she requires,
and she instinctively answers, "*Rest*."   All nature
demands a time of complete quietude.

Mr. Peccavi is announced by Florence.

"I suppose, Alcia, that we will hear some news from
him in regard to our pending suit," said Mrs. Dale, as
she arranged her tie before entering the parlor.

"Good morning, Mrs. Dale," said Mr. Peccavi; "I
only called to inform you, madame, that as I have had
some heavy transcripts copied, I will require about four
or five hundred dollars more, and that will be *all* I will
need for the present to carry on this "*mammoth*" litigation.   I am surprised myself to see how expensive this
suit has been."

Mrs. Dale answered him in the most positive manner,
saying: "Mr. Peccavi, I can stand this drainage upon
my purse no longer.   This suit, sir, has now cost me
three thousand dollars, and you call upon me for still
more money.   Mr. Peccavi, your demands are very
unreasonable.   I shall be compelled to throw up the
entire business.   I am hopelessly ruined, sir.   I can
stand it no longer.   All that you have left me is my
home, sir."

"Mrs. Dale," he said, "why do you grudge a few thousand dollars when I am going to recover for you over one hundred thousand dollars? You should not be annoyed. You can dispose of your home, for you will soon be in a position to purchase a more elegant and suitable house, when your just rights are restored to you."

"Oh, Mr. Peccavi, why do you advise me to do such a rash act? Suppose you should not be successful in this suit, as I have repeatedly suggested before, what could I then do? I would be homeless and penniless. I am not calculated to go out into the world to earn my own support, for I have been reared in the lap of luxury, amidst great wealth, and I am not the person to come in contact with this heartless world," she sorrowfully replied.

"But, Mrs. Dale, you paint a gloomy picture, when you should only think of the glowing future that awaits you upon the termination of this 'famous' suit. You will have all that is necessary to render one content and happy. So, madam, try to raise me five hundred dollars by next Thursday, if possible."

"Mr. Peccavi, I do not like to dispute your word, but a small, still voice constantly whispers in my ear that you are not going to be successful in the Cheatem lawsuit. I cannot explain to you any particular reason that causes me to form such a conclusion, but an evil forboding haunts me constantly."

"You should not allow yourself to give way to any doubts, but have full confidence in your lawyer and his ability to win a case, and, madame, you will come out all right," said Mr. Peccavi, as his gloated eyes viewed in imagination the five hundred dollars already before him. "We are now so near the trial and settlement of this famous suit that you must brave up, madame; you will shortly be in possession of your rights."

"You are very encouraging, and I pray to God that all your sanguine expectations may be realized. Since we are so near the close of this long and disagreeable litigation, I will, if possible, try to raise the amount of money you say that you require, 'though it will place me in some financial embarrassment," said Mrs. Dale.

"Good morning, madame," said Mr. Peccavi, and his tall, angular figure was soon making strides to his office; but he would have to halt at a saloon to take a little something to *build him up*, as he had but a small amount of flesh upon his wiry bones.

Mr. Peccavi became the laughing-stock of Mrs. Dale's entire family, and many who met him pronounced him either in his dotage or a consummate villain.

Mrs. Dale, with a great effort, tried to have confidence in his ability and honesty, notwithstanding the battery daily brought to bear against her credulity. She could only look hopefully forward to the termination of this long and hotly contested lawsuit. She felt that, either for or against her, the decision alone could ease her mind; but that for her dear children and faithful Florence, life would have but few attractions; every happy moment was almost invariably obscured by a dark cloud that seemed to haunt her very existence. No one could ever doubt Enola's generous im-

pulses, for she rarely let an opportunity pass when
presented to her that she did not come to the relief of
the distressed, especially her own sex. It was always
the joy of her life to mitigate the suffering in mind or
body. As an instance, we will relate upon one occasion
poor old Mrs. Dilwith came to her in great distress of
mind, wringing her hands and weeping bitterly. "Oh,
Mrs. Dale!" she said, "the sheriff is in my house and
is going to attach everything I have, and, oh, tell me
what am I to do!"

"Dry your tears, Mrs. Dilwith," said Enola, "and
I will go at once and stop this proceeding against your
property. I will assume your indebtedness, Mrs.
Dilwith, and you shall be allowed to retain your furniture."

She straightway sought the sheriff and gave him a
check for the full amount of the claim. Words cannot
express the seemingly thankful spirit Mrs. Dilwith displayed toward Enola, and for a brief time she certainly
felt a full appreciation of the kindness; but, as time
wore on, the favor reflected back only the shadow.
of the past. Ingratitude, ingratitude, she thought,
had completely seared the heart of Mrs. Dilwith. It
pained her to see these infirmities in human nature.

Alcia looked queenly, robed in a heavy combination
of green and gold velvet, richly draped, and garnished
with exquisite point lace. Her golden hair, dressed
high upon her swan-like neck, with flashing jewels,
vieing with the brilliancy of her dark brown eyes, she
was indeed a picture to behold. Florence bore upon a

silver salver two handsome visiting cards: "Bentley Cushing" and "Auguste Manwell."

"This is my cousin, Miss Vernon, Mr. Manwell."

"Very happy to meet you, Mr. Manwell," said Alcia.

"I feel that I am not meeting a stranger," said Mr. Manwell, "as I have so very frequently heard our friend Bentley speak of you. Indeed, Miss Vernon, I have had so many graphic descriptions given me of yourself, that I should have known you had I met you in the streets of New York."

"Indeed," replied Alcia pleasantly, "I am happy to know that my friends remember me sufficiently well to give a description of me. I like to think of not being forgotten."

After passing a most charming evening, interspersed with music and wit, the two gentlemen departed.

Once out into the street, Bentley remarked: "Auguste, how do you like my cousin Alcia?"

"Why, Bent., old fellow, she is the most transcendentally beautiful girl that I have ever beheld; and so bright and versatile, full of humor and wit. Why, that young lady could entertain twenty beaux as easily as one. Wonderful girl. My heart is gone. I am in the same boat with everybody else that is fortunate enough to meet her. I am infatuated; yes, in love, my old friend."

"Well, Auguste, before you become hopelessly gone, investigate your pathway, and see whether it lies among roses and violets, or if thistles and thorns hedge it up. Be careful, old boy, there are at least one hundred love-sick swains now imploring a smile from my cousin. Don't become stranded upon the shores of *love*. She is callous to all their ardent protestations, so guard well your approach. Now, who knows but that *you* may be the very man to win her heart. I know that she *has* a heart, and that it is frank, warm and noble.''

''I believe, Bentley,'' said Auguste, ''that you are in love with your fair cousin yourself.''

''I have never denied that accusation, Auguste, but she only regards me with a cousin's affection, and, really, hardly that. But you continue nourishing the flame that is now burning within your bosom, and maybe Cousin Alcia may quench it herself.''

''You give me great encouragement, I must say, Bentley. You are a queer fellow; always was. Now don't tell your cousin how greatly I am infatuated with her at first sight. Leave that for me, Bentley. I desire that pleasure myself. I could gaze into those grand eyes of hers forever; and did you ever see such pearly teeth? Faultless.''

''Good night, Auguste,'' said Bentley, as he approached his residence.''

Let us return to Alcia. Seated in her mother's room, before a cheerful fire, she exclaimed: ''Mamma, Mr. Manwell is the most elegant gentleman that I have met since my return home. I do admire his quiet, dignified manner, yet he is not stiff, but easy and graceful.''

CHAPTER XI.

MR. MANWELL became a frequent visitor at the home of Mrs. Dale. Alcia admired his proud, determined style, and very frequently commented upon his independent spirit. He was an only son of a family whose ancestors figured extensively in the French Revolution, and gained for themselves a most enviable reputation for valor and faithfulness to their country's cause; which distinction has descended from generation to generation, and made illustrious several members of the Manwell family.

Mrs. Dale had a lady relative, of whom she was very fond, who had importuned her upon several occasions to consent for her daughter to accompany her abroad. As she had been partially educated in a European school, she believed that she would not only be of great assistance to her in speaking the foreign languages, but it would be exceedingly pleasant to *chaperone* so beautiful and accomplished a young lady. Mrs. Gilford persisted in having Alcia join her for a year's travel in Europe, till her yielding mother at last consented.

Dr. and Mrs. Gilford were very dear to Enola, and she felt that no better opportunity could have presented itself; for whilst at school Alcia did not travel as much as she desired through many parts of Europe; that now she could enjoy with them the many historic

(216)

portions of the old world—always full of interest to
the observing traveler and appreciative mind.

" I never heard you express yourself in such language before, about any of your gentleman friends,"
said her mother. " What has come over you?"

" Mamma, I am not an enthusiast over anybody or
anything, but I somehow do like the appearance of Mr.
Manwell. He seems unlike any of my gentleman
friends. I admire odd people, but they must be cultured. I don't admire the oddity of such as old man
Peccavi, reminding me more of an ape than a man;
but I think Mr. Manwell can be classed among the
pleasing odd people. He is not handsome, but polished
and refined."

"Well, my dear," said her mother, "we know that he
belongs to a very old and aristocratic family, and I
think, my child, that ancestral lineage has much to do
with a person's innate refinement ; for, using a common
expression, ' blood will tell.' "

" I agree with you, mamma. I could not marry a
man of low origin. Still, many of our greatest and
most gifted men descended from obscure parents. I
have great respect for a self-made person — a meretori-
ous man or woman — but I love the high-born still,"
she said.

" I think, Alcia, a person with an abundance of *will-
power* can make and form the man. Force of character
guides us on through life, aiding us in the accomplishment of great purposes. It conquers foes; it drives
the coward back to shame ; and, behind that strong
fortification, has subdued nations, and restored peace

to a country verging upon war.   All will readily admit,
that without will or firmness, a general on the field of
battle would soon be vanquished; and hence all should
cultivate that trait of character especially."

As the " Acacia " was advertised to take her depar
ture for Liverpool upon a certain day, and Dr. Gilford
was anxious to secure passage upon that particular
steamship, Alcia had but little time to prepare for the
voyage.

When Mr. Manwell learned that she was about to
leave for a foreign land, he seemed greatly distressed,
and then and there made a full confession to her of his
passion.   He urged her to become his betrothed.

"I cannot think of such a long separation.   A year
is a great while to be absent from those we love; and
then, who knows but—well, I will not express myself
just now upon the subject, but I wish you to promise
me, Miss Vernon, that you will not give your heart
and hand away to any of those titled beaux that you
will be sure to captivate," said Auguste Manwell.

" Mr. Manwell," said she, " I am very certain that
no one abroad can ever win my affection.   Indeed, I
am proof against this passion you call ' love;' yet, no-
body understands fully his or her own heart until
tested," she replied with a thoughtful smile.

" Then, Miss Vernon," said Auguste, " permit me to
test yours, will you?"

"Certainly, Mr. Manwell; only tell me how you
propose to go about it?"

"Well," replied Mr. Manwell, " if your heart does
not yield to some one of your many admirers, you

must allow me to try to win your love, Miss Vernon.
Think seriously of this conversation, won't you," he
said.

"Mr. Manwell, I have a sure way of testing one's
heart. As you are fond of the wild frontier country,
and have often expressed your intention of making it
your home, now, Mr. Manwell, if you will remain away
five years, and are true to your 'first love,' as you
say, and I find no one I am willing to bestow my affection upon in the meantime, and still regard you as I
now do, I will then look favorably upon your declaration. How do you like that test?" she asked.

"Miss Vernon, though you are severe and exacting
in your request, my love for you is of that true devotion and sincerity, that I am willing to be banished, by
you, to a lonely isle in the Ægean sea, if by such
banishment I can win your love, my beautiful girl. I
am willing to wend my way, and pitch my tent nearer
the setting sun, among the savages and wild beasts of
the forest, and there remain until your command bid
me return. When you are gliding over the broad
bosom of the Atlantic with your friends, enjoying to
the fullest extent the pleasures of life, I shall be rushing on to new scenes, and a life that is to be henceforth
solitary and alone; but I shall have your lovely image
engraven upon my heart, and that will be all the society
I require during our separation."

"Am I asking too much of you, Mr. Manwell?" she
said.

"By no means; your desires are my pleasure. I
prefer to be alone when thinking of you, and as my

thoughts are constantly upon you, it is necessary that I should be to myself."

With many promises to correspond, and keep remembrances of each other fresh in their hearts, Auguste Manwell bade her farewell. He felt very sad, and was really convinced in his own mind that no one but his idolized Alcia could ever claim his affections. He was a man of great intensity of feeling, but to the stranger seemed cold and indifferent. His true character he concealed from the outside world, but to know him was to appreciate his worth, merit and ability. He was not a man to win friendship easily, but when once an attachment existed, with him it was as firm as the sea-washed rocks of the Dardanelles. Auguste Manwell was a man of sterling integrity—a good man.

Enola sat musing alone in her quiet chamber, after the departure of Dr. and Mrs. Gilford with darling Alcia. "Yes, I have a lonely, sad life; many, very many trials to bear. I cannot look for much sympathy from Wickliffe. He is of the world, and carried away by its pleasures and follies. Poor boy! I hope he will learn by experience the inability of earthly enjoyments to satisfy the cravings of the soul. I wish that my fate had been different, and that my lot had been cast among none but the honest and upright of earth. Alas! this could never be. To the christian, life has its thorny paths; for through great suffering and affliction the heart is purified and made perfect to receive the crown that awaits the immortal saints. It is a sweet sadness to review the past. But, hark! what noise is that I hear in the hall?"

Enola sprang to her feet, and in a moment Florence was by her side, wild with excitement, trembling from head to foot.

"Miss Enola, come, for God's sake ; poor little Baring is killed !"

Mrs. Dale attempted to descend the stairs, when she fell fainting to the floor. The hall was crowded with friends, anxious to know the worst. After some time she regained consciousness, and was told by the attending physicians that little Baring would live, but he would require perfect quiet, and such nursing as only a mother's anxious heart and gentle hands can bestow.

The dear little boy had been playing out in the broad street, with other children, in the deep, soft snow, unconscious of any passers-by, when a large two-horse carriage, belonging to some liveryman in the city, came rolling down the grade, when one of the fiery horses struck and knocked him senseless under the wheels of the vehicle, bruising him fearfully. He was lifted into the house, covered with gore, bleeding profusely from his wounded face. Fortunately no internal injury had been produced by the dreadful accident. It only caused the little sufferer many long, weary nights of pain.

"Baring bore his affliction bravely, and with remarkable patience ; but with the assistance of good nursing he slowly began to recover. His schoolmates kept the sick room continually supplied with beautiful and fragrant flowers.

"Patient little sufferer," said Dr. Armstrong, "you will soon be well, my boy."

"I know I am improving, for I am not so sore now when Florence moves me in my bed," said Baring. "If I could only see my sister Alcia I would recover so much faster, Doctor."

Frequent letters came from her, giving glowing accounts of their travels. They attended several brilliant court receptions, and Mrs. Gilford always exclaimed that "Miss Vernon was considered the most beautiful lady in the room."

After visiting many places of interest, viewing the wonders of the great cities, the rural, mountainous scenery of Switzerland, climbing to the most noted points of the snow-capped peaks of the Rega and Matterhorn; visiting old castles full of historic interest, from age and exposure now tottering and crumbling to the earth; ruins and bastiles that, could their decaying walls speak, they would tell to the inquiring visitors truths that would curdle their very blood; ruins that are now the abode of bats, with the venomous reptile and screeching owl as companions. These once palatial mansions are now infested with loathsome creatures; where an occasional brigand seeks shelter to escape the fury of some midnight storm, but as quickly as the elements become quiet, hies himself beyond the dreaded place, fearing the apparition of some holy martyr who had lived long ages ago.

This happy party were soon to return to their native soil. Mrs. Dale's anxious heart longed to be with her child again, for always her presence was a source of great comfort to her, and alleviated, to a great extent, her sorrows. Her bright, sunny smile added delight to the entire household, causing her mother to feel less the responsibilities that constantly crowded upon her. She longed to press her to her bosom once more.

A messenger boy bore a telegram to Mrs. Dale, reading thus:

"We will be in St. Chelsea Tuesday morning.
H. Gilford."

What inexpressible joy filled the heart of the fond mother. Baring could scarcely contain his emotional delight; he proudly ran from room to room proclaiming the joyful tidings, "My sweet sister will be home on Tuesday." Each member of the household were anxious to welcome her return, and every preparation necessary to her comfort and pleasure was fully arranged for the expected arrival of the friends and loved ones.

The happy morn brought the party safely to St. Chelsea, Alcia looking the picture of health and perfected loveliness from her year's sojourn abroad. The brilliancy of color suffusing her plump, round cheeks certainly added a charm to her rare beauty—perfect health verifying the picture.

The famous Cheatem litigation drags slowly through the mills of law. Old Mr. Peccavi was still positive of final success in his "mammoth case," as he invariably termed it.

Mrs. Dale's hopes were still bright. Her anticipated recovery of her lost fortune added a few rays of sunshine to a life that had been so full of sorrow.

After many conversations with her daughter upon this cursive subject, each time the strong mind of the incredulous girl persistently refusing to listen to any promise of success that might attend Mr. Peccavi's efforts, "Mamma," she at length said, "can you expect a court to give to a man bearing the reputation Mr. Peccavi does a verdict in his favor? No; my dear mother, that poor old man, as I have repeatedly told you, could have no weight with such a dignified body *as a court.*"

Alcia spoke with a great deal of vehemence and felt all that she had said.

" My daughter, you may misjudge Mr. Peccavi. We cannot believe all that a wicked, gossipping world might say of him. At the same time, I do not consider him the very soul of honor. Still, he may have his enemies, and they may be trying to ruin him. I yet have confidence in his ability as a lawyer."

" Yes, mamma; when the bridge has carried you over safely, then you can praise it; and I will wait, myself, till then, before I commence my exultations."

" Well, my child, let us be patient, and time will develop and bring with it the fruits of his labors. It were well that future events were not revealed to the obscure mind, for there would be many tear-stained pages in the ' Book of Knowledge.' God's wisdom in concealing and throwing a veil over the coming events of life certainly cannot be disputed. In all His seeming mysterious acts, His great wisdom stands out in bold relief, showing mortal man his utter insignificance and dependence."

"Mamma," did you know that I had received a letter from Mr. Manwell very recently, in which he stated that he expected to visit St. Chelsea in a few days? I shall be quite rejoiced to see him again," she continued.

"Indeed," said Mrs. Dale; "I do not think he has been here for more than a year. I should, myself, be pleased to see him, for I view him as a most sensible man; so positive and dignified in his bearing, that I cannot but admire him. He will remain some time, I suppose," she said.

"No," said Alcia. "He will be on his way to California."

"Is Mr. Manwell of a roving disposition, my child?" asked Mrs. Dale.

"By no means, my dear mother. He is a man that has traveled extensively, and has a knowledge of many things necessary to a life of research and business, and his heart craves to acquire more and more information upon subjects that will benefit him in the future." Alcia continued: "He always said that his local attachments were very strong, and that his firmness knew no bounds; that when his mind was fully convinced of a fact, it required a strong effort on the part of friends to eradicate his decision."

"I admire a man of such force of character, and can now begin to realize the *fatal mistake* of my life—it was credulity," said Enola sorrowfully.

"Mamma," she asked, "if you could recall the sands of time, place back the sun's dial, subtract thirty years of your life, and begin to tread the pathway of

15

your existence anew, what would be the first change that you would make?"

"My daughter, "replied Enola, "you have put a strange question to me, but I shall not be confounded over it, so will answer according to the dictates of my heart. The first thing that I should change, my child, would be my confiding, credulous nature. I would change many of my imperfections, and try to assimilate our blessed Redeemer's character."

"Well, mamma, you have answered my question well. I agree with you. I have always told you that credulity was your failing; that some day you would be greatly disappointed in human nature, as you have always considered everybody sincere and honest."

"You speak, Alcia, like one who had been in the world and traversed its rugged pathway many years, and you are not yet twenty years old, my daughter, nor have you ever known one sorrow or disappointment in your young life. God forbid that the wrongs may ever be visited upon you that have been my sad experience to endure," she said, with a sigh.

"You may rest assured, mamma, that were I to marry and be left a widow with a fortune, that no administrator would ever control my money. Never, never;" stamping her tiny foot upon the carpet.

"But, my daughter, suppose you could not defend your interest, and had not sufficient executive ability to manage an estate, what would you then do, Alcia?" asked her mother.

"I would soon make myself proficient in business; sufficiently posted, at least, to keep my means from

' ghouls,' as my deceased grandparent styled the robbers of the widow and orphan. A good and appropriate epithet," she . said.

" I think every woman should know something about business," replied Mrs. Dale. "My father never taught me anything but to look upon the beauties of life, not the stern realities that come to many. He always tried to impress upon my mind that he would leave me an abundance of ' filthy lucre ' as Mr. Cheatem called it, to place me independently above the cold frowns of the world. I wish very much that I had been taught to be suspicious of every body, until they had proven themselves worthy of my confidence ; what an age of anxiety and care it would have spared me ; but I must not harrow up the ground sown with tears and sorrow, for my heart would burst with disappointed and crushed hopes," said Enola.

"My darling mamma," said Alcia, tenderly placing her head upon her mother's shoulder, " let us not talk upon so unpleasant a subject; but our conversation inadvertently drifted upon the painful theme ; it was no fault of mine ; cheer up, all will yet end well, and in the decline of your life you will be bright and happy. Beside, mamma, you know how firm your faith in Christ is, and how you trust Him, and you may live to see that these trials, that now seem so burdensome, have proved blessings in disguise."

" Alcia, you are truly a comfort to me," said her mother.

After kissing her mother fondly, and whispering words of solace to her, she withdrew to her room to

arrange her toilet to receive Mr. Manwell, who was
expected to call in a few hours upon her.

Sweeping majestically into her mother's room to im-
print a kiss upon her lips before going into the parlor,
Alcia stood in front of Mrs. Dale, a perfect picture.
Her light golden hair fell loosely from beneath a rich
band that confined it, while her great lustrous brown
eyes looked lovingly upon a mother that almost idolized
her.

"Welcome to St. Chelsea" was the greeting Alcia
gave Auguste Manwell. After an hour's conversation
with him her mother came into the room, receiving him
with a warm welcome. He had improved wonderfully,
during his frontier life; his cheeks were bronzed by
the dry hot prairie winds that sweep over those vast
fields, adding a healthy appearance that greatly enhanced
the complexion.

Alcia thought: "I have never seen him look so
handsome. Indeed, I never considered him even good-
ing before."

"Miss Vernon, you are looking well," said Mr. Manwell. "I rarely pay compliments, as you know; but
really, you remind me of some Peri queen. I am entranced, so forgive me if I seem to gaze too admiringly
upon your face. Anyway, Miss Vernon, I am rejoiced
to see you. I have been in the western wilds, shooting
the buffalo and game that abound in that country,
whilst my queenly Miss Vernon has been gracing the
courts of a foreign land. Quite a contrast in our lives,
don't you think?"

"Yes; I am sure your frontier life has not detracted

any from your dignity. But were you not happy in your uncivilized home?''

''Certainly, Miss Vernon. I would not return to this country, only to secure the consummation of my fondest hopes and promises, made to me by yourself, when we separated. Have you forgotten those vows, my angelic girl? I hope not. They are with me as fresh and sacred as on the day we made them.''

Alcia, in a taunting manner, asked him how long he expected to remain in the city.

''That is with you, Miss Vernon. If you desire me to continue my journey at once, say so, and I will obey your command; but I would not have left my far-away home at this particular time, but for the exquisite pleasure of seeing you, the only woman that ever stirred my heart. You have awakened all my ardent nature, and I love you as never woman was loved.'

''The same old story,'' thought Alcia, ''that I have listened to so many times, and as carelessly cast aside. I wish I could meet a man who would express his vows of undying love a little differently,'' she thought. ''I do not admire this sameness in all my beaux.''

Mr. Manwell, almost a ''mind-reader,'' with quick perception, continued: ''I am of that peculiar temperament, Miss Vernon, that unrequited love would not place me in the grave, with a green, grassy mound o'er my head.''

Alcia's heart was touched. She looked at him a moment in silence. She could not understand why *he* should express himself to her in that manner, when every other admirer that had ever made a declaration of love to her would certainly die without a reciprocity of affection. "I like that man," she thought, "for his independent spirit. I am sure he will never be ruled by a woman, and that is the kind of man to win my heart, love and respect."

"Miss Vernon," he continued, "I have boldly, truthfully and sincerely declared my love for you. I have asked you in all frankness to become my wife, and it is now for you to say what you will do. You have told me in all candor, that whilst you were traveling with Dr. and Mrs. Gilford you had kept your heart secure from love's attacks. Did you test your affections, and have you found them true to me, Miss Vernon? Answer me now, or never."

"Mr. Manwell, I think you too hasty in requiring or demanding an answer from me upon so grave a subject. You remember that I was to test your love for me five years, and then, at the expiration of the appointed time, if we found ourselves faithful to the test, the outcome of the waiting would be a marriage," said Alcia, haughtily.

"But why require such a length of time to ascertain whether you have any love for me?" asked Mr. Manwell. "I know my own heart now; knew the very moment I saw you that I would love you and none other. Oh, Miss Vernon, I am afraid you are a cold-hearted girl. You have received such adulation that it has destroyed all the sentiment in your nature. Am I not correct, Miss Vernon?"

"If you think me a heartless girl, Mr. Manwell, why ask me to become your wife?" she replied haughtily.

"Because I love you," sternly replied   .

"I think, Auguste Manwell, that we are unsuited to each other. You have always, no doubt, controlled your family, and I mine, hence we might assert more than our rights. I would not yield, and I am sure that you would not."

"Miss Vernon, you misjudge me. I did not say that you were heartless. I simply asked you the question. You do not yet know Auguste Manwell. When you know and appreciate me, you will come to the conclusion that we are perfectly suited to each other," he said calmly. "I am just the man to be your husband. You do not know the intensity of my devotion to you. It is no idle fancy of an imaginative brain. You are the only woman I have ever addressed, and never again shall I make vows of love to another. You can believe me or not. I shall never deceive you, Alcia, in anything. Do let us come to some understanding in this all-important matter. You certainly can answer me the plain question, do you love me or do you not? Very plain questions, Miss Vernon," said Auguste Manwell.

"Mr. Manwell, I never confessed to any man my love, or had I ever"-

"Let me finish the sentence for you. I insist," he quickly replied.

"What would you say to complete the speech, Mr. Manwell?" she asked.

"Do you really have a curiosity to know? If so, I will give it to you in full. You said that you had never confessed your love to any man, or had you loved any one before you met me," laughingly replied Mr. Manwell. "Am I correct in your answer? Answer me truthfully," he continued.

"I like your presumption," she replied sarcastically. "The impudence of the man."

"You may dissemble; you may call me impudent, or what you please," he replied, "but I know you, Miss Vernon, better than you know yourself. I know that I am correct. I am sure that you love me, and your modesty, together with your independence, prevents you from confessing or committing yourself in any way."

"You must be a professional mind-reader, Mr. Manwell, since you know my thoughts," she replied.

"Your last expression, Alcia, confesses *all*, and I am the happiest man on earth. I only wish that I could persuade you to marry me, with your mother's consent, at once, and go with me to California. What do you say to such an arrangement, my own dear girl?"

"Mr. Manwell, I could not leave my poor mamma now, when she is in so much trouble over her business. She needs my constant sympathy and encouragement."

"What a noble, self-sacrificing daughter you are, Alcia. You must be very dear to your mother. I see that she is very fond of you. I wish you would broach the subject to her. Will you not, my noble girl?" he continued.

"I will when my dear mother becomes more reconciled to the heavy losses she has sustained," she replied.

"I will then remain a few weeks in St. Chelsea, and return home. I shall not take my California trip alone, for I wish you to accompany me, and will defer it until I can claim you as my wife."

CHAPTER XII.

ANOTHER year has passed in the eventful life of Enola Dale. To many, years bring trials and sad experiences, and an afflicted heart frequently causes the silvery locks to appear. Enola's once raven hair is prematurely gray. With a deep, abiding faith in Christ, she has long since ceased to grieve over her heavy losses, and lives to obtain, through patience, an inheritance in that beautiful world, "where thieves cannot break through and steal." "How much wiser to lay up for ourselves treasures in heaven," she thought.

Florence announced that Mr. Peccavi wished to see Miss Enola in the hall.

"Why did you ask him into the hall, Florence?" asked Mrs. Dale.

"Because he was quite intoxicated, and looked so untidy I thought that I would not invite a man in that condition into the parlor," said honest Florence. "You know, Miss Enola, that I have the parlors to attend to, and this old man looked so untidy I feared to take him into such nice rooms."

"Well, well, Florence, you are a great girl — one among a thousand."

As soon as Mrs. Dale entered the room, with one glance she discovered that poor old Mr. Peccavi was indeed in an unfortunate condition. She disliked to remain in the same room with him, but she thought that some very important business had brought him out through the inclement weather.

"Did you wish to see me, Mr. Peccavi?" said Mrs. Dale.

"Yes — y-e-s" (hiccough), stammered the old gentleman. "Mrs. Dale, it becomes my painful duty to inform you that I — I — hic — hic — I — your suit is gone up, madam."

"What, sir?" exclaimed Mrs. Dale, in a most excited manner. "I did not understand you, sir," viewing his loathsome appearance from head to foot. "I did not understand you, Mr. Peccavi. Please repeat what you said," continued Mrs. Dale.

"Why, madame (hic), your—your suit is lost. The (hic) miserable old judge has decided against me at (hic) last."

Had a thunderbolt just then fallen from heaven and struck her, she could not have been more astonished.

Mr. Peccavi continued: "I (hic) thought to the very last that I would win." Sobering himself up a little he continued: "I hope, madame, that you will not — reflect upon me. I must say it is the first case I ever lost."

Mrs. Dale knew that he was telling an untruth, for there is no lawyer that has not been at some time unsuccessful in his legal business, however just their cases might be, and their talent among the finest in the land. His untruthfulness only aggravated her, and so thoroughly convinced her of his perfidy, that she could with great forbearance continue the conversation.

"Mrs. Dale," he said, "it was no fault of mine. I did all I could, but you see this man, Cheatem, had so much money, and money, you know, wields its power (hic), madame, and can influence the highest men of the (hic) land."

"You do not pretend to say, sir, that Mr. Cheatem *bribed* the judge, do you?"

"It (hic) looks that way now, ma'am," Mr. Peccavi said.

"Your revelation is astounding, sir, and I can scarcely credit your language. I thought that men in whom the people had sufficient faith to confer on them almost the highest position within their power to bestow, neither would nor could do such a dishonorable act. Why, Mr. Peccavi, would a judge accept a bribe? Is there money sufficient in our treasury to tempt him? No, Mr. Peccavi, a judge cannot be bribed, and you should not frame that excuse for your lack of success. The disappointment is great, but my strength is sufficient to bear it, for I am convinced that God will yet open the way, at some future time, for me to recover all that justly belongs to me. He permits the wrongs to go just so far, and, at His own proper time, His mighty hand will be raised in the defence of the widow and the orphan. Who can stand when the great Creator sits upon His throne of justice? Can His Court be bribed?"

Mrs. Dale turned to Mr. Peccavi, and he had fallen asleep in the large arm chair. Whiskey had deadened his sensibilities, showing the ruinous and debasing influence of its nature.

She retired from the room and left the sleeping attorney to himself. She immediately sought her daughter, and told the disappointing news to her.

"Mamma, I am not at all surprised at the decision, for I anticipated nothing else. You should have consulted your friends in regard to this man and his ability and merit. You must bear up under your trials; all will yet be well. I feel for you, my darling mother. Trouble seems to follow you like a phantom, but a bright day is dawning, and we must bear bravely the ills of life. I will be your comforter. Oh, mamma, do not weep; you have shed too many tears in your early life; the lachrymal fountain must now cease to flow. You must not weep, kind mamma," said Alcia fondly, wiping the tears from her mother's eyes.

"No, my darling; your words of sympathy are soothing to my troubled heart, you precious child. I love you more than tongue can tell, and I pray that my darling child may never be subjected to such wrongs, but that flowers and sunshine may ever be your portion."

As soon as Mr. Peccavi aroused himself from his drunken stupor, he quietly wended his way through the hall, and as stealthily passed out.

So ended this "mammoth suit."

Enola felt that her money advanced to him was utterly lost, as he was considered beyond the reach of law, courts or judgment, being proof against everything. She had sustained through his rascality many losses, placing her in such a financial condition as to compel her to sacrifice her beautiful home and luxurious furniture. Reverses came upon her thick and fast, but like a true woman she bravely bore them with christian resignation.

"Mamma," said Alcia one day, "did you know that I am engaged to Auguste Manwell? I did not confide the secret before, fearing it might distress you just now ; he has been writing and urging me to consent to a consummation of our solemn vows, and I can only reconcile his mind to a delay, by telling him what a comfort I am to you, and that I cannot leave you just yet. Now he writes again, and informs me that he has waited so long and anxiously that his determination now is to claim the fulfillment of my promise within a few months, and that I must consult with you and arrange for the wedding. Now, if you say that you cannot live without me, I will not leave you. I know that Mr. Manwell will be kind, and that he loves me with an intense devotion, and if I do not marry *him* I will never marry any one. He is just the style of man I admire, and the only one I ever met with whom I could be happy."

"Oh, Alcia, however painful it might be for me to be separated from you, I feel that your own happiness is mine. I regard Mr. Manwell most highly ; consider him a man of sterling worth, and free from any vices. You have had some very wealthy offers of marriage, my daughter, but as he is your choice, I will not say a dissenting word."

"Then I shall let him know, when I write again, that I will marry him at the time he so earnestly desires. I do not wish any wedding, simply a marriage ceremony.

I detest these great crowded weddings; so does Auguste," said Alcia.

"You shall be married just as you please. I have always yielded to your wishes, and, really, it has made you a shining light in our household; some persons might consider you too much petted, but you accept it with such a good grace that I almost feel that you deserve more love than my poor heart can offer you."

"Baring," said his sister, "what would you say if I were to marry?"

"I would not like it, sister. Why do girls always want to marry as soon as they get to be grown ladies?"

"Baring, you have put a difficult question to me for my solution, and I can only answer for myself. Before I met Mr. Manwell I frequently thought that I would never leave mamma; and Baring, some of these days you also will be marrying some pretty blue-eyed girl."

"No, sister," he exclaimed, "I would not desert my mother for any girl on earth. I don't love girls. What is love, sister, anyway?"

"You little mischief," said Alcia, "why do you wish to know what love is? Well, I shall try to explain to you *my* solution of the problem. Love is a passion, a quenchable flame, that when once ignited burns on and on, until perchance through long neglect and deception it may finally and utterly be extinguished. Alas! alas! how many there are who never consider the solemnity of the marriage vow, thoughtlessly made and lightly broken. How do you like that definition, my little brother?" said she.

"Splendid, sister, splendid," he replied. "You seem to understand the question. Where did you learn so much; in the school of love?" he innocently asked.

"Yes, my little Baring, every young lady before she marries attends *Love's School*," Alcia laughingly answered.

"Do young gentlemen attend this school, too, sister?" he playfully asked.

"No, my cute little brother, the young gentlemen are the teachers in the school," she replied, filled with amusement at the questions that he had asked her.

"Well, when I grow to be a big, tall man, I intend to try for a place in that school."

"I think, Baring, that you will be competent to make a first-class teacher, judging from your large brown eyes and manly expression."

"Mamma will have to consent first to my accepting such a place, for if it does not pay well I can't take it, for, sister, when I get to be a big man, you know that I am going to make lots of money, and give it all to mamma; I am going to. take care of her before anybody else, and if that position don't pay well, why, all about it is, that I won't have it," said Baring, excitedly.

"Do not become so nervous over it, Baring," said his sister. "Let me tell you that some teachers in that school make it pay well, and others do not. If you should captivate a very rich girl, and marry her, then the position becomes profitable to the fortunate teacher. So, Baring, it will be within your power to make your position lucrative."

"Sister, I have learned so much from you; can't I find a girl in that school that is as good-looking as you are?" he asked, wishfully.

"Oh, Baring," she answered, "you will find in the 'Love's School,' many, very many, much better-looking girls than your sister."

Baring could not understand that any one could presume to be more beautiful than his idolized sister. He was firm in his belief.

"Baring," said Mrs. Dale, "it is your school hour. Come, get yourself in readiness. When you can claim a few moments of your sister's time you almost talk her to death."

"Well, mamma, sister entertains me so nicely. I like to talk with her, but you always appear to be in a deep, thoughtful mood, and won't pay any attention to what I say, because you think, mamma, that I am a little boy; but sometimes little boys have more sense than grown men. Don't you think they do?"

"Oh, yes, Baring, there you go; talking again. Hurry, and be off to school," said his mother, "or you will receive a mark for tardiness."

"No I won't, mamma," he merrily answered, and bounded off to school.

"What are you doing, Alcia, looking through the secret apartment of my escritoire?" said Mrs. Dale; "you will only find some business papers and old deeds, maybe an old diary, kept many long years ago."

"Yes, my mother, here is one now; an ancient diary, judging from the color, for it is darker than saffron. May I look at it, my dear mamma?" she asked beseechingly.

"I hardly know whether it would edify you, so many long years have intervened since I wrote those faded lines—when I was not as old as you are now, Alcia."

"Oh, do let me just run through it, I so much love to read old books and diaries."

She could not refuse her, although it flashed across her mind that there might be some things that she had kept esoteric.

"I think this old diary is the most interesting piece of literature I have come across for a long time. It takes one away back to the days when you left your handsome home to marry my father, so much against your parent's wishes. I do not think that anything could induce me to leave my home to marry, for I don't believe that any runaway match ever resulted in good," said Alcia firmly.

"I would rather you should not read that old forgotten diary, my child."

"Do, mamma, permit me to read it. There is nothing in its tarnished pages that can affect me in the least. Past events that you desire not to remember should be forgotten. Please let me continue reading," she said.

Her too yielding mother consented, and she proceeded.

"Are these large spots on the leaves tear-drops, mamma?" she asked, sympathetically.

"Yes, my dear child. At that time my books,

16

pillow and your little baby face were drenched with tears. It will only cause you to feel sad, Alcia.''

But woman's curiosity prevailed. '' No, these old sorrows are long since forgotten, mamma, are they not?''

Her mother did not reply, but great swelling tears rushed to her eyes, unobserved by her daughter, which would have answered the question more plainly than words.

'' June 10 — Alcia is three months old to-day. June 11 — A desire to send mother and baby to heaven,'' read Alcia from the time-stained pages of the diary.

'' Mamma, who was it that wanted to send you and me to heaven?'' innocently she asked.

'' I would not read those reminiscences of the past, for you could not understand them without an explanation of everything you read,'' answered her mother.

'' Well, just explain this to me, and I will not ask you any more questions.''

Sadly and quietly Mrs. Dale commenced her story:

'' Your dear, dear old grandfather Vernon, who lived with us, had a terrible attack of illness. It was an affection of the brain. He was, when in health, one of the most honorable of men, beloved by everybody. I don't think, my child, I ever could have loved an own father more tenderly, for he was the soul of honor and goodness, generous, and as gentle and considerate in his disposition as any woman, and he in return loved both you and me most devotedly. Indeed, his attachment for *you*, my child, was perfect idolatry. He was old and feeble, had drank to its dregs the cup of sor-

row, and wanted and craved you to love, an innocent
little infant only three months old. He would sit and
watch your sleeping little face, and when in your baby
slumbers you would smile, he too would smile, and
say : ' Hush ! hush ! Enola; the angels are whispering
to her, and with love stories have amused her little
mind, and she is smiling in return.' Poor father Vernon
became dangerously ill with a distorted brain and
burning fever. He cautiously secreted a loaded pistol
beneath the folds of his loose flowing gown, one sultry
evening in midsummer, and proceeded to your little
bed, where you were sleeping, unconscious of any
danger. In a moment more I heard the click of the
pistol. I sprang to the crib, and immediately realized
the perilous position we were in. God came to my rescue, giving me firmness. I spoke to him gently, putting my hand in his, saying: ' Father Vernon, why did
you get out of your bed of illness to awaken the baby?
She is sleeping so sweetly ; do not disturb her.' Trembling, and palsied with fright, I did not know what terrible catastrophe the next moment might usher in.

" Looking me steadily in the face, with a wild, vacant
stare, he spoke to me: ' Enola, you are not happy.
You spend your days and nights weeping over the
youthful follies and neglect of my son, and I am here,
now, to send you and my precious little Alcia to
heaven, where I too am soon going, and will join you
there. And oh, won't we all be happy, my child?' I
saw that I had not a moment to lose, but all the presence of mind that I ever possessed rushed to my rescue
at that instant, and I gently led him away from you,

saying: 'Father Vernon, you would not send us to heaven before Alcia awakens? That would not be right.' He instantly grasped the idea, and was led away as gentle as a lamb. The pistol fell to his side. I conducted him to his room, promising to get him some cooling ices if he would lie down and compose himself, which he did, saying at the same time: 'Oh, Enola, why did you not let me send you and your little babe to heaven, where we could have been so free from suffering? Well,' he continued, in his delirium, 'as soon as she stirs I will be ready. We will all go, won't we, Enola?' 'I will now go and get you a cooling drink, Father Vernon,' I replied.

"I went into my room and bolted the doors. I then stepped out upon the upper verandah and that moment saw poor dear Harry coming in through the front gate, and from the upper gallery I spoke to him: 'Come, Harry, come quickly; there is no one in the house but father Vernon, the baby and myself. Father Vernon is very wild and delirious; he is ill — so dangerously ill that something must be done to relieve him. I promised him some refreshing ices, and as soon as one of the servants returns I will send for them. Harry, our duty is to nurse him faithfully, for he is ill, and requires constant attention. Claude is still down street. It is now ten o'clock at night; you will remain with him, Harry, until Claude comes home.' "

"Oh, mamma," said Alcia, "what a thrilling story; and how much presence of mind you displayed in saving our lives. What a dreadful thing, if grandpa had sent us, then and there, as he thought, to heaven."

"Too appalling to think about. Your grandfather was one of the noblest of men, and I love his memory; but it causes a sadness to come over me when we wander back to those years, so full of misery."

"Well, mamma, I promised I would not read any more in your diary, or worry you any longer with explanations. I suppose that in honor bound I must keep the promise; but, mamma, I would so much like you to explain one more item to me that I see here in your diary. It reads thus: 'March 20 — Saw my solitaire diamond ear-rings in Mrs. Marie Churchill's ears, across the table at a hotel. Wonder how she come into possession of them?' I am anxious to know that myself. Can you explain it to me, my patient mother?"

"No, my child; I never could ascertain how Mrs. Churchill came to possess them. I only know that they graced her ears; but I was helpless. I could do nothing but weep over my wrongs. I, of course, had many theories about them, but could not vouch for the truthfulness of any of my imaginations. I only know that I never recovered my diamonds."

"I have amused myself investigating the mysteries of your escritoire, and will now close it and place everything just where I found it," said Alcia. "Old mementoes and antiquated jewelry I would dearly love to own, and intend, if ever I have a home, to fill it with the curious antiquities of every country. I want a grandfather's clock, an old weaver's loom that our forefathers' clothes were woven in, and a spinning-wheel, with flax and tow. The student of archæology must enjoy his knowledge."

"Have you heard anything lately from Wickliffe, mamma?"

"No, my child, he rarely writes to me, he is wholly given up to the world and its allurements. I made a mistake in rearing him. I was entirely too indulgent. Boys should have a father's vigilant eye over them; and then they should be firm and positive, but kind and reasonable. Mothers are too yielding to have the responsibility of training sons. Baring is not a difficult child to manage; he is so obedient to all my commands that I find it. a very pleasant duty to instruct him in all things. I hope he will always continue as faithful to my precepts. There is much wholesome good in the little fellow, and he reminds me so much of his lamented father."

Just then a letter was handed Mrs. Dale from Wickliffe's physician, telling her of her son's dangerous illness, and urging her to come as quickly as possible.

After a hasty preparation for the journey, she was soon upon the steam cars being rapidly carried away to his bedside, whom, judging from the physician's letter, she expected to find dangerously ill. She was soon with him, and he was a very sick man; all hope of his life having been despaired of, but Enola, true to her devotion to her children, nursed him for nine long weeks, not knowing at the close of each day's weary watching that the morning sun would find him living. The first ray of hope during his illness gave her great encouragement and new strength to continue her faithful vigil. After great prostration and intense nervousness, leaving his system in a relaxed condition, he slowly recovered. Enola, with the physician's advice, attempted to remove him to her home. His emaciated form seemed scarcely equal to the emergency, but with proper care and attention she hoped to be able to reach their destination with him safely. Once at home, she thought that he would soon build up his weakened constitution, but it took many months for him to recuperate and become strong. He seemed indifferent to the allurements of the world, and was certainly a changed man. During his extreme illness, when all hope of his recovery was despaired of, Enola sent his father a telegram, announcing to him his son's dying condition, but no response came from him. He no doubt allowed resentment to fill his bosom, overcoming the better part of his nature. Maternal affection is ever ready to accept any sacrifice for the benefit of her offspring, though it might be carried to the extreme, her constant appeal being, "Spare, oh spare my child!" ready to yield up her own life that he might live.

As soon as Wickliffe had entirely recovered, he again left his mother and returned to take his position in business. He was very much in disposition and appearance like his father. He had his quiet manner and admiration for the beautiful, especially in the fair sex. He often remarked: "I will endure suffering, anything; only, let me behold a handsome woman." He reflected the father's image and character to so great an extent, that the latter preferred to withdraw from his child reminders of himself and his eccentricities.

Mrs. Dale sought Mr. Peccavi several times, and urged him, as an honorable man, to cancel the large amount of his indebtedness, but he thought it a most preposterous idea for him to ever think of paying a *debt*.

"Why, Mrs. Dale, I could not consider the obligation binding, of paying or refunding any money you may have advanced to me. No, madame, that suit cost a great deal of money to conduct it properly, even though I did lose it. Besides, when a man has a fee paid him, win or not win, he must hold on to it; you must learn to practice that theory too."

" But, Mr. Peccavi, do you consider that you are acting as an honest man to take my money, sir, without fulfilling your part of the agreement? No, Mr. Peccavi, it is anything but honorable, and no man that had a grain of principle would be guilty of such bold robbery, sir."

As she said this, Mrs. Dale felt a sense of righteous indignation pervade her whole being, and she prayed in her heart that God would have mercy upon so wicked a man. In despair and disappointment she returned to her home, not knowing what course to take that would guarantee to her a collection of her just claim. She held nothing against him to prove the validity of the debt, but had solely depended upon his honor, and legion pronounced that long since buried in the ruins of gain and corruption. "Thou, too, Mr. Peccavi, must stand soon before the great Judge to give an account of all your dishonest deeds."

" I wish you had been with me last night, mamma,"

said Alcia, as she slowly entered the breakfast-room. "The play was grand, sublime. The great tragedienne did credit to her talent, to *your* native State, Kentucky. You should be proud of her as an actress, and I think that all Kentuckians should reverence her. She has elevated the profession, and by her pure and modest deportment won the respect and love of all good people. Mary Anderson is a gifted woman. I do not deny my great admiration for her, as an artiste, possessing purity of character, with extraordinary dramatic talent. Col. N. Smith, acknowledged to be the most handsome man in the United States—not encroaching upon his egotism ; no, no !—wisely remarked that 'Mary Anderson could be styled a classic beauty.' I think that she possesses wit, beauty and genius, and she should be well satisfied with her earthly attainments. Don't you think so, mamma?"

" The accomplishments you mention do not always insure a contented spirit, or do such persons live free from the anticipated cares incident to this transitory existence of ours. I cannot but think, though," said she, " that Miss Anderson is as happy as the majority of worldly people. She has the assurance that her talent has yielded her a fortune, and can and does feel her power of self-reliance."

"I once traveled up the Mississippi River with Adelina Patti when she was making a tour through our country, when quite young, and I was greatly interested in her peculiar manner in private life, as well as amused at her dictatorial commands given to those under her control. She was punctilious, guarded her voice carefully, and

ate only those articles of food that were not injurious
to the expansion of the lungs. She required acid
food, such as pickles, cauliflower, dressed with vinegar
and salads. She too is one that God has endowed
with an unmistakable gift, yet delve into the privacy of
that life and will your search be fruitless for the skel-
eton?''

Alas, there are too many households that contain
the ghastly monster, to cumulate sorrow and discontent
upon their inmates. The heart of man yearns for. an
indescribable *something*, that is beyond the power of
earthly gifts. What is the searching, longing heart
anxious to obtain? The gift of God, which is eternal
life. Oh, my dear friends, that every one of us might
shape our course through this life of probation so as
to receive the unspeakable gift as our inheritance.
Usquebaugh has been the ruination of this little world
of ours. It swells the annals of crime at home and
abroad, until blood almost toucheth blood.

Who can extinguish this heinous curse? Not by the
influence of man can this demon be destroyed, but by
the Holy Ghost pervading our entire land. That alone
could conquer this deadly foe. But alas! man will not
permit the reign of the Holy Spirit in the world.

"Mrs. Annan," said Enola to her kind friend, "I
believe that my nature is losing much of its natural
credulity. I am less confiding, and I fear since the
many wrongs that I have experienced that I am becoming just a little suspicious. Is it right to cultivate
such a spirit, Mrs. Annan?''

Mrs. Annan was the minister's consort, a most de-

vout christian; whose every act in her life spoke
plainly her character. She was kind, benevolent, and
certainly tried to live up to the fulfilment of every
christian duty. Mrs. Dale was remarkably fond of her,
and in her darkest hours of despair sought her motherly
advice and soothing influence. She regarded her as
one of the earthly saints, traveling through the world,
striving to be the means of bringing souls to Christ.
She could appreciate with the keenest perception the
wrongs of others, and would mingle her tears with
theirs, and suffer equally the acute pangs of sorrow
and trouble that they experienced. Her mission was
to soothe the dying, and comfort the afflicted in heart.

It was not to be wondered that Enola should seek
her. Mrs. Annan's christian graces were acquired by
a half century of untold trials and anguish; they had
purified her heart and cleansed it from the earthly
dross of wickedness, until it shone, reflected by her
acts of kindness, like the morning star.

"Am I committing a sin, Mrs. Annan," asked
Enola, "by allowing myself to become suspicious of
people?"

"No, my dear friend; caution toward all cannot be
imputed to be sinful; you have not been cautious
enough. You have allowed the wicked to rob you,
when you should have regarded all their acts with a
suspicious eye until they had proven themselves entirely worthy of such confidence as yours. From all
that I can learn from the outside world, Mr. Cheatem
and old Mr. Peccavi, with several of the learned profession, combined to absorb your entire estate, root and

branch. I am thankful to know that there is a righteous *judge* to sit in judgment upon such men. When
they are called to give an account for robbing the
widow and the fatherless, there will be a dreadful doom
meted out to them," said Mrs. Annan.

"Mrs. Annan, I wish I understood the Bible as thoroughly as you do, my friend. What a consolation it
would be to me."

"I have made that sacred Book my study since
fifteen years of age. I certainly ought to know something of its teachings by this time, as I am now sixty
years old," replied Mrs. Annan. She continued: "I
see new rays of light every day from the prophetic
lamp shining around my feet, and if we take heed
to it, will burn with an ever-increasing light, unto the
perfect day. The Bible is a wonderful book, pre-
eminent over all other printed works, and none that
search diligently within its sacred pages for its hidden
treasure, ever fail to find them. The christian's life,
my dear Mrs. Dale," continued Mrs. Annan, "'midst
all the cares, trials and afflictions that fall to the lot of
mortal man, should be a life of extreme joy and happiness, feeling the full assurance of God's pardoning
power and mercy to forgive, and by such forgiveness
to become joint heirs with Him, in the establishment of
the new earth."

CHAPTER XIII.

SUMMER is again upon us, with its crisping, scorching heat, and Arabia's simoon winds to fan our feverish brow. In vain we go from room to room to seek a cooling breeze. The very air seems charged with electricity, waiting to burst and do its deadly work. The listless, languid animals stand in pools of cooling water, panting to catch a stray breeze that may be wafted from some snow-capped peak. The fowls seek shelter from the burning rays of a midsummer's scorching sun, beneath the heavy foliage of the forest elm or cypress' mourning boughs, with drooping wings, feeling the burden of their downy crest. The doleful trill of the melancholy locust is wafted in the open casement, speaking of " more heat, more heat," to be expected. The parched earth seems to gaze wishfully up to the flying, fleecy clouds that rapidly pass and repass in a tantalizing manner, till at last in vapory substance they dissolve, and leave the azure sky to taunt poor longing nature. Oh, for a cooling shower, to water the wilted plants. The agriculturist in despair prays for rain, " rain, or all is destroyed ; my yearly labors perish without refreshing dews to enliven the germ." The beasts of the forest traverse for miles their solitary pathways to some cool running brook, fed by an ever-flowing spring, and drink to heart's content, unmindful of the great anxiety the long drouth is causing the tiller of the land.

(253)

With what ecstatic joy the farmer eyes the gathering semblance of a cloud, hoping to gain a spark of information that with its density rain may come. It passes on and leaves him in despair. The truthful locust still sings its little song, "more heat, more heat, more heat;" as long as his chirping notes are heard the tedious drouth continues.

Heavy, curling, rolling clouds gather, until the very heavens seem blackened by their immensity. The anxious farmer gazes constantly upward, hoping to see the welcome fluid pouring upon the famished fields and perishing nature. The animals bask beneath its shadowy darkness, for it cools them from the burning rays of the summer's sun. But, alas! no rain. Whirling and blowing, the expected storm has passed over; and thus it is, until tired, disappointed nature droops, to hope again and again. It is ever so with all our earthly hopes, built upon a transitory foundation, to crumble and fall with every varying scene in life.

> And thus our dreams of happiness,
> Our visions bright, our prospects gay,
> And all our little world of bliss,
> Will perish like these fields of hay.

The summer's heat becoming so oppressive, Mrs. Dale decides to seek some cool, quiet, inexpensive place, where she and her family can spend a few months away from the heated walls of the city. She longs for some retreat where she can forget the existence of wicked, dishonest men, and with her dear children, she can have the birds and flowers as her com-

panions, with the *Bible* as her *friend*. Alas! the term
"friend," has almost lost its force in this age of scepticism and delusion. Friendship bears not the sacredness
imposed upon its individuality. No matter how strong
the affection between individuals, the chilling, blighting
intensity of self-interest creeps into the soul, and by the
tinted visions of *gain*, allows that tie to be severed, and
nothing remains but the *name*. The substance has vanished. Speak cautiously that cherished name *friend*.
What are so-called "summer friends" worth? They
drink the sweetness from your hospitable board; they
accept the proffered hand of full enjoyment tendered
them; they revel in rich and gorgeous entertainments,
and sip from prosperity's gilded cup the envied name;
but, alas! should adversity overtake the poor unfortunate, and wrest from him, in his cold, iron grip, all his
earthly ambitions and estate, where, oh, where can
those summer friends be found? They have been carried away, as it were, upon the wings of the tinted
butterfly to seek new fields of conquest, to sip the
honey and sweetness from the freshly developed flower,
and enjoy the friendship of newly made and highly
favored acquaintances. Go ask the millionaire how
many friends he claims, and legion stands up in bold
relief. Ask the man of poverty how he numbers his
friends since he grasped adversity's hand, and his sad
reply will be, "none;" but, if a christian, with a beaming, happy face, he will answer: "I have one *friend*,
worth all the world to me, and that is *Christ*. He
never violates His promise to fallen man; He is true
to those who keep His commandments.

The calm, deep waters of the placid lake had a most soothing effect upon Enola. Baring, with his sister, would spend hours upon its shelly banks, drinking in the cooling zephyr that was wafted across the glistening waters. The barques, with their snow-white sails, glided along, unconscious of the idle spectators that constantly thronged the piers. Baring was wild with joyous excitement over the various sailing boats that dotted this beautiful body of water, and kept his mother in anxious fear, as she could see, from the oriel, his venturesome pranks upon the pebbled shores.

Alcia and Baring came in from a long stroll beside the sandy beach, Baring with his pockets laden with sea-shells, and his sister, a bouquet of seaweed and grasses.

" I have a letter for you, Alcia,' said her mother, handing it to her at the same time.

She broke the seal, and found the letter to be from Auguste Manwell. After carefully reading it, she turned to her mother, saying:

" Mr. Manwell will be here to join us very shortly, and he urges me to marry and return home with him; indeed, he declares that he will remain here until I consent to become his wife. He said that he had waited almost five long years for me, and he must now claim his promise and the consummation of his earnest desires. So, I suppose, now, my dear mother, that I must make all the necessary arrangements for our marriage, which, with your consent, will take place here when Mr. Manwell comes.''

Baring was dressed in a handsome new suit, and felt

A LAKE OF CLEAR WATER.

quite consequential, with his boutonniere and buff kid gloves. He felt that he was dressed for a particular occasion, and his little witty sayings amused every one. Mrs. Dale was arrayed in a handsome, heavy black satin, richly trimmed in lace, which contrasted well with her iron-gray hair. She wore a thoughtful expression, and frequently, from deep emotion, tears would came rushing to her eyes, and as rapidly be brushed aside. It was a trying hour for her—it was Alcia's wedding day.

A tranquil, azure sky and a golden sun heralded the happy event, dispelling all doubts of an ill-mated pair, or a life of woe to the high contracting parties. With rain comes tears, and sunlight brings joy. Happiness is promised them in the uncertain future. What a struggle it was to her to give up her idolized child. No one can doubt but that her heart was sad, for in taking a retrospective view of her past life, she could well say with the poet:

> "O, ever thus, from childhood's hour
> I've seen my fondest hopes decay;
> I never loved a tree or flower,
> But 'twas the first to fade away."

She felt that dear little Baring alone was left her; all other ties torn from her, either by the ruthless hand of death, or alienations more painful than the grim monster. Living sorrows feed upon the soul as the gnawing cancer-worm eats on and knows no satiety. She felt convinced in her own mind that Auguste Manwell would make a model husband, that his love for her

17

daughter was of that pure and holy nature that could but ensure great happiness to both, yet she felt that in giving Alcia to him she was losing her child. Still, with a prayerful heart, she yielded to the desires of her daughter, and placed her happiness in the keeping of the man of her choice.

The solemn vows are consummated that bind forever the hearts of Auguste and Alcia. When the divine words were spoken, making them husband and wife, Enola could control her feelings no longer, but gave vent to her tears. Alcia stood statue-like, her face pale and calm. She tried to soothe her distressed mother ; and their tears flowed and mingled together. The bridal party were driven from the marriage altar to the railroad depot to take the eastern-bound train. It was a farewell long to be remembered. With little Baring's hand clasped in hers, Enola stood transfixed to the spot where she had kissed her precious daughter farewell, and watched the car that bore her away from sight. It was well that she had something to divert her distracted mind. She returned, and busied herself in having the great number of exquisite bridal presents carefully packed, marked and shipped to their destination. It was a responsible undertaking, as the gifts were numerous and valuable. The wedding was private, only the very near relatives and a few most valued friends being present.

After spending a couple or more months upon the lake shore, Enola and little Baring wended their lodely way back to St. Chelsea.

"In calling me by the strange name of 'Enola,' I wonder if my dear departed parents received a glimpse of the future life of their child in a camera, speaking to them of her life of loneliness," mused Enola, "for truly I am alone, with the exception of my little Baring, who is so dependent."

She felt since her great financial robbery, that it was very important for her to live most economically, as Mr. Cheatem had advised her years ago, when she first discovered her great wrongs, that she would be cut short of a large revenue, but that she must not care for "filthy lucre," the thought would frequently come into her confiding heart: "Does he (Mr. Cheatem) care for 'filthy lucre?' Surely he grasps the shining coin and presses it to his heart; he has a large amount of the dross, purloined from trusting natures. And poor old Peccavi, does he love 'filthy lucre," too? He must adore the precious stuff, since he ignores the just payment of it."

Enola's common sense constantly prompted her to ostracise all mercenary wicked men, and devote the remainder of her life to the cause of Christ, and religious works necessary for the accomplishment of noble and charitable purposes. She found in her trusted friend and co-worker in Christ's cause, much comfort and spiritual felicity. They held their Bible instructions together, and she seemed to have the veil lifted from her eyes, and could but praise God for having led her through so many dismal paths and thorny hedges; dark days bordering on despondency, even to the very brink of despair. She had the assurance that those God loveth He chasteneth, and she bore the soothing unction to her soul. From the deepest recesses of her heart thanked the Almighty Father for every heartache she had experienced; thanked Him for the knowledge that He had given her, contained in His sacred Book; thanked Him for giving her sufficient grace to forgive those who should have comforted and loved her in her declining years.

She realized each day that she was permitted to live, that the Great Jehovah doeth all things well. Her now insignificant trials were simply bubbles upon the great ocean of eternity; a moment seen, then lost forever in the glorious work of redemption. Out of Christ, worldly trials are very, very hard to bear. They try the soul, they cause the doubting heart to become rebellious, they contaminate the mind of frail, weak man, until all good is obscured, and reason is swallowed up in a contortion of scepticism. Optimism seems lost to them, and darkness and despair pursues their unbelieving souls until even their orgies cry for rest from the weary things of earth. In Christ, all is peace, love and harmony. The ship of sin may roll, toss and heave, until the planks of corruption creak and break; but the christian fears not, knowing that his barque of salvation is anchored to a rock that cannot be shaken. In Christ, our very thoughts are hallowed, and softened by that sweet peace of mind that never comes to the wicked or blasphemous man. In Christ the dying struggle is bereft of its agony, and the dark valley is lighted with His glory. The new earth is viewed afar off, and thus the righteous pass away, full of hope and the beautiful visions of home in store for them.

The clouds of adversity still enveloped the life of Enola Dale, and pursued her with the same vigilance that the wild beasts of the African jungles hunt their prey. She had an extensive field opened to her to test all her former friends; many proved recreant to her truest friendship, and a few were firm and faithful. Their hearts knew no change, but loved her for her own worth and merit.

Faithful Florence was a self-sacrificing and true friend. She had no sinister motive to prompt her; none but the most sincere feeling of love and kindness. It were well that events should occur in one's life to afford the test, so mysterious and wonderful, concealed behind a bulwark of wealth, fame, and perhaps regard, bereft of these prerequisites, to form the chain of so-called friendship, and the test is forever lost and sinks into insignificance.

It is a difficult matter to study the human heart. There are so many varied causes that prompt its action for good deeds or wicked demonstration toward those claiming sacred affinity, and the transformation of the heart is so boundless, so puissant in its developments, that the mind is engulfed in bewilderment, as to the theory of the causes of all these changes. We cannot be the correct judges of our own hearts. We try to persuade ourselves of our knowledge of perfection and imperfection, but fall very short of obtaining the true condition of our minds. We believe that God implants within the bosom of every truly converted soul, a feeling of security from the follies and temptations of the world. He possesses them with a longing and thirsting after righteousness, and convinces them, in their helpless condition, that he has forgiven them ; but further than that, no one can know their own heart.

We would not be a misanthropist, for there is much in mankind to love and revere ; still, God's Book declares that the heart of man is deceitful and desperately wicked above all things, but capable of great improvement and changes through sanctification. By a constant exertion to overcome the wicked propensities in our natures, and cultivate with diligent attention the good and honorable, we arrive at a purer condition of heart, mind and impulses.

Perfection of character is an art to be cultivated and tended with as watchful an eye as the gardener nurses the delicate, tender exotic plant, and guards it against the chilling winds or burning midday sun. As the anxious young mother, regardless of all else, watches her innocent firstborn, and eagerly looks for the daily development of face, disposition and growth, so it is with a perfected character. Innocent babe, in all thy purity, mother longs for greater perfection, and promises, in her loving heart, for her child, many strides up the ladder of fame, when maturity is obtained, should he arrive at an age capable of receiving instruction, and developing into a great and worthy personage. "As the twig is bent, the tree inclines." Sow the seed of truth, mixed with honesty and fidelity, in the garden of righteousness, tended with sincerity and sprinkle with the water of life, and an upright, good and honest person is reared, to be a joy and comfort to the loved ones.

Frequent letters from Alcia and Auguste bring joyful tidings of health, contentment and perfect bliss. The dutiful daughter writes freely and fully of her happy condition in life, saying:

MY DEAR MOTHER: I could not have found greater perfection in man. Auguste is all that I could expect, to constitute a good and worthy husband. His ardent attachment for me is unlike the ordinary love that, from my own observation, I have discovered lurking in very many apparently happy and congenial households. A full display of outward affection, made public by extraordinary demonstrations of unalloyed sincerity, too frequently causes the observant mind to think, and with thought comes investigation of many facts that would have hitherto been buried in some deep recess of the heart, and been kept inviolate from the prying public. Auguste is a man of few words. He makes no outward display of his affection, but it is of that pure, self-sacrificing type that renders it greatly to be appreciated. In a word, mamma, he is a kind and gentle husband, and I only wish my darling absent mother's mind was as free from all care and responsibilities as your own devoted daughter's,

ALCIA VERNON MANWELL.

Enola felt consoled and reconciled to the separation, when she knew how inexpressibly happy and cneerful her daughter was in her new relation as wife. Her kindred ties were most pleasant, and his mother and sisters were lovable women.

Auguste was blessed with any amount of "filthy lucre," as Mr. Cheatem pronounced it ; hence the cares of struggling existence would be greatly diminished, for money satisfies mankind with the life's necessaries, and places the possessor above the frowns of a mercenary world. It provides for the luxurious liver a gorgeous, palatial earthly home, but even within its gilded walls it does not insure happiness ; beside, wealth is like the fleeting snow: it comes, it melts, it disappears. Go ask the sacred records imprisoned within the iron and mortar vaults, where many dead men's accumulated wealth has gone, and there, upon their damp and time-stained pages the startling revelation is given to the inquiring mind, and in holy horror he departs from those walls of silence *a wiser man.* The toiling, sleep-less nights of the widow, the appeal of the wronged orphan, so free from guile, cry to the courts of equity to right their wrongs and empty the pockets of corrupt and defrauding men, and return that which in all jus-tice belongs to them—perhaps money acquired through long years of manual toil and strict economy by de-voted parents, long since slumbering in the lonely graveyard, their hard earnings now in the possession of strangers. It is well that the dead know not anything, for restless would be the sleep of many now reposing quietly, unconscious of right or wrong. Could. they awaken to a full realization of the suffering of their offspring, how vigorously would they resist the barriers that confine them. But happily their profound sleep is

undisturbed, not to be broken until that awful blast of
the trumpet shall sound that alone can awake the sleeping dead. Only the dead in Christ are made partici-
pants in that glorious resurrection call, when all wrongs
will be righted by Him who is the God of the widow,
the father of the fatherless and a judge of the quick
and the dead.

Enola long since gave all her wrongs to the Lord,
and with that firm *faith* that characterizes the true
christian at heart, that abounding omnipotent *faith*,
the firm *rock* upon which all our hopes are centered,
she holds on to with the same tenacity that a drowning man grasps at a twig, and clings to it for rescue
from his impending fate. God knows his children better than they know themselves. It requires severe and
long chastisements to bring some of His perishing ones
to Him. He does not take delight in using the heavy
rod of affliction upon .His people; but, alas! human
nature is so wicked that, in order to save, He cannot
withhold the discipline necessary for their salvation.
My dear friends, we are constantly reminded that our
present existence is not lasting. Each day the solemn
funeral dirge is sung in the presence of some surviving
dear one, and as the years roll on the number is constantly increasing of those who are borne to the cities
of the dead, and who of us can tell the day, the month
or the year when our appointed time will come to
answer the summons that calls us to our rest?

"Baring, you will soon be a man," said Enola,
"and you do not know with what pride your mother
watches your development into mature manhood. God

willing, you will be my comfort and protector in my declining years."

"Mamma," he replied, "I am now as tall as sister, and I am going to study and apply myself diligently to my books so that I can fully understand all about business, and when I feel that I am competent, and with the assistance of some well-balanced head, I am going to do something that may no doubt astonish you all, but mamma, this esoteric scheme I am not going to confide to you or the fakirs either for safe-keeping, but I am going to take my sister Alcia and my new brother into my confidence and relate to them my views and purposes."

"I am surprised to hear you talk in that manner; what sort of a crotchet have you got in your head?" said his mother. "Would you have a secret and conceal it from me, Baring? I would have no concealments from you. You must always tell me your little joys and sorrows."

"But, mamma, this is no trouble or joy connected with me; only I don't wish to tell *you*, yet. I would confide all my thoughts to you if you desired me to do so," he replied, a little quietly.

"No, my son, any secret that you may have and are willing to entrust to your sister for safe-keeping must be all right, and no doubt she could guard it more cautiously than I could, my little son."

"Well, then, we will let my little *secret* rest for a time, until sister comes in to visit us; then she and I will have a good old time together. I am so fond of talking with her, for she is so entertaining and says so many funny things; her expressions are all original," said he. "Will sister and my new brother be here this spring to visit us?"

"Yes, my son, I am expecting them in May, the beautiful month of May. Our hearts will give her a warm welcome; she has been absent a great while. Florence, you must arrange Mrs. Manwell's room, and place in it beautiful vases of flowers, for she is passionately fond of roses, and Mr. Manwell loves the modest, unobtrusive little pansy; 'tis his favorite of all the flowers in the vocabulary of the botanist. I wish, Florence, that I had not lost so heavily by Mr. Cheatem, Mr. Peccavi and a few others connected with my business; *then* I would have been in a condition to decorate the rooms and furnish Alcia's apartments more handsomely, so that she might be reminded of her once beautiful home; but, Florence, I have made a vow to let the past be forgotten, for I have placed my wrongs in the hands of the great God, who is the adjuster of all things, and who has promised to defend the widow and the fatherless."

"Miss Enola," said Florence, "I, too, as you well know, have suffered great wrongs; but mine was of a different nature from yours. Me, a poor servant, Miss Enola, had no money to steal; but, excuse me, Miss Enola, treacherous people, with bitter malice, have sought to rob me of my good name, and have tried to influence you against me; but, Miss Enola, the whole world could not turn me against you or any of your family."

"Well, Florence," said Mrs. Dale, "You must let

bygones be bygones, or God will not assist you out of your difficulties."

" That is true, Miss Enola ; but some people have persecuted me so long, and fiercely, that it has made me sinful. I was once a good, true christian, Miss Enola, and tried to live near to God, but I am I fear, far from being a christian now," she said.

" You must remember, my poor Florence, how St. Paul was persecuted and how bravely he bore up under' his many trials ; let him be an example to you, as a monument of patience, goodness and forbearance, so think no more of the past," said Mrs. Dale.

Baring and his mother were at the depot as early as the dawn of day, for Alcia and Auguste were expected to arrive on the first eastern train. Enola, so full of true happiness, could scarcely wait to see the rolling, curling smoke of the locomotive appearing in the distance, with most vivid imagination, wondering if her daughter would be the same pretty girl that she was when she saw her last. 'Twas but a moment, and mother and daughter were folded in each others embrace. With many expressions of happiness the little family wended their way to their mother's house, comfortable, though plain in style, to what she had been accustomed to.

Baring's acme of happiness was reached. He and his sister enjoyed many long conversations together, and no doubt he imparted his *secret* to her, just as soon as she had recuperated from her long and tiresome journey. Their mother was kept in total darkness as to the purport of the great secret existing between himself and sister. They would not permit a careless word to escape their lips; *caution* was the watchword with them. An extensive correspondence seemed to be circulating. Various letters from Kentucky, Wyoming and other places would be brought to the house by the postman, still all was an enigma to Mrs. Dale. Whenever their mother would make her appearance, and they were having their caucus meeting as she termed them, they would quickly separate, and be as indifferent as though all things were publicly known to her. Auguste was let into their *secret*.

After several months charmingly passed in the society of her mother and various relatives, Auguste and Alcia returned to their far-away home.

In making Gene Baring a visit upon one occasion, a singular occurrence, as well as a dangerous position to be placed in, was related to Enola by the family. His homestead was an old-fashioned wooden structure, upon the plan of a cottage house. The residence was erected upon the slope of a range of miniature mountains that reached almost to the very doors of the building. It was a picturesque spot, around which so many dear memories clustered and dwelt in the heart of Enola.

The tall sage-grass twined and matted together, until it completely formed a network over the scraggy hills. The wild strawberries grew in great profusion upon portions of these, and in flavor and sweetness were more dainty than the cultivated berry. The wild, sweet-scented jasmine climbed and tenaciously clung to shrub and cliff, scattering its fragrant odors into the surrouuding atmosphere, to mingle with that of the violet. " There is no rose without a thorn," is an old and true adage. This cliff of roses, wildwood vines and flowers, so romantic to view, freighted with its berries bright and red, had, too, its " thorns."

'Twas in the sultry month of August. The oriel window stood open to catch a stray breeze that might, perchance, spring up, for the evening was exceedingly sultry and stifling. The family had retired, feeling perfect security from all danger. The sweet little songster, the canary bird, a pet with all the household, was snugly snoozing within his gilded cage. In the quiet of the night, Mrs. Gene Baring was startled by a peculiar noise in the room, as though something heavy was being slowly drawn across the carpet. She listened attentively for several moments. The night being so oppressive, and, hearing no other sound, tired nature came to her relief, and she was soon again in a profound slumber. Only a · short time she enjoyed sleep, when she was again aroused by something falling sluggishly, apparently from her · very bed. She remained quiet a moment, when she was startled by a solid fall. She sprang from her bed, struck a light, and soon discovered that her sweet little singer was dead. She, of course, thought that some vicious stray cat had killed it. Deeply grieved at her loss, but not being able to do anything further in the premises, she soon began to enjoy her morning nap. As the sun arose behind the range of miniature mountains, she concluded to arise, and bury, with much solemnity, her favorite little birdie.

Gene vowed vengeance upon the wilful murderer of the innocent songster, and searched the premises, with shot-gun in hand, to annihilate the wicked destroyer — some straggling cat, as he supposed — when a terrible shriek from his wife brought him into their bedroom, where, lo and behold! a huge rattlesnake was concealed underneath a large arm-chair, and defied to be touched or assailed by any one; but Gene, being accustomed to the slaughter of reptiles, soon made quick work with the creeping, venomous monster. The serpent had crawled down from these flower-decked hills, crept slyly into the chamber, and, in the stillness of this sultry August night, sought the little caged bird, crushed it with his poisonous fangs, and dropped again to the floor beneath. The snake had crept to a safe retreat from view, as he thought; a perfect miracle that his deadly work did not continue.

Gene, fearing that the serpent's mate might seek its slain companion, decided to put a torch to the heavy, crisp, waving grass, and burn the reptiles up.

To the northeast of this rural homestead there lies a range of hills, a stranger to agricultural purposes. At their base a crystal stream of water flows, playing in the versatile sunlight, laughing musically as infants do in the heyday of their childish happiness. This stream was on the sunny side of this range of miniature mountains. Wild roses and forest shrubs grew in tangled confusion upon the water's very edge. A rustling noise within these bowers caused Gene Baring to suspect the rattler's mate could be found secreted in the tall rank undergrowth. Glancing in the direction

from whence the sound emanated, he witnessed a sight
that gave him a series of cold chills.   There were cop-
perheads, blacksnakes, rattlers and blue racers, all
apparently holding a caucus.   For the moment Gene
Baring was unable to decide the best course to pursue.
Returning to his residence, he concluded to put a torch
to the dry prairie grass, made unusually inflammable
by the continued summer's heat.

Snake stories generally cause a disposition to laugh,
but if the reader will converse with Gene Baring con-
cerning these loathsome reptiles, all hilarity will cease.

Almost one hundred different species fled from the
burning, crackling undergrowth, and many perished
in the rushing, spreading flames.   It was a snake battle,
and grew to be alarming, from the great number that
were living and crawling through the prairie grasses.

By constant prayer, and an entire submission to the
will of God, Enola began her field of labor.   With the
assistance of faithful Florence, and counsel, with pecu-
niary aid from one or two friends, she began to see
the heavy clouds scattering, and the silvery lining from
within peeping out to cheer and gladden her weary pilgrimage, for she realized fully that her entire life had
been an eventful one, with many hedges and thorns
along the wayside.   The sorrows largely overbalanced
the joys; but this school of probation must be varied
and terse, the discipline of each one necessarily changing according to the disposition, sensibility and control-
ling element of the subject.   God knows *just* how to
reprove and chastise, and He never gives us greater

burdens than we are able to bear. Many obdurate sinners require the chastening rcd of affliction to be applied over and over again before they yield in humble obedience to His almighty will.

Enola was convinced, in her own mind, that her inordinate *pride* was her besetting sin. She had, by serious reflection and careful study, investigated her faults, and was not ignorant of them. She was trusting and generous to a fault; was never known to refuse alms to the poor and needy. In her early life her attachments were strong and firm; but, as the sombre days of adversity dawned upon her, she withdrew from the gay world and sought something more tangible. She thirsted for that love and confidence that knows no deception. She had long since ceased to think of the early blight of her young life that Claude Vernon had brought upon her. Remorse, remorse, so cruelly had been his portion. He long since became a chronic invalid. He regarded the universe as the result of chance, and thought that it would eventually sink or be resolved into chaos. The truths that Enola had in vain sought to instill into his doubting mind were now swallowed up in scepticism, with remorse dangling from every point of his various cisms. He grasped with eagerness the latest religious craze — Esoteric Buddhism—trusting to quench the burning flame that seemed to be consuming his very soul and life. He sought Vedar's Ancient Philosophy, and delved into oriental religion with an abandon and enthusiasm even unknown to the student of God's Book, nourishing what he considered a beautiful and celestial belief—Indian Theos-

18

ophy—until the infatuation took possession of his entire
nature. Buddha's teachings he claimed were correct.
He became cynical in the extreme, regarding science
as his only friend. Poor deluded mind, with such con-
tradictions speaking in unmistakable words from the
Bible refuting any such idea or belief.

Mrs. Vernon, Sr., died at a very ripe old age, and
'tis to be hoped that "she sleeps in Jesus." 'Tis painful to think that many of the aged die in unbelief, with
no Redeemer to go with them through the "dark valley and shadow of death."

Poor Claude Vernon, it seems that his life has been
a blank. His children are far away from him, and as
he has never filled the position of father to them since
their birth, they know him not, only in name, "and
what is in a name?"

Mrs. Thorne passed into the silent grave many years
ago. It were folly to attempt to say that her conscience
ever rebuked her for the advice she gave to Enola long,
long ago, which unhappily wrecked her young life.

Had Enola never met Claude Vernon her fate would
have been different. But it was thus to be, and the
mandates of fate must be obeyed. There is no escaping
the decree. But perhaps Col. Baring's curses were
placed upon her for her acts of disobedience to him, the
reader will say. Enola felt that they were, and it frequently caused her to view in a lugubrious manner her
sad history.

A gentle rap at the door, and much to Mrs. Dale's
surprise, old Aunt Tilly was ushered in. She had
not seen the old colored woman for a great·many years.

She was delighted to once more look into her honest, wrinkled face, for her age was speaking loudly, " Thy race is almost run."

" Well, well, Aunt Tilly," she said; " you don't know how rejoiced I am to see you. Be seated and rest yourself. Where did you come from?"

"La bress yer, chile, I just cum from Louisville. I hern yer was in truble, that a rich man they call 'ministrator got 'way wid all ole massa lef' yer, which was big money, an' jist as soon as I herd that I jist tole my gran'sun: ' Wat,' sez I, ' Wat, I'se gwine to see poor Miss 'Nola 'fore I died,' and h'ar I is, mighty poorly off in health though, but bro't a little money wid me fur yer, pore chile. Yer knose, Miss 'Nola, wa' back yonder, in ole massa's kitchen, I tole yer; I 'vised yer not to marry that thar man, way off. He was kinder stranger, an' yer didn't suit him, nether. I'se gwine to tell yer sumpin, Miss 'Nola. Ole massa did put his vingance on yer, yas he did, pore chile. Does yer bleve ole Tilly now?" she asked.

" Aunt Tilly, since I last saw you, very many changes have taken place in my life, and all trials I regard as blessings in disguise."

" Now yer 'gins to talk like a christen. Did the bressed Lord whip yer wid truble 'til yer sot Him?"

At that moment Alcia entered the room and greeted the old colored aunty.

" Miss 'Nola, that thar girl is like yer was when yer use to come in ole massa's kitchen, and pick over my vituals, an' then I'd jist drive yer out. Dose yer 'member them plentiful days, Miss 'Nola? An' how

Jack stole the watermilon out of ole man Jones' patch, and how'ern the dog bit him? Oh, Miss 'Nola, I 'members all them thar incistants."

"How old are yer now, Aunt Tilly?" asked Alcia.

"La bress yer butiful sole, my chile, they tell me I am ninety-two years ole next watermilon time, but I dunno think I's that ole, for I don't feel mor'n eighty years ole. But bress yer sole, I'm ole, fur sumtimes I's purty shaky."

"Make yourself at home, Aunt Tilly; I know you are weary, and Florence will show you to a room where you can lie down and rest," said Mrs. Dale.

"Yas, Miss 'Nola, Tilly is mighty tired, but seein' yer all has kinder made me frustrate, but I's all right when I rest, so I's gwine to lay down, fur my bones is tired."

With Mrs. Dale's instructions, Florence conducted her to a room.

CHAPTER XIV.

THERE is joy in Mrs. Dale's household, for a son is born to Auguste and Alcia Manwell. Baring is jubilant at the thought of being an uncle, and Mrs. Dale feels her matronly position still more, and bears, with graceful dignity, the title "grandmother." The little darling received a warm welcome, and previous to his appearance upon the stage of life, a name was given him—Vernon Henry Manwell. An infant in the family is a pleasant institution, and Vernon was a sweet, attractive little pet, sharing alike the adulation with other infants. The very life of Mrs. Dale seemed to be absorbed in the dear little creature, and at times, from her contented, satisfied appearance, the stranger would never imagine that she had ever experienced one heartache in her life.

Alcia felt very proud to be the young mother, and filled the position with great affection and solicitude for her firstborn. From the day of his birth, she resolved to rear him with a great deal of firmness, and instill into his tender mind the principles on which to lay the foundation of a noble, useful character.

Vernon, though an infant, already knows that his mother intends that he shall obey her in all things, and love, as well as fear her. The present is an age of progress. Knowledge of the fine arts and sciences have almost reached perfection. The youth of to-day

is seemingly never a child. He springs from babyhood
to manhood; there is no intermediate state in his life.
Boys are not to be found; girls are out of the order of
things. From infancy they seem to spring into manhood
and womanhood. To the investigator, the scientist and
philosopher, the nineteenth century has opened to them
a field so broad and extensive, for research, invention
and investigation, that nature itself is bewildered at the
wonderful genius of man, and his accomplishments.

Fabrics of every variety were never so beautifully
designed, or of such exquisite texture. The antiquated,
grotesque style of the early ages was greatly admired
by the connoisseur, but compare any of them with the
artistic workmanship of the present age, and he can
readily discover that our tastes and designs far excel
the primitive execution of ancient workers and invent-
ors. The agriculturist rejoices in the facility that
man's invention has achieved, to lighten manual labor
of all kinds, where in former years the busy plough-
man, from dawn of day to twilight's sombre hour, followed, with his steady tread, the plough and horse that
uprooted and laid the soil open to receive the grain.
In primitive times the preparation of the earth for cultivation was a laborious task. Then the agriculturist
obeyed the divine mandate, earning his bread by the
"sweat of his brow."

A century or more since, the harvest season, in the
rural districts, was considered a time of great interest,
and busy, generous neighbors offered their assistance
to each other, toiling and cleaning the threshing floor,
and assiduously working with hands, until the entire

THE HARVEST.

grain that had been gathered was freed from chaff and securely garnered in rustic buildings to protect it from the weather. How is it in the present age? Vast fields of golden grain, covering hundreds of acres, are cultivated and gathered by the assistance of two or three men. Machinery does the labor and man guides the invention. It is a wonderful and interesting sight to watch the great locomotive, charged with steam, and all necessary appurtenances, skillfully separating the grain from the chaff; carefully placing each apportioned part into its designated place. And thus it is throughout the civilized world. Man has surely put his inventive genius to the utmost test to facilitate labor of all kinds. Is the human race growing more indolent and slothful? This may be so. God's Book tells us that this is the age when knowledge shall increase, and wisdom be engrafted within the hearts of many. This is an age of wisdom. Read the astrologist's predictions; and the astronomer's scientific knowledge given to the world, through constant study and research, and the mind readily grasps the conclusion. Go ask the renowned astronomer Richard A. Proctor, of our time, and if you please, consult the works of the German scientist Kepler, as to what of the sun, moon and stars? and they will, by their wonderful astronomical wisdom, satisfy the most inquisitive mind. Such scientific knowledge is appreciated throughout the entire land.

True science does not conflict with the Bible. The former harmonizes with the latter when correctly understood. Science gives much light upon the relative positions of the heavenly bodies, the velocity of

their movements, but we doubt if any scientist has
ever been able, by any scientific means in his power,
to ascertain that they are inhabited by beings like
ourselves.

We have been discussing the "clouds of sorrow"
that have obscured a bright and beautiful life, that
afforded food for meditation. How many clouds have
darkened the horizon of other valuable lives. There
are clouds *too* real, not figurative, that we will now
contemplate.

The clouds in the *heavens*, from whence descend the
rain and the snow; they are beautiful to look at as
we watch their varied changes, some fleecy, some
golden, some crimson.

There is exquisite and artistic loveliness in the richly
tinted clouds; the blending of the delicate colors,
beyond the reach of man's inventive genius. No
fancy touch of his brush can equal the grand and brilliant hues that are seen in nature's handiwork. The
funnel-shaped cloud deals death and destruction to all
that come within its whirling, deadly grasp. When
seeing the approach of such a cloud it sends an agoniz-
ing thrill of horror into the heart of the beholder, for a
funnel-shaped cloud means a *cyclone*. There is beauty
in the fleecy cloud, the mackerel cloud—indeed, the
clouds prognosticate what should be expected. There
are very many star-gazers, but give us the cloud-gazer.
Clouds "move in a mysterious way, *their* wonders to
perform," can be truthfully said of the modern clouds
that form and combine to sweep with destruction all
things before them. Clouds upon an April day seem to

pass, repass and kiss before shedding their tears upon a fallen world.

Finally, our Saviour, when He left this earth, went up in a cloud, and when He comes again it will be in the "clouds of heaven, with power and great glory." Surely those clouds will be more beautiful than any ever seen by mortal eye.

"Baring," said Mrs. Dale, "did you know that you have never imparted to me the secret that you and your sister have so carefully guarded these many months? I have a small amount of curiosity left in my nature yet, my little boy. Will you give to me the secret?"

"Mamma," he replied, seemingly much troubled, "I would prefer that you should not insist upon knowing it; but, my dear, dear mother, it is a scheme — an honest scheme — that, when fully accomplished, will interest you. It is nothing that will in the least injure you or annoy you, for both sister, brother and myself know full well that you have passed through sufficient annoyances to be free from care, and we intend that you shall be; so you must content yourself to let our 'secret' rest in peace for a time."

"Baring," said his mother, "you talk like an old experienced man. You are a plain, matter-of-fact boy, and I know the day is not far distant when I can find in my little son a world of comfort; when I can consult you in all my business arrangements. Won't that be bliss, to realize in you your mother's fondest hopes? I feel that age is creeping upon me, and, God willing, I shall have you as my staff to lean upon."

"You shall have a strong cane to rest upon," said he, "if you will trust my strength, mamma."

"You are my darling boy."

Baring continued: "If I had been a grown man when my father died, neither Mr. Cheatem, Mr. Peccavi, nor any one else would have ever taken any advantage of your interest or ours. How old was I, did you say, when my papa died?"

"You were not quite five years old, my child."

"I wish that I had been a man," he independently answered; "I would have looked after all our interests. I am growing fast, and will soon be your protector."

Seated around a table in the library were Mrs. Dale, Alcia and Auguste, in earnest conversation.

"Well, Auguste, it was no fault of mine," demutely answered Mrs. Dale. "I had very shrewd, designing men to deal with, and, unfortunately, I was created with a most trusting, confiding disposition. I had never in my life wronged anybody, and I did not suppose for a moment that any man would defraud me or my children. I believed everything that Mr. Cheatem or others told me; and as he had upon various occasions declared to me, in the most vehement manner, that he would never wrong the widow or orphan child of his old departed friend Vivien Dale, I believed all that he said. He went even farther, to say that if he were the corrupt man that many gave him the credit of, that he would rob or take advantage of large corporations; but he vowed that he was *honesty intensified*, and would not be guilty of doing a dishonorable act. Now you see how beautifully he talked. How could I suspect one who expressed himself in that manner?"

Mr. Manwell replied: "Did you not have some interested relative that could have convinced you of the true character of the man before you entrusted everything belonging to you and your children to such a person?"

"I had a brother who warned me, but I thought him prejudiced against Mr. Cheatem. The court accepted the man, and I could do nothing but agree."

"A deplorable outrage upon my mother's credulity," said Alcia, at the same time winking at little Baring as he entered the room.

"Come to me, Baring," said his sister; and whispering something to him, he hastily left the room. He was absent perhaps ten minutes, when he returned, carrying in his hand a large full envelope, which he handed to his sister. She said: "Mamma, do you see this envelope that I hold in my hand? It is valuable, for it contains a life policy that Mr. Dale left for Baring's benefit, and at the death of his father, before an administrator had been appointed, some wicked person purloined it, hoping that they would be benefited by this dishonest act; but thanks to good friends who have investigated the wrong, to-day he has ten thousand dollars in this sheet of paper. We all kept our knowledge and plans a profound secret from you until we had everything arranged, so as to collect the money at once. Now, my dear mamma, this is the great *secret* that Baring and I have kept inviolate."

Mrs. Dale was astonished, as well as much pleased, at recovering the long-lost policy, and she felt that God was instrumental in restoring some of their just claims back from dishonesty's grasp.

"Auguste," she said, "I will get you to attend to the collection of this policy for Baring," handing the paper to him.

"Certainly," he replied.

Then Mrs. Dale, catching up the thread of their conversation, continued: "I feel the great injustice that Mr. Peccavi did me as keenly as I did Mr. Cheatem's, although his wrong was upon a smaller scale. He resorted to so many contemptible devices to extort money from me, that I could but have the most disgusting opinion of him. As I have left everything in the hands of a God full of justice and mercy, I feel assured that He will deal with these wicked people according to their acts. I am happy, Auguste, in having placed all my injuries in the hands of such a judge; a judge that was never known to deceive, or acquit the wicked without just punishment; a judge, from time immemorial, that has promised to hear the cry of the widow and the fatherless. 'Come unto me,' saith the Lord."

"My mother speaks pathetically on the subject," said Auguste, "and had you been less trusting, you no doubt would have escaped the depletion of your purse. I feel very much for you, and have no fears but that, through your great faith, you will in the end triumph."

Alcia felt that she had sat so quietly listening to the conversation between her husband and mother, that it was now her turn to express her opinion upon this very important matter.

"Mamma," she said, in her own peculiar way, "I am delighted to hear you say that you have now placed your troubles and financial losses into the hands of the Infinite Judge, for your mind will be forever free from worldly annoyances, and what you have cast aside and given to the Lord, I may at some future day, years to come perhaps, gather together and see what success Alcia Manwell will have. I believe that I was born in a lucky month, but you, poor mamma, never realized much good to come to you from the ides. Did you?"

"No, my dear child, I was, when very young, disobedient to my father. I married greatly against his will; and a true saying, worthy to be observed by all, 'As you sow you must reap.' And I assure you, my children, it did appear to me that the harvest field was extensive, and required a great length of time to reap it, for until very recently I have been reaping, reaping, reaping, when only a few seeds of disobedience were sown; but they grew and grew, and it was quite impossible to choke out the seed by repentance and faithfulness to an injured parent. I drained the cup of remorse for my youthful disobedience, and tossed upon my bed of anguish for the wrong I did my unsuspecting father. I wept, I prayed; I longed to have the burden lifted from my offending heart; but the seed of disobedience was sown to grow and flourish like a green bay-tree. Oh, I am sure, Alcia, could I have secured my tears, as is the custom of some heathens,

I could have filled and refilled the lachrymatory with the outgushings from my bursting, penitent heart. Had I listened to my father, had I heeded his interested counsel, and not married Claude Vernon, my entire life would have been different; even Claude would have respected me more for my fidelity to my parent."

Alcia replied : " Well, all those dark days and thorny by-paths have been traversed, and you can never travel over the same road again—the stranded shores of life. Hedge up the thorny paths of disappointment, make bright the days, and, now that your harvest of disobedience is ended, let all be buried in the deep, deep well of forgetfulness. You can now begin a new existence, and live a new life in your children and my precious babe, Vernon Henry."

" You are very poetic in your expressions, my dear wife," said Auguste.

" The field is an extensive one to labor in," she quickly retorted.

" I am now happy and content, my children, and had not our conversation drifted upon this subject, I am sure that I never should have alluded to the past history of my life; reminiscences are sad, anyway. Troubles and trials only prove blessings in disguise. Who that has not shed a tear? Cold must be the heart that cannot feel emotion's softening touch sufficient to bring tears. The sympathetic chord is easily reached in my heart, and I weep when I see others weep."

" It requires a great deal to make me weep. I do not shed my precious tears over anticipated sorrow, for

in course of time it will visit all. Then it will be time
enough to waste our lachrymal fluid upon disappointed
hopes,'' said Alcia ironically.

Auguste replied, in his dignified manner, '' Thou
should'st not paint the devil upon the wall.''

'' No,'' said Baring, '' for once when I was very sick,
I saw a little devil upon the wall, and I am sure that he
came, in my fevered imagination, without paint or
brush.''

'' What ever became of the old, grim-looking gentleman that related to you the wonderful adventure he
had in Wyoming, years ago?'' asked Auguste.

'' To whom do you refer?'' asked Mrs. Dale.

'' I scarcely remember his name, as it was a most
peculiar one. The euphony, if I remember correctly,
was harsh.''

'' I know whom he is trying to remember,'' said
Alcia. '' It is old Mr. Peccavi. Is it not, Auguste?''
she asked.

'' Yes; that is the very name, Peccavi. Did you
ever get your money out of him?'' he asked in a quizzi-
cal manner.

Laughingly Mrs. Dale replied, '' Auguste, did you
you ever pour wine from an empty decanter?''

'' Of course not.''

'' Then I will answer your question in like manner:
' of course not.' Mr. Peccavi soars above this groveling earth; he would not stoop to pay an honest
debt, especially money that he has treacherously purloined from some unsuspecting widow. No, Auguste, my son, Mr. Peccavi has never paid me

one cent. I have heard that the poor man's mind was almost gone ; that he imagined he was the happy possessor of millions of acres of land in many States in the Union. I have lost trace of him, since so many years have elapsed. Poor old gentleman may be long since dead. Who knows? and we should let the ashes of the dead rest in peace."

" What became of Dr. and Mrs. Scott—May Thorne, that was?" Alcia inquired.

" They are still living in some remote southern clime, and May has a large family of children ; but several have died with consumption. I believe May, too, has had her own sorrows, and we are both gliding down the stream of life."

Florence came in and interrupted this family *tete-a-tete*, with the announcement that a gentleman was in the parlor, and desired to see Mrs. Enola Dale on very important business. Mrs. Dale, upon entering the room, soon discovered that she was in the presence of an entire stranger.

" Did you wish to see me, sir?" inquired she, in her dignified manner.

" Have I the honor of addressing the widow of Vivien Dale, madame?" he replied.

" I am his widow," she thoughtfully responded.

" Then, madame, I have been searching for you or your children for nearly two years. It was merely accidental that I discovered your whereabouts. It was through a gentleman that I met at the hotel that I received the information that you and your family were residing in this city, and that if I would examine the directory that I could ascertain the exact number of your residence, which I found most successfully. I am Charles Henry McIlvain, and my business with you, madame, is to show you papers where you and your children are the rightful heirs of a large fortune in Scotland, the native country of one of your grandparents. He had a brother, dying without issue, and leaving an estate of ten millions of dollars. There are nine heirs, madame, with yourself. I have the highest references in the country, and with very little difficulty this vast fortune can be claimed, and satisfactorily adjusted by all the rightful heirs. My business is to attend to these matters, and I will give you full assurances of the exact amount of money, with the location of the lands, as there are several large domains, and a castle where the old gentleman resided and spent his last days and hours."

She listened with astonishment to all that he had to say, and wondered if this could be an illusion. She called in her daughter, and the trio discussed the subject freely.

"Yes," she said, "my grandfather on my mother's side was from Scotland, and frequently my grandmother (now long since dead) had spoken of the vast wealth of her husband's family in Scotland."

"Yes, madame," said Mr. McIlvain, "I have all the convincing proof — papers, all — down at the hotel in my trunk. And now, that I have discovered the party I have been so long searching for, I feel that I will soon be able to progress with my labors, and in the course of a few weeks purpose to sail for Scotland. Madame,

19

it may be necessary for you to come to Glasgow, and
if so, I will advise you."

Mrs. Dale liked his honest manner of talking, and
she lost no time in discussing the whole affair with
Auguste, who did not seem to pay much attention to
the subject; but she knew more about her own family
than any one else.

Alcia and her mother had many conversations regarding this Scotland fortune, and early the following
morning Mr. McIlvain called, with all the papers.
They appeared very plain and concise.

Mr. McIlvain was delighted at having found Mrs.
Dale, and felt that he would now make all the necessary
arrangements for his departure across the briny deep
as soon as he possibly could.

Mrs. Dale, although having been robbed of nearly
all that she had inherited, did not appear to be much
elated over the prospect of getting another fortune.
She had learned to look at life differently, and felt
that really man's wants were few in this transitory life,
for she remembered that God had said, "The gold and
silver are mine." She knew that all our worldly possessions were simply loaned us, and that He could at
any moment call upon us to yield them up. She was
conscious of her true conversion, and had ceased to
grieve about her financial losses, or rejoice over
financial prosperity. She had graduated in the school
of affliction, and become enured to all the disappointments pertaining to a life like hers. It was alone for
the comfort and interest she felt in her dear children,
that prompted her to use any effort to regain worldly

possessions. She was striving to lay up for herself treasures in heaven.

" Mamma," said Alcia, " see how the Lord blesses you, and what perfect peace of mind you enjoy. Worth all the frivolities of life; are they not?"

" I am happy to hear you express yourself in that way. I hope that my darling child will realize how uncertain are all earthly things, and how important it is for the young to turn to God, and have that beautiful, intensified faith in Christ, our Redeemer, that will smooth the rugged pathway, and lead them gently to the river of life," said her mother.

"You do not know," replied Alcia, "how many serious reflections I have, and I trust that the time is not far distant when I can feel in my heart that God has forgiven all my sins, and that I can yield myself up wholly to Him. I do not desire to be sinful, I have been fond of society, fond of amusements and gaiety, but I think there is a time in everybody's life when the heart yearns for something better than this poor hollow world can give,"

" Oh, what joy it gives me to hear you express yourself in that way. I have a few lines here from Mr. McIlvain," said Mrs. Dale; " he writes as follows:

NEW YORK CITY, 18—,

MRS. ENOLA DALE:

RESPECTED MADAME:—I have everything now in readiness for my departure to Scotland, and should anything of interest transpire after my arrival in Glasgow, I will advise you. I feel very hopeful that my

trip will prove satisfactory to all parties. My address
I will send you, upon my arrival.

Very respectfully,
CHARLES H. McILVAIN.

" It begins to appear," said Alcia, " that something
good will come from the trip to Scotland."

" I am greatly encouraged myself, encouraged for
the sake of my children. This is no surprising fact,
for I have heard my ancestors speak of the Scotland
branch of the family as being extremely wealthy.
Had my grandmother been spared, she intended to
visit Scotland, and I expected to accompany her ;
Had she lived, I doubt very much if I should ever have
married."

" You might not have chosen my father, but I rather
think that you would have united your fate with some
congenial person, for your nature is one of dependence
and you could not have lived alone. What do you
think of marriage, anyway ? Give us your own private
views upon that subject, won't you, mamma ?"

" My daughter, my ideas are still the same. I have
my own opinions in regard to the marriage relation.
First, no man should marry until he is in a condition to
support a wife. No young lady should ever consent to
become the wife of a man until she had thoroughly investigated his private character, and I think it very
necessary to know the family and its antecedents. The
marriage vow should not be taken lightly or unad-
visedly by either of the parties. It is a subject that
should be fully considered, then both assume the sa-

cred obligation with a full determination to make each other happy, and abounding faith, permitting *no one* to interfere with the divine relationship of husband and wife. I think, by adhering strictly to these rules, that the divorce courts would not be so thronged with anxious, heart-broken subjects. The great number of unhappy marriages in the present age is appalling. It is truly difficult to trace the exact cause of the demoralization that is spreading throughout the wedded community."

"Don't you think," said Auguste, "that the great cause is, the reckless extravagance of both men and women, incident to this nineteenth century? It is so much more difficult to obtain a handsome support, and the cost of living is so much greater, the discontented mind, not feeling secure in its own possessions, becomes distorted, and from bad grows to worse, until utter dissatisfaction takes the place of contentment."

"Your theory is correct, Auguste, and the vital question at issue now is, how to remedy the great evil that is about to engulf our moral law and prosperous government. The pride and covetousness of the people is increasing at such a fearful rate; ambitious love of display in homes, dress and living are causing the ruin of many happy households, often ending in bankruptcy, suicide or lunacy. I feel, that something should be speedily done to stem the tide of extravagance, threatening to ruin every civilized country on the face of the globe," said Mrs. Dale.

"Man's accumulation of wealth is so rapid and boundless in this age, that easily won, as quickly spent.

He goes forth with the intention of outdoing, in grandeur and display, all his social friends, exciting, in their once-contented hearts, envy and a desire, if possible, to excel the pompous neighbor at the peril of honor and life. Finally, not succeeding, he sinks into the gloomy vale of despair." replied Auguste.

Mrs. Dale said: "Oh, that men and women could realize that this fleeting existence was not all of life, but only the first stepping-stone to a higher and a better one that will never end—the life none but the good can ever reach.

"The successful and prosperous speculator has a perfect right to use his money, honestly acquired, any way he pleases," said Auguste Manwell, quite sharply, "although he should not rush headlong into foolish extravagances that may prove his own ruin."

She responded: "But you must remember from whence cometh such gifts, such a talent. God endows him with the power to gain, and some of the gifts received should be returned to the Lord."

He answered: "That precept will not hold good with every one, although many wealthy men have no doubt been kind benefactors to the poor and needy, and many persons entirely unappreciative of all acts of kindness bestowed upon them; and so goes the world until the long and final destruction, and so it will be until the end. Ages upon ages will roll on in their cyclopean wonderment, rivers will change their courses from the flowing channels, hills and mountains will move out of their places, but this old earth of ours will move on and on through all eternity."

"Auguste," said Alcia, "you could not change my mother's views in relation to her Bible knowledge, for she has studied it faithfully, and much of the inspired light has been given her through years of constant prayer."

"Well," said Auguste, "we will not have any controversy over religion; we will lay that subject, important though it may be to us all, upon the table for some future discussion. I am anxious to draw you out, Mother Dale, upon the facts contained in the Bible, as you seem to know what you are talking about whenever we touch on responsibilities and duties toward one another."

"Yes, Auguste, it is only by studying that most wonderful of all books, and living up to its precepts, that man in his fallen condition can fully realize the duty he owes to his fellow-man. If each one of God's creation to-day would come to a determination to keep every one of the ten commandments, or decalogue given to man for his instruction and good, and not fail to do so, there would be no more murders committed, no more defrauding the widow and the orphan, no more broken hearts, no more misery, no more devastated homes, no more civil wars and no infidelity. What a glorious state of affairs. The now thronged prisons would be empty; the bat would build its nest in the murderer's cell; the mercenary man, that gained his spoil from the wicked promptings of dishonesty, would return to the rightful owner the ill-gotten wealth; the prodigal son would return to the bosom of his family a better man. There would be no more disobedient children to whiten the heads of their anxious parents; no more jealousies; no more rancor.''

Enola Dale, happy and peaceful in the society of her children, who add joy and comfort to her declining years, feels in the deep recesses of her heart *now*, no resentment toward any. She is supremely happy, with many assurances from her past *eventful* life, that although the punishment of disobedience to her father had caused her rugged pathway to be o'ershadowed by almost impenetrable darkness, yet with the smile of God upon her, with faith and hope to cheer her, she trusts ere long to reach the haven of perfect and everlasting *peace*.

FINIS.

Printed by BoD˜in Norderstedt, Germany